Pfeiffer
& COMPANY

THE 1996 ANNUAL: Volume 1 Training

(The Twenty-Sixth Annual)

Edited by
J. William Pfeiffer, Ph.D., J.D.

Pfeiffer
& COMPANY

Johannesburg • London
San Diego • Sydney • Toronto

PREFACE

The Pfeiffer & Company *Annual* series has been a success since its inception in 1972. One key to this success has been how well the *Annuals* meet the needs of human resource development (HRD) practitioners. The contents of each *Annual* focus on increasing a reader's professional competence by providing materials of immediate, practical use.

In 1995, Pfeiffer & Company began to publish two *Annuals* each year. Volume 1 is focused on training, and Volume 2 is focused on consulting. For the purposes of the *Annuals*, we consider training to be that which has an impact on individuals and consulting to be that which has an impact on organizations. Obviously, it is difficult in some cases to place materials strictly in one category or another, so there will be some overlap in what the two volumes cover.

Results have shown that our readers need and use both volumes. We are delighted to have the opportunity to showcase twice as much of the finest materials available in the HRD field.

The 1996 Annual: Volume 1, Training is the twenty-sixth volume in our *Annual* series; its contents reflect our intention to continue to publish materials that help our readers to stay on the cutting edge of the field. In keeping with this objective, users may duplicate and modify materials from the *Annuals* for educational and training purposes, as long as each copy includes the credit statement that is printed on the copyright page of the particular volume. However, reproducing Pfeiffer & Company materials in publications for sale or for large-scale distribution (more than one hundred copies in twelve months) requires *prior written permission*. Reproduction of material that is copyrighted by some source other than Pfeiffer & Company (as indicated in a footnote) requires written permission from the designated copyright holder. Also, reproduction on computer disk or by any other electronic means requires prior written permission.

For the *Annual* series, we actively seek materials from our readers as practicing professionals in the field. We are interested in receiving presentation and discussion resources (articles that include theory along with practical application); inventories, questionnaires, and surveys (paper-and-pencil inventories, rating scales, and other response tools); and experiential learning activities (group learning designs based on the five stages of the experiential learning cycle: experiencing, publishing, processing, generalizing, and applying). Contact the Editorial Department at the San Diego office for copies of our guidelines for contributors, and send submissions to the *Annual* editor at the same address.

I want to express my heartfelt appreciation to the dedicated people who produced this volume. First, I offer my genuine thanks to Dr. Beverly L. Kaye, who served as an acquisitions editor for the 1996 volumes. Her contacts and her talent enabled us to have many submissions from which to choose the pieces that are published here. Also, I am very grateful to Dr. Beverly Byrum-Robinson, who once again has reviewed all of our experiential learning activities. Her perspective as a facilitator and her insightful recommendations are irreplaceable in our quest to publish activities that meet the high standards of Pfeiffer & Company. I recognize and applaud the efforts and accomplishments of our Pfeiffer & Company staff: project manager Marian K. Prokop; graphic designer and page compositor, Judy Whalen; cover designer, Lee Ann Hubbard; and the members of our editorial and graphics staff, Arlette C. Ballew, Dawn Kilgore, Shana Lathrop, Marion Mettler, Carol Nolde, and Susan Rachmeler. Finally, as always, I extend my sincere gratitude to our authors for their generosity in sharing their professional ideas, materials, and techniques so that other HRD practitioners may benefit.

ABOUT PFEIFFER & COMPANY

Pfeiffer & Company is engaged in human resource development (HRD) and business book publishing. The organization has earned an international reputation as the leading source of practical publications that are immediately useful to today's facilitators, trainers, consultants, and managers. A distinct advantage of these publications is that they are designed by practicing professionals who are continually experimenting with new techniques. Thus, readers benefit from the fresh but thoughtful approach that underlies Pfeiffer & Company's experientially based materials, resources, books, workbooks, instruments, and tape-assisted learning programs. These materials are designed for the HRD practitioner who wants access to a broad range of training and intervention technologies as well as background in the field.

The wide audience that Pfeiffer & Company serves includes training and development professionals, internal and external consultants, managers and supervisors, team leaders, and those in the helping professions. For its clients and customers, Pfeiffer & Company offers a practical approach aimed at increasing people's effectiveness on an individual, group, and organizational basis.

CONTENTS

---

*See Experiential Learning Activities Categories, p. 5, for an explanation of the numbering system.

GENERAL INTRODUCTION
TO THE 1996 ANNUAL

The 1996 Annual: Volume 1, Training is the twenty-sixth volume in the *Annual* series. Each *Annual* has three main sections: twelve *experiential learning activities;* three *inventories, questionnaires, and surveys;* and a series of *presentation and discussion resources.* Each of the pieces is classified in one of the following categories: Individual Development, Communication, Problem Solving, Groups, Teams, Consulting, Facilitating, and Leadership. Within each category, pieces are further classified into logical subcategories, which are explained in the introductions to the three sections.

The *Annual* series is a collection of practical and useful materials for human resource development (HRD) practitioners—materials written by and for professionals. As such, the series continues to provide a publication outlet for HRD professionals who wish to share their experiences, their viewpoints, and their procedures with their colleagues. To that end, Pfeiffer & Company publishes guidelines for potential authors. These guidelines, revised in 1996, are available from Pfeiffer & Company's Editorial Department in San Diego, California.

Materials are selected for the *Annuals* based on the quality of the ideas, applicability to real-world concerns, relevance to current HRD issues, clarity of presentation, and ability to enhance our readers' professional development. In addition, we choose experiential learning activities that will create a high degree of enthusiasm among the participants and add enjoyment to the learning process. As in the past several years, the contents of each *Annual* span a range of subject matter, reflecting the range of interests of our readers.

A list of contributors to the *Annual* can be found at the end of the volume, including their names, affiliations, addresses, telephone numbers, facsimile numbers, and e-mail addresses (if available). Readers will find this list of contributors useful if they wish to locate the authors of specific pieces for feedback, comments, or questions. Further information is presented in a brief biographical sketch of each contributor that appears at the conclusion of his or her article. These elements are intended to contribute to the "networking" function that is so valuable in the field of human resource development.

The editor and the editorial staff continue to be pleased with the high quality of materials submitted for publication. Nevertheless, just as we cannot publish every manuscript we receive, readers may find that not all of the works included in a particular *Annual* are equally useful to them. We invite comments, ideas, materials, and suggestions that will help us to make subsequent *Annuals* as useful as possible to our readers.

Pfeiffer & Company

Introduction
to the Experiential Learning Activities Section

Experiential learning activities should be selected based on the participants' needs and the facilitator's competence. A good way to begin to select an activity is with the goal in mind: What do I want to accomplish with the participants as a result of this activity? Many activities address similar goals and can be adapted to suit the particular needs of a group. However, in order for the activity to meet the needs of the participants, the facilitator must be able to assist the participants in successfully processing the data that emerge from that experience.

All experiential learning activities in this *Annual* include a description of the goals of the activity, the size of the group and/or subgroups that can be accommodated, the time required to do and *process*[1] the activity, the materials and handouts required, the physical setting, step-by-step instructions for facilitating the experiential task and discussion phases of the activity, and variations of the design that the facilitator might find useful. All of these activities are complete; the content of all handouts is provided.

The 1996 Annual: Volume 1, Training includes twelve activities, in the following categories:

Individual Development: Life/Career Planning

Living Our Values: Checking for Congruence Between Values and Actions, by Maureen Wilson Dücker (#548, page 25)

Career Roads: Mapping the Journey to Your Goals, by Peter R. Garber (#549, page 35)

---

[1] It would be redundant to print here a caveat for the use of experiential learning activities, but HRD professionals who are not experienced in the use of this training technology are strongly urged to read the "Introduction" to the *Reference Guide to Handbooks and Annuals* (1994 Edition). This article presents the theory behind the experiential-learning cycle and explains the necessity of adequately completing each phase of the cycle to allow effective learning to occur.

Communication: Awareness
Bugs: Improving Customer Service, by James W. Kinneer (#553, page 73)

Communication: Feedback
Lines: Understanding Goals and Performance Feedback, by Michael R. Larsen (#551, page 59)

Communication: Styles
Enhancing Communication: Identifying Techniques to Use with Diverse Groups, by Robert William Lucas (#550, page 51)

Problem Solving: Information Sharing
Bean Counters: Analyzing Production Errors, by W. Norman Gustafson (#552, page 67)

Problem Solving: Action Planning
The River of Change: Exploring Coping Skills, by Mary Sue Barry (#555, page 93)

Groups: Competition/Collaboration
The Property Game: Exploring Motivation to Work, by Tom G. Geurts and Austin J. Jaffe (#554, page 77)

Teams: Roles
Tasks, Skills, and Commitments: Building a Cooperative Team, by Robert C. Preziosi (#546, page 15)

Teams: Problem Solving/Decision Making
Team Checkup: Monitoring and Planning for Progress, by Michael L. Mazzarese (#547, page 19)

Consulting and Facilitating: Facilitating: Opening
Bingo: Getting Acquainted, by Patrick Doyle (#545, page 9)

Consulting and Facilitating: Facilitating: Closing
Feedback Letters: Achieving Closure, by Gary Wagenheim and Gary Gemmill (#556, page 99)

Other activities that address goals in these and other categories can be located by using the "Experiential Learning Activities Categories" chart that follows, or by using our comprehensive *Reference Guide to Handbooks and Annuals*. This book, which is updated regularly, indexes all of the *Annuals* and all of the *Handbooks of Structured Experiences* that we have published to date. With each revision, the *Reference Guide* becomes a complete, up-to-date, and easy-to-use resource for selecting appropriate materials from *all* of the *Annuals* and *Handbooks*.

Pfeiffer & Company

EXPERIENTIAL LEARNING ACTIVITIES CATEGORIES

Vol. Page

INDIVIDUAL DEVELOPMENT

Sensory Awareness

	Vol.	Page
Feelings & Defenses (56)	III	31
Lemons (71)	III	94
Growth & Name Fantasy (85)	'72	59
Group Exploration (119)	IV	92
Relaxation & Perceptual Awareness (136)	'74	84
T'ai Chi Chuan (199)	VI	10
Roles Impact Feelings (214)	VI	102
Projections (300)	VIII	30

Self-Disclosure

	Vol.	Page
Johari Window (13)	I	65
Graphics (20)	I	88
Personal Journal (74)	III	109
Make Your Own Bag (90)	'73	13
Growth Cards (109)	IV	30
Expressing Anger (122)	IV	104
Stretching (123)	IV	107
Forced-Choice Identity (129)	'74	20
Boasting (181)	'76	49
The Other You (182)	'76	51
Praise (306)	VIII	61
Introjection (321)	'82	29
Personality Traits (349)	IX	58
Understanding the Need for Approval (438)	'88	21
The Golden Egg Award (448)	'88	89
Adventures at Work (521)	'95-1	9
That's Me (522)	'95-1	17

Sex Roles

	Vol.	Page
Polarization (62)	III	57
Sex-Role Stereotyping (95)	'73	26
Sex-Role Attitudes (184)	'76	63
Who Gets Hired? (215)	VI	106
Sexual Assessment (226)	'78	36
Alpha II (248)	VII	19
Sexual Values (249)	VII	24
Sex-Role Attitudes (258)	VII	85
Sexual Values in Organizations (268)	VII	146
Sexual Attraction (272)	'80	26
Sexism in Advertisements (305)	VIII	58
The Promotion (362)	IX	152
Raising Elizabeth (415)	'86	21

	Vol.	Page
The Problem with Men/Women Is...(437)	'88	9
The Girl and the Sailor (450)	'89	17
Tina Carlan (466)	'90	45

Diversity

	Vol.	Page
Status-Interaction Study (41)	II	85
Peer Perceptions (58)	III	41
Discrimination (63)	III	62
Traditional American Values (94)	'73	23
Growth Group Values (113)	IV	45
The In-Group (124)	IV	112
Leadership Characteristics (127)	'74	13
Group Composition (172)	V	139
Headbands (203)	VI	25
Sherlock (213)	VI	92
Negotiating Differences (217)	VI	114
Young/Old Woman (227)	'78	40
Pygmalion (229)	'78	51
Race from Outer Space (239)	'79	38
Prejudice (247)	VII	15
Physical Characteristics (262)	VII	108
Whom To Choose (267)	VII	141
Data Survey (292)	'81	57
Lifeline (298)	VIII	21
Four Cultures (338)	'83	72
All Iowans Are Naive (344)	IX	14
AIRSOPAC (364)	IX	172
Doctor, Lawyer, Indian Chief (427)	'87	21
Life Raft (462)	'90	17
Zenoland (492)	'92	69
First Impressions (509)	'94	9
Parole Board (510)	'94	17
Fourteen Dimensions (557)	'96-2	9

Life/Career Planning

	Vol.	Page
Life Planning (46)	II	101
Banners (233)	'79	9
Wants Bombardment (261)	VII	105
Career Renewal (332)	'83	27
Life Assessment and Planning (378)	'85	15
Work-Needs Assessment (393)	X	31
The Ego-Radius Model (394)	X	41
Dropping Out (414)	'86	15
Roles (416)	'86	27
Creating Ideal Personal Futures (439)	'88	31

	Vol.	Page
Pie in the Sky (461)	'90	9
What's in It for Me? (463)	'90	21
Affirmations (473)	'91	9
Supporting Cast (486)	'92	15
Career Visioning (498)	'93	13
The Hand You're Dealt (523)	'95-1	23
Living Our Values (548)	'96-1	25
Career Roads (549)	'96-1	35

COMMUNICATION

Awareness

	Vol.	Page
One-Way, Two-Way (4)	I	13
Think-Feel (65)	III	70
Ball Game (108)	IV	27
Re-Owning (128)	'74	18
Helping Relationships (152)	V	13
Babel (153)	V	16
Blindfolds (175)	'76	13
Letter Exchange (190)	'77	28
Dominoes (202)	VI	21
Blivet (241)	'79	46
Meanings Are in People (250)	VII	28
Mixed Messages (251)	VII	34
Gestures (286)	'81	28
Maze (307)	VIII	64
Feelings (330)	'83	14
Synonyms (341)	IX	5
In Other Words (396)	X	55
Taking Responsibility (397)	X	62
Pass It On (398)	X	68
Shades of Difference (417)	'86	35
E-Prime (440)	'88	39
Words Apart (464)	'90	29
Supportive Versus Defensive Climates (474)	'91	15
Let Me (511)	'94	31
Bugs (553)	'96-1	73

Building Trust

	Vol.	Page
Dyadic Encounter (21)	I	90
Nonverbal Communication I (22)	I	101
Intimacy Program (70)	III	89
Dialog (116)	IV	66
Dimensions of Trust (120)	IV	96
Dyadic Renewal (169)	V	116
Disclosing & Predicting (180)	'76	46
Current Status (196)	'77	57

Pfeiffer & Company

545. Bingo:
Getting Acquainted

Goals

- To offer the participants a chance to become acquainted in a nonthreatening way.

- To generate involvement in an upcoming training event.

Group Size

Up to twenty-five participants.

Time Required

Forty-five minutes.

Materials

- One copy of the Bingo Card for each participant. (*Note to the facilitator:* The cards are easier to handle if they are copied on card stock.)

- A pencil for each participant.

- A copy of the Bingo Caller's List, completed prior to conducting the activity. The facilitator either may ask the participants to fill in the information on the list as they arrive or, if the information is available in advance, may complete the list before the participants arrive. (*Note to the facilitator:* If the group is small, one or more spaces on the Bingo Card may be declared "free spaces," meaning that the space is considered filled.)

The 1996 Annual: Volume 1, Training.
Copyright © 1996 by Pfeiffer & Company, San Diego, CA.

- Prizes (optional).

Physical Setting

A room large enough to allow the participants to circulate freely.

Process

1. The facilitator announces that this will be a getting-acquainted activity and gives each participant a copy of the Bingo Card and a pencil. (Five minutes.)

2. The participants are told that they will have twenty minutes to mingle, during which time they are to introduce themselves to one another and "collect" the initials of the people they meet. One set of initials is written in each box on the Bingo Card, and the boxes may be filled in any order the participant chooses. The facilitator instructs the participants to begin mingling. (Twenty minutes.)

3. After twenty minutes the facilitator calls time and explains that he or she will call out initials from the Bingo Caller's List. The participant whose initials are called stands and introduces himself or herself to the group by repeating the initials, followed by his or her name and organization or department. (*Note to the facilitator:* If more than one participant has that set of initials, they introduce themselves in the same round, in any order.) The remaining participants check their Bingo Cards; if they have met that person and collected his or her initials, they draw an "X" through the box containing those initials. The facilitator continues to call out initials until a participant fills a row (horizontally, vertically, or diagonally) of five boxes with X's. At that time, the participant calls out "Bingo" and is declared the winner. Prizes (optional) are awarded at this time. (Ten minutes.)

4. The facilitator leads a concluding discussion by asking the following questions:

   - How many of you met more than half of the participants? Less? How do you account for the difference?

   - What about this activity made it easy to meet people? Difficult?

   - What did you learn about the getting-acquainted process?

   - How might this be useful to you in the future?

   (Ten minutes.)

Variations

- Participants may be directed to record names in the "B," "I," "N," "G," or "O" column, depending on which letter is included in the person's first or last name (e.g., "Henry James" in the "N" column, "Carly Smith" in the "I" column, etc.).

- Participants may record both the person's name and organization or department.

- When a participant's name is called, each may be asked to respond to the following question: "What nonathletic games—other than bingo—do you play and why?"

Submitted by Patrick Doyle.

Patrick Doyle is the principal of High Impact Training Services and a professor of Training and Development at St. Lawrence College in Kingston, Ontario, Canada. He is active in the field of human resource development in business and public health organizations. Mr. Doyle's specialty is management techniques during periods of technological change.

Bingo Card

B	I	N	G	O
1	1	1	1	1
2	2	2	2	2
3	3	FREE	3	3
4	4	4	4	4
5	5	5	5	5

Bingo Caller's List

Name	Initials	Organization / Dept.

546. Tasks, Skills, and Commitments: Building a Cooperative Team

---

Goals

- To increase the team members' awareness of one another's tasks and skills.
- To encourage the team members to commit to assisting one another in performing tasks and using skills.

Group Size

All members (at least three and not more than twelve) of an ongoing team or a temporary team (for example, a product-development team or a task force). This activity is intended to be used soon after the formation of a team or when new members or new responsibilities are acquired.

Time Required

One hour to one hour and forty minutes, depending on the number of team members.

Materials

- A felt-tipped marker for each team member.
- A pad of large Post-it™ Notes for each team member.
- A newsprint flip chart.
- Masking tape for posting newsprint.

Physical Setting

A room with movable chairs. Plenty of wall space is recommended for posting newsprint. Tables are helpful (for creating newsprint lists) but not essential.

Process

1. The facilitator introduces the goals of the activity.

2. Each team member is given a felt-tipped marker and a sheet of newsprint and is asked to make a newsprint list of the major *tasks* that he or she performs on the job. The facilitator explains that after completion the task lists should be posted on the wall, with at least enough space between lists to accommodate another sheet of newsprint. (Approximately ten minutes.)

3. After all lists have been posted, the team members take turns presenting the contents of their lists. After each presentation, the facilitator encourages the members to ask questions about any information that they need clarified. (Five to fifteen minutes.)

4. Each team member receives another sheet of newsprint and is asked to list on it the *skills* that he or she uses in performing work tasks. The facilitator announces that the completed skill lists should be posted on the wall, next to their respective task lists. (Approximately ten minutes.)

5. After the new lists have been posted, the team members again take turns presenting the contents. After each presentation, questions are asked and answered as necessary. (Five to fifteen minutes.)

6. Each member is given a pad of large Post-it™ Notes so that he or she can write a note to every other team member about a way in which he or she might assist or support that member in performing tasks and using skills. Each Post-It™ Note is placed on the other member's newsprint list (task or skill) where appropriate. (Five to fifteen minutes.)

7. The team members take turns reading aloud the Post-it™ Notes attached to their own newsprint lists so that the entire team knows what assistance and support have been offered and what commitments have been made. (Five to ten minutes.)

Pfeiffer & Company

8. The facilitator leads a discussion on reactions to the process as well as how to follow up on the commitments that have been made. The following questions may be helpful:

  - What was your reaction to writing lists of your tasks and skills and then presenting them to the team? What was your reaction to hearing about others' tasks and skills?

  - How did it feel to offer assistance and support? How did it feel to receive assistance and support?

  - What have you learned about your team's tasks and skills? What have you learned about its assistance and support?

  - What have you learned about making commitments?

  - How can you ensure that the commitments made today are met— that the assistance and support are, in fact, given? What can you personally do to ensure that you meet the commitments you have made to others?

  (Fifteen to twenty minutes.)

9. Before dismissing the team members, the facilitator informs them that all posted information will be reproduced and distributed to them as a handout. The facilitator also recommends that the team members review their tasks, skills, and commitments every few months.

Variations

- The team members may be instructed to list only those tasks and skills that they need or want assistance with.

- After Step 8, the team members may assemble into pairs to make contracts to assist each other.

- When developing their skill lists, the team members may list only those skills and resources that they bring to the team. The team members who can benefit from those skills and resources may then use the Post-it™ Notes to match their needs with the resources offered.

Submitted by Robert C. Preziosi.

Robert C. Preziosi, D.P.A., is a professor of management education in the School of Business and Entrepreneurship at Nova Southeastern University in Fort Lauderdale, Florida. He is also the president of Management Associates, a consulting firm. He has worked as a human resources director, a line manager, and a leadership-training administrator and has consulted with all levels of management in many organizations, including American Express, the Department of Health and Human Services, John Alden Life Insurance, Siemens, and many hospitals and banks. Dr. Preziosi has been training trainers since the 1970s; his areas of interest include leadership, adult learning, and all aspects of management and executive development. In 1984 he was given the Outstanding Contribution to HRD Award by ASTD; in 1990 he received the Torch Award, the highest leadership award that ASTD gives.

547. Team Checkup:
Monitoring and Planning for Progress

Goals

- To offer team members a way to evaluate and monitor the progress of their team.
- To encourage team members to devise priorities and action plans for improving their team.
- To encourage team members to execute action plans for team improvement.

Group Size

All members of an ongoing team.

Time Required

One hour and forty minutes to two and one-half hours (excluding prework), depending on the size of the team.

Materials

- A copy of the Team Checkup Questionnaire for each team member.
- Newsprint sheets listing the team members' responses to the questionnaire items (prepared in advance). A separate sheet (or sheets) should be created for each item.
- A newsprint flip chart and a felt-tipped marker.
- Masking tape for posting newsprint.

Physical Setting

A room in which the team members can work without interruption. Movable chairs should be provided, and plenty of wall space should be available for posting newsprint.

Process

1. *Prework 1:* The facilitator distributes copies of the Team Checkup Questionnaire and asks each team member to complete this questionnaire and return it to the facilitator at least twenty-four hours before the activity session. In explaining the activity, the facilitator states that undergoing a team "checkup" will help the members to form a picture of the team's present situation; then they can decide in which direction they want to move in the future. The facilitator says that he or she will be recording the team members' responses from the completed forms, but assures the members that those responses will remain anonymous. (Five minutes.)

2. *Prework 2:* Once all members' completed questionnaires have been collected (approximately a day before the activity session), the facilitator records on sheets of newsprint all responses to each individual item so that everyone's views can be displayed during the activity session. (A *minimum of one hour* to record data.)

3. At the beginning of the activity session, the facilitator posts all newsprint sheets with the members' recorded responses. The facilitator leads a discussion of each item, striving for understanding and consensus on each. (One to one and one-half hours.)

4. The facilitator instructs the team members to focus on suggestions for improvement (item 4 on the questionnaire) and asks if there are now additional improvement ideas. Any new ideas are recorded on newsprint and clarified as necessary. Then all improvement ideas are reviewed, and similar ideas are assembled into categories. The members may want to eliminate any plans for improvement that are already in motion or that are not within the team's control. From the remaining list the team members choose the top one to three priorities. (Note: The team should not work on too much at once; one to three improvement items are enough. After the initial items have been tried and modified as needed, other items may be tackled.) (Twenty minutes.)

5. The team members are assisted in devising action plans from the list of priorities. The four critical elements (*who* will commit to action,

what will be done, *by when,* and *how you will know your actions are working*) are determined and recorded on newsprint. The facilitator keeps the newsprint action plans so that he or she can create a handout from them and distribute a copy to each team member. (Twenty to thirty minutes.)

6. The facilitator leads a discussion of the activity based on questions such as the following:

   ▪ What did you learn about yourself as a team member?

   ▪ What did you learn about your fellow team members?

   ▪ What did you learn about working together as a team?

   ▪ How can you use what you learned to address team issues in the future?
   (Ten minutes.)

7. The facilitator encourages the team members to meet every few months to fill out the questionnaire again, to review progress, and to modify goals as necessary.

Variations

▪ Instead of administering the questionnaire, the facilitator may interview each team member separately and record his or her responses to the items on the questionnaire form. The facilitator should clarify for everyone that responses will be shared but will remain anonymous. Subsequently, all responses to each item should be recorded on newsprint. The activity then begins at Step 3.

▪ The facilitator may, if appropriate, encourage the team members to own their responses during the discussion of the questionnaire items. (However, the members must not feel pressured to relinquish the anonymity of their responses.)

Submitted by Michael L. Mazzarese.

Michael L. Mazzarese, Ph.D., heads Mazzarese & Associates of Westfield, New Jersey, a firm specializing in the retention of executive and key talent in organizations. He coaches individuals and teams by linking personal effectiveness and change to strategic business results. Dr. Mazzarese has extensive international experience in industry, healthcare, and education. He consults, writes, and speaks frequently about executive development, leadership, organization development, change, and the strategic alignment of human resources.

TEAM CHECKUP QUESTIONNAIRE

1. How would you describe the interactions when the members of your team get together to plan, solve problems, or make decisions?

   Have interactions improved or worsened in the past two or three months? What have you observed that tells you this?

2. How would you describe the team's relationships with outside groups (for example, other teams or units, other organizations, suppliers)?

   Have these relationships improved or worsened in the past several months? What have you observed that leads you to this conclusion?

---

3. What are your team's greatest strengths?

How can you build on these strengths?

4. What two or three things does your team need to improve?

What are you as an individual doing to improve these things? What is the team as a unit doing to improve these things?

What could you and the team do that you are *not* doing now?

5. How would improving the things identified in item 4 benefit your team's planning, problem solving, decision making, member interactions, or relationships with outside groups?

548. Living Our Values: Checking for Congruence Between Values and Actions

Goals

- To have participants identify their values on five predetermined items.
- To have participants identify actions they have engaged in that support or violate their values.
- To allow participants to examine the degree of congruence between their values and actions.

Group Size

Twenty participants in subgroups of four or five members each.

Time Required

Approximately one hour and five to twenty minutes.

Materials

- A copy of the Living Our Values Chart for each participant.
- A copy of the Living Our Values Behavioral Checklist for each of the participants.
- A copy of the Living Our Values Follow-Up Sheet for each participant.
- A copy of the Living Our Values Discussion Sheet for each participant.
- A pencil and a clipboard or other portable writing surface for each participant.

The 1996 Annual: Volume 1, Training.
Copyright © 1996 by Pfeiffer & Company, San Diego, CA.

Physical Setting

A room in which participants can spread out and write in relative privacy; no participant should be able to see another's paper. When subgroups are formed in Step 5, each needs to be able to work without disturbing the others.

Process

1. The facilitator introduces the goals of the activity and informs the participants that they do not have to show what they write to others.

2. The facilitator distributes copies of the Living Our Values Chart, pencils, and clipboards or other portable writing surfaces and then reads the handout directions aloud. Participants are asked to complete their charts individually. (Fifteen to twenty minutes.)

3. After the participants have completed their charts, the facilitator distributes copies of the Living Our Values Behavioral Checklist and reads the directions aloud. Participants are asked to complete their checklists. (Ten to fifteen minutes.)

4. After the participants have completed the checklists, they are asked to compare their responses on the Living Our Values Behavioral Checklist to their responses on the Living Our Values Chart. The facilitator also distributes copies of the Living Our Values Follow-Up Sheet, explaining that this handout offers some information that might be useful in making comparisons. (Ten minutes.)

5. Subgroups of four or five members each are assembled. The participants are given copies of the Living Our Values Discussion Sheet and are asked to discuss the questions in their subgroups. The facilitator calls the participants' attention to the guidelines listed under the questions on the handout and suggests that the participants follow these guidelines in their discussions. The participants are encouraged to challenge themselves, but are also told that there is no requirement to share information that is uncomfortable. (Twenty minutes.)

6. The facilitator reassembles the total group and leads the participants in a concluding discussion. The following questions are helpful:

   - What have you learned about why people make decisions or engage in behaviors that are inconsistent with their values?

- What have you learned that can help you live your values more consistently?

- What is an action you can take to help you live your values more consistently in your personal life? In your professional life?

(Ten minutes.)

Variations

- An inexperienced group may need a lecturette on identifying a value and learning how to articulate it.

- A group may benefit from a discussion of particular values not identified on the Living Our Values Chart. The activity may be adapted to address those values.

- To shorten the activity, the facilitator may use either the Living Our Values Chart or the Living Our Values Behavioral Checklist.

Submitted by Maureen Wilson Dücker.

Maureen Wilson Dücker is a Ph.D. student in higher education and student affairs at Ohio State University, Columbus, Ohio. She also serves as an academic adviser for undergraduates in University College at Ohio State. Her special interests include adult development, ethics and professionalism, and women's issues. She has published articles in the Journal of College Student Development *on a capstone seminar for graduate students and on educating staff in issues connected with ethics and professionalism.*

LIVING OUR VALUES CHART

To help you clarify your values and the actions you take in connection
with those values, complete the following steps:

1. In the "Values" column, briefly define each item (what it means to
   you).

2. In the "Actions That Support My Values" column, list specific behaviors you have engaged in *within the past year* that support each of your
   stated values.

3. In the "Actions That Violate My Values" column, list specific behaviors you have engaged in *within the past year* that violate each of your
   stated values.

Values	Actions That Support My Values	Actions That Violate My Values
Self-Care		
Truth		
Theft		
Cheating		
Relationships with Others		

Living Our Values Behavioral Checklist

To help you further determine the consistency between your values and your behavior and why some actions may not be consistent with your values, complete the following steps:

1. For each numbered statement, place a check mark in Column A under "Yes" if the statement is true for you *in the past year* or under "No" if the statement is not true for you *in the past year*.

2. If your response in Column A *is* consistent with your values, place a check mark in the column labeled "Consistent with My Values"; if your response in Column A is *not* consistent with your values, put a check mark in the column labeled "Not Consistent with My Values."

3. If you indicated that your action was *not* consistent with your values, list the reason(s) in the last column.

In the Past Year...	Column A		Consistent with My Values	Not Consistent with My Values	Reason(s) for Actions Not Consistent with My Values
	Yes	*No*			
1. I have exercised at least three times a week.					
2. I have taken advantage of a friend or coworker.					
3. I have stolen money or property from a business or organization.					
4. I have maintained an appropriate weight for my height and build.					

The 1996 Annual: Volume 1, Training.
Copyright © 1996 by Pfeiffer & Company, San Diego, CA.

In the Past Year...	Column A		Consistent with My Values	Not Consistent with My Values	Reason(s) for Actions Not Consistent with My Values
	Yes	No			
5. I have told another person what a friend told me in confidence.					
6. I have used a personal connection to gain an advantage over competitors.					
7. I have taken money or property from a close friend.					
8. I have lied to protect a friend's feelings.					
9. I have cheated in a competitive event or sport.					
10. I have gotten adequate sleep every night.					
11. I have taken office supplies from work for personal use.					
12. I have been unfaithful to a committed partner.					

Pfeiffer & Company

In the Past Year. . .	Column A		Consistent with My Values	Not Consistent with My Values	Reason(s) for Actions Not Consistent with My Values
	Yes	No			
13. I have eaten a well-balanced diet.					
14. I have taken some-thing that was not mine when I thought I could not be caught.					
15. I have lied to gain an advantage.					
16. I have falsified data for a report, assignment, or study.					
17. I have gossiped about other people.					
18. I have lied to avoid a confrontation with a close friend or partner.					
19. I have stolen to assist someone in need.					
20. I have cheated on an assignment or test.					

In the Past Year. . .	Column A		Consistent with My Values	Not Consistent with My Values	Reason(s) for Actions Not Consistent with My Values
	Yes	No			
21. I have overindulged in alcohol.					
22. I have voluntarily performed community service or charitable work.					
23. I have lied to a business or organization.					
24. I have used someone else's work as if it were my own.					
25. I have embellished my résumé or a job application.					

Pfeiffer & Company

Living Our Values Follow-Up Sheet

It may be helpful to you to know which items on the Living Our Values Behavioral Checklist correspond to the values on the Living Our Values Chart. The following is a list of values and corresponding checklist items:

Self-Care: 1, 4, 10, 13, 21

Truth: 8, 15, 18, 23, 25

Theft: 3, 7, 11, 14, 19

Cheating: 6, 9, 16, 20, 24

Relationships with Others: 2, 5, 12, 17, 22

LIVING OUR VALUES DISCUSSION SHEET

Discussion Questions

1. How consistent did you find your values and actions to be? What was confirmed for you? What did you find puzzling? What did you find upsetting?

2. When your actions violate your values, why is that? How might you account for your behavior on such occasions?

3. When your values and actions are in conflict, would you prefer to change your values or your behavior? Why? Which of your values might need changing? Which behaviors might need changing?

4. How do you make decisions when your values are in conflict (e.g., truth versus loyalty)?

Discussion Guidelines

1. Challenge yourself to examine your own values and how you support or violate them through your actions.

2. Respect differences of opinion.

3. Maintain the confidentiality of all participants.

4. Strive for openness with yourself and others.

The 1996 Annual: Volume 1, Training.
Copyright © 1996 by Pfeiffer & Company, San Diego, CA.

549. CAREER ROADS:
MAPPING THE JOURNEY TO YOUR GOALS

Goals

- To encourage participants to determine their career goals.
- To allow participants to examine past career choices and whether these led toward their goals or not.
- To help participants to evaluate the "costs" of attaining their career goals.
- To help participants to assess their current positions in terms of their career goals.
- To encourage participants to plan for action choices that further their career goals.

Group Size

Up to twenty participants in small groups of four or five members each.

Time Required

Two hours to two and one-half hours.

Materials

- A copy of the Career Roads Task Sheet: Destinations for each of the participants.
- A copy of the Career Roads Task Sheet: Directions for each participant.

The 1996 Annual: Volume 1, Training.
Copyright © 1996 by Pfeiffer & Company, San Diego, CA.

- A copy of the Career Roads Task Sheet: Tolls for each participant.
- A copy of the Career Roads Task Sheet: Signs for each participant.
- A copy of the Career Roads Task Sheet: Conditions for each of the participants.
- At least two pieces of newsprint flip-chart paper for each participant.
- Several colors of felt-tipped markers for each participant.
- Several strips of masking tape for each participant.
- A newsprint flip chart and felt-tipped markers for the facilitator.
- Masking tape for posting newsprint.

Physical Setting

Sufficient table space or clean, smooth floor space for each participant to work. If tables are provided, a chair for each participant. Wall space on which to post newsprint sheets.

Process

1. The facilitator introduces the activity and states its goals. The facilitator gives each participant a copy of the Career Roads Task Sheet: Destinations, two sheets of newsprint flip-chart paper, masking tape, and several colors of felt-tipped markers. The participants are divided into groups of four or five members each, and the groups are positioned around the room. (Ten minutes.)

2. The facilitator directs the participants to read the Career Roads Task Sheet: Destinations. The facilitator tells the participants to answer the questions for themselves and then to create their own career road maps on the newsprint sheets. The facilitator says that two sheets of newsprint may be joined with masking tape, if necessary, to create a longer map surface and allow room for additions. (Ten to fifteen minutes.)

3. The facilitator gives each participant a copy of the Career Roads Task Sheet: Directions and draws the participants' attention to how the directions are added to the career road map. The participants are then instructed to read the task sheet, answer the questions at the bottom of the task sheet for themselves, and add their own directions to their career road maps. (Ten minutes.)

4. The members of each group share their career goals, any important features of their career road maps, and their most pertinent answers to the questions on the task sheets. (Fifteen minutes.)

5. The facilitator distributes copies of the Career Roads Task Sheet: Tolls and directs the participants to read it. The participants answer the questions at the bottom of the sheet for themselves and add their personal tolls to their career road maps. (Ten to fifteen minutes.)

6. The members of each group share their insights and observations about the tolls they have paid or expect to pay along their career roads. (Ten minutes.)

7. The facilitator distributes copies of the Career Roads Task Sheet: Signs and directs the participants to read it. The facilitator tells the participants not to worry about using all the road signs or selecting the perfect ones, just to use the ones that make the most sense to them in terms of their career roads. The participants are instructed to answer the questions at the bottom of their sheets for themselves and to add their personal road signs to their career road maps. (Ten to fifteen minutes.)

8. The members of each group share their insights and observations about the road signs they have added to their career road maps and how they have heeded or ignored such "road signs" in the past. (Ten minutes.)

9. The facilitator distributes copies of the Career Roads Task Sheet: Conditions and asks the participants to read it and to answer the questions on the sheet for themselves. (Ten minutes.)

10. The participants are instructed to post their career road maps around the room. (Five minutes.)

11. The entire group is reassembled. The facilitator asks for comments and insights about each of the segments of the activity, in turn, making notes of important points on the newsprint flip chart and posting completed pages for all to see. The following may be included in the debriefing:

   ■ What similarities were there in identifying your destinations or career goals? What were the differences?

   ■ What similarities were there in making choices and decisions about career directions? What were the differences?

- What similarities existed in the "tolls" that had to be paid along the way? What differences were there?

- What similarities existed in the "signs" that you have followed or missed? What were the differences?

- What similarities existed in the external conditions that affected your careers? What were the differences? How were these conditions managed?

- What are the most helpful things you have learned from the concept of career road mapping?

- How do you plan to use your insights from this activity in managing your careers in the future?

(Thirty minutes.)

Variations

- The example (sales) can be changed to fit the group.

- To shorten the activity, participants can do the entire mapping process individually and then share important insights with their groups.

- Participants can make actions plans after the final processing step.

Submitted by Peter R. Garber.

Peter R. Garber *is the manager of teamwork development for PPG Indus-tries, Inc., in Pittsburgh, Pennsylvania. He has held various positions in human resources and has developed training programs in the areas of safety, quality improvement, and teamwork. He is the author of* Coaching Self-Directed Workteams, 25 Skill-Building Activities, Diversity Explorations, *and* 30 Easy-To-Use Reengineering Activities, *and his experiential learning activity, "Adventures at Work: Experiencing Work As a Movie," appears in* The 1995 Annual: Volume 1, Training.

CAREER ROADS TASK SHEET: DESTINATIONS

In the poem, "The Road Not Taken," the poet Robert Frost ponders the path he did not choose and where it might have led. We travel along many roads on our way to our career destinations. Some of these roads we choose and some are chosen for us. Each plays an important part in our lives.

Often, it is helpful to see where these roads have already taken us. Knowing where we have been can help guide us to where we are going. We can see which roads led toward our goals and which did not.

An old proverb says "Even the longest journey begins with the first step." We actually begin preparing for our eventual careers at very young ages. Our performance in school and in other activities may lead us toward or away from certain career possibilities.

Destinations

Another old proverb says "If you don't know where you are going, almost any road can take you there." That is like beginning a journey without a destination or a road map; you are likely to end up driving around in circles and never getting anywhere. Career goals may not always lead you to your destination, but they help to guide your choices and decisions and improve your chances of ending up somewhere where you want to be.

In the example that follows (page 41), a person begins a career as a sales trainee. You can see the progression of jobs leading to the career goal of marketing manager. Notice the scale of time; it will take about nine years to reach this career goal. Of course, a lot of things could happen in those nine years, and the person will have to make some career decisions along the way.

Tasks

Think about how your journey began. Did you make a conscious choice regarding your career?

What led you to this choice?

Would you make that choice today? If no, why not?

State, in a few sentences, what your career goal is now.

Now draw a map of your career road, as you see it, including your likely or chosen destination and the milestones along the way. You may use color in any way you choose.

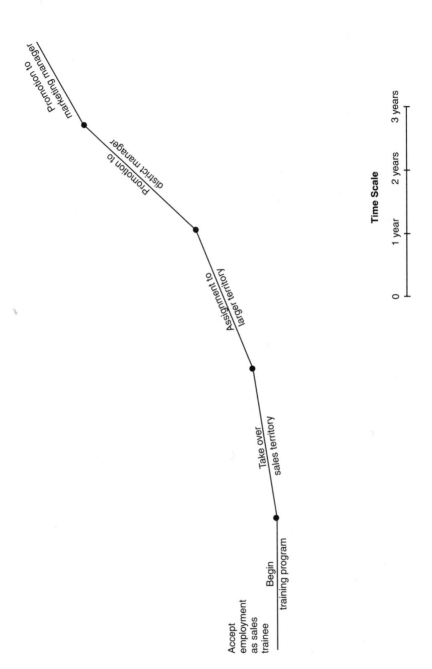

Time Scale

0   1 year   2 years   3 years

CAREER ROADS TASK SHEET: DIRECTIONS

Each choice we make can have far-ranging consequences. In the illustrated example, the salesperson might decide in the fourth year to stay in his or her present location rather than relocating to a larger territory.

Sometimes the best directions are not obvious. Also, some careers may have many roads to choose from and others have relatively few. In each case, it is important to attempt to know the direction in which each road leads. When making career decisions, it can be helpful to actually draw a map of where you believe each road will take you.

Tasks

Do you feel that you have exercised much choice in the direction in which your career has gone?

How has taking or changing a direction affected your expected career path?

Are you on a path that is likely to lead to your stated career goals?

How do you typically make such decisions?

Do you think that is the best way for you to make such decisions?

Now add your directional possibilities and choices to your career map.

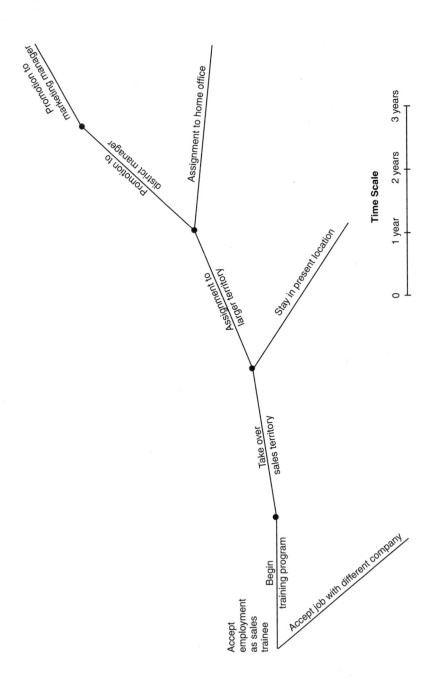

Accept employment as sales trainee

Begin training program

Accept job with different company

Take over sales territory

Assignment to larger territory

Stay in present location

Promotion to district manager

Assignment to home office

Promotion to marketing manager

Time Scale

0   1 year   2 years   3 years

Career Roads Task Sheet: Tolls

Like many roads, the career road often includes tolls that must be paid. A toll may be simply completing a training program or it may involve moving to a different city or state or country. Some career roads require changing jobs or gaining experience in several different organizations or earning an advanced degree. Other tolls include working long hours, which, like relocating, can have a detrimental effect on family relationships. As one's career progresses, the tolls may seem to be more "expensive," as is shown in the example of the salesperson.

Tasks

What "tolls" have you "paid" on your career road?

What have been the rewards and benefits of paying these tolls?

Do you know what the next tolls are to reach your career goals?

Are you willing to pay these tolls to get there?

On your career map, indicate the tolls that you have paid and the ones that you expect to have to pay in the future. Put a plus sign by the tolls that you believe are worth the price and put a minus sign by the tolls that you feel ambivalent or negative about.

The 1996 Annual: Volume 1, Training.
Copyright © 1996 by Pfeiffer & Company, San Diego, CA.

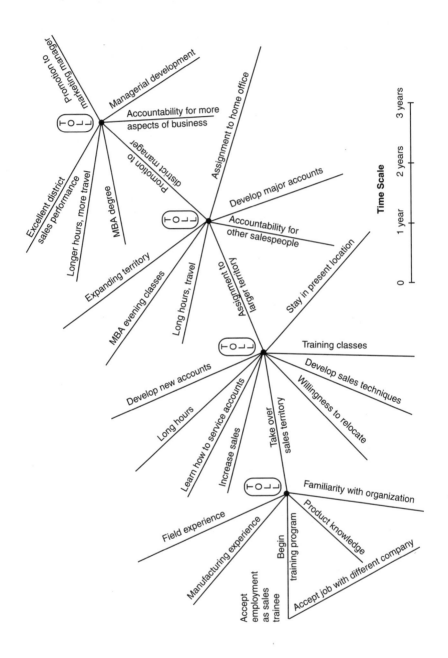

Time Scale

0   1 year   2 years   3 years

Promotion to marketing manager

Managerial development

Accountability for more aspects of business

Assignment to home office

Excellent district sales performance

Longer hours, more travel

MBA degree

Promotion to district manager

Develop major accounts

Accountability for other salespeople

Expanding territory

MBA evening classes

Long hours, travel

Assignment to larger territory

Stay in present location

Training classes

Develop sales techniques

Develop new accounts

Long hours

Learn how to service accounts

Increase sales

Take over sales territory

Willingness to relocate

Field experience

Manufacturing experience

Accept employment as sales trainee

Begin training program

Product knowledge

Familiarity with organization

Accept job with different company

Pfeiffer & Company

CAREER ROADS TASK SHEET: SIGNS

In the continuing example of the salesperson, signs have been placed on the career roads. These signs serve many of the same purposes as those found along a highway: they tell us where we are and where we are going. They warn us of roadblocks or hazards ahead. They often tell us how we should proceed.

Career road signs help us see which roads we can travel the fastest [55] and which roads are most difficult to travel [≦] . They let us know when we are entering an area where the results take a long time to see [◉] . They warn us of dangerous intersections ⬦ and caution [◎] us about traveling in directions [↑ Detour] [Alternate Route] away from our career goals. These signs tell us the type of road we are on and when we are nearing [→ Career Goals Next Exit] our career goals.

Road Under Construction	Single-Lane	Highway

In the example of the salesperson, the career road signs might look something like the example on the next page.

Many times, signs are all around us but we do not see them or do not know how to read them.

Tasks

What are some of the signs you have read along your career road?

What are some of the signs you might have missed or ignored?

What crossroads, detours, or roadblocks might you encounter in the future?

Add the appropriate road signs to your career road map.

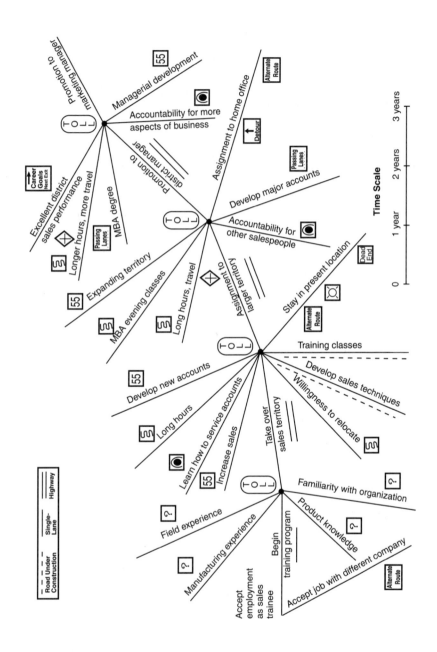

CAREER ROLES TASK SHEET: CONDITIONS

Travel conditions can greatly affect a journey. Business climates, company policies, internal and external competition, economic conditions, technology, and many other factors can influence your career. Sometimes it is fair and clear; conditions such as organizational growth and career opportunities can make your journey smoother, faster, and more enjoyable. Like the weather, there is often very little one can do about many of these conditions and, like the weather, these conditions are constantly changing. Therefore, it is important that you keep informed about existing and anticipated conditions as you travel along your career road.

Tasks

What are some of the "uncontrollable" conditions that have affected your career?

How might you have prepared for or handled some of them more effectively?

How are you preparing for those that might occur in the future?

550. Enhancing Communication: Identifying Techniques to Use with Diverse Groups

Goals

- To enhance awareness of the need to use certain techniques to enhance communication with diverse types of people.

- To identify techniques that can be used in order to clarify communication.

Group Size

Three to six groups of approximately four members each.

Time Required

One to one and one-half hours.

Materials

- A copy of the Enhancing Communication Sheet for each participant.

- A newsprint flip chart and felt-tipped markers for each group.

- A copy of the Enhancing Communication Lecturette for the facilitator.

- A newsprint flip chart and felt-tipped markers for the facilitator.

- Masking tape for posting newsprint.

Physical Setting

A room large enough for subgroups to work without disturbing other groups. Provide a chair for each participant. Tables for the subgroups are optional.

Process

1. The facilitator introduces the activity and delivers the Enhancing Communication Lecturette. (Five minutes.)

2. The facilitator asks the participants, "What are some of the diverse types of people that could cause problems in communicating with them?" If needed, the facilitator may give one of the following as an example:

   - Those people from other cultures who have difficulty speaking the language,

   - Those people who have different orientations because of their cultural backgrounds,

   - People who have hearing or speech disabilities,

   - People who have learning disabilities or people who are illiterate/uneducated,

   - Members of the opposite sex from the speaker, and

   - People who are angry or have an argumentative attitude.

   The facilitator lists the participants' responses on a flip chart but does not discuss them in detail at this time. (Five minutes.)

3. The participants are divided into groups of approximately four members each. Each group is provided with a newsprint flip chart and felt-tipped markers. Each group is instructed to select a "scribe," who will be responsible for listing all ideas presented by group members on the flip chart and reporting them later to all participants. (Five minutes.)

4. The facilitator either assigns to each group one of the types of people identified in Step 2 or instructs each group to select a type (with no duplication among groups).

5. Each group is asked to take five minutes to brainstorm a list of techniques for communicating effectively with people in its particular type, then to take five minutes more to select its top ten tech-

niques. The group's scribe lists these on newsprint. The facilitator gives time warnings during this period. (Ten minutes.)

6. The facilitator tells the groups that they have an additional ten minutes to discuss why they would use each technique. The group scribes take notes and create lists on newsprint. (Ten minutes.)

7. At the end of the allotted time, the total group is reassembled, and the groups report on their discussions. The following procedure may be used:

   ■ Each group's scribe, in turn, announces the group's "type," one of his or her group's techniques, and the reason for it.

   ■ The facilitator lists all ideas under each "type" on newsprint. If an idea is duplicated, a check mark is placed next to it.

   ■ When all scribes have presented one idea, each presents a second. The facilitator records all ideas under each group's type.

   ■ The process is repeated until all group items have been presented and recorded.

   (Fifteen minutes to one-half hour.)

8. The facilitator notes that in most situations like the ones addressed by the groups, there are some common techniques that can aid in making communication more effective. The facilitator distributes the Enhancing Communication Sheet and discusses any items not addressed by the groups. (Five to ten minutes.)

9. The facilitator leads a discussion of the activity. The following questions may be asked:

   ■ How did it feel to focus your attention on diversity among people?

   ■ What do you now understand about potential communication difficulties with diverse types of people?

   ■ What techniques seem to you most useful to try with diverse types of people?

   ■ How can you use these techniques in your back-home and on-the-job situations?

   (Ten to fifteen minutes.)

Variations

- If the participants deal with diverse customers in their work, the focus of the activity can be on identifying customer needs and responding to them.

- The activity can be focused on working with others in a diverse work force.

- If the participants are managers or trainers, the activity may be focused on what techniques they could teach employees that would aid in communicating effectively with a diverse customer base/work force.

Submitted by Robert William Lucas.

Robert William Lucas is the manager of professional development at the national office of the American Automobile Association in Heathrow, Florida, and is the president of Bob Lucas & Associates. Mr. Lucas has over twenty-three years' experience in the training and development and management fields, is president of the Central Florida Chapter of the American Society for Training and Development, and has authored four books. His areas of expertise include management and training program development, interpersonal communication, adult learning, customer service, and employee and organizational development.

ENHANCING COMMUNICATION SHEET

Communicating with a wide variety of people is a challenge. There are numerous types of people with whom conversing and extracting meaning may be difficult. The causes of communication problems may be physical (e.g., ineffective use of the voice, eyes, arms, or hands), or skill-based (i.e., lack of knowledge about verbal and nonverbal communication skills), or emotional (e.g., issues related to culture, age, sexual preference, gender, or disability).

To effectively present information and identify the other person's needs, the following general techniques can help.

Listen actively. Take the time to practice effective listening skills by focusing on what is said by the other person and rephrasing it in your own words to see if you have interpreted it accurately. Check for understanding before making assumptions or decisions.

Act responsively. Decide whether an action is required and select the appropriate response or action.

Reduce your rate of speech. When dealing with people who have a hearing, learning, or speech-related disability or who are not native speakers of your language, slow your rate of speech. This allows better comprehension and formulation of a response.

Speak audibly and clearly but not patronizingly. Communication with people who have difficulty understanding your verbal communication can be enhanced if you clearly enunciate your words. Do not shout or exaggerate your pronunciation. This may distort your words or confuse your meaning. If the person does not have a hearing disability, it may also offend him or her.

Look directly at the person. When communicating, face the other person so that he or she can see you speak the words and watch your nonverbal facial expressions and gestures. This aids comprehension and verification of your message. Even if the person is using an interpreter or companion to assist in communication, speak to the person, not to the assistant.

Be concise. Eliminate unnecessary words and expressions and say exactly what you mean. Ask simple, open-ended questions (those that allow more than a "yes" or "no" response). In some cultures, the word "no" is used sparingly or not at all, so allow the other person to communicate unwillingness or disagreement in another way.

Have patience. Take time when communicating; do not rush the other person or interrupt or finish his or her sentences. Encourage the other person to continue.

Repeat or rephrase. If necessary, repeat your message, ensuring that it is spoken clearly and slowly. If appropriate, select shorter words. It also may be helpful to give an example, illustration, or demonstration.

Watch for nonverbal cues. Watch the person's facial expressions and body language to help gauge his or her reactions and comprehension. For example, frowning may indicate lack of comprehension as well as disagreement. In some other cultures, the typical North American speaking distance is "too close" or "not close enough" for interpersonal communication.

Keep hands and objects away from your face. Avoid masking your speech or facial messages. Obstructing the other person's view of your face may send the message that you are embarrassed, lying, or uncertain about what you are saying (or that you are rude). Keeping your face in view also makes it easier for hearing-impaired people to read your lips.

Use standard language. Avoid using contractions (e.g., don't, shouldn't, can't), slang, technical terms and jargon, acronyms, or other verbal short cuts that may be unfamiliar or annoying to the other person.

Use pauses. Allow time for comprehension and for the other person to respond or react. Also allow opportunities for questions.

Use inclusive language. Ensure that your language does not omit anyone or any group (e.g., do not refer to a group of men and women as "you guys").

Avoid demeaning terminology. Do not use terms that have negative meanings when referring to individuals or groups (e.g., handicapped, girls, retard). Do not make slurs about other cultures or beliefs.

Put messages in writing. In addition to verbally transmitting messages, provide written copies. This aids people who have difficulty interpreting spoken language by allowing future reference or translation from the material.

ENHANCING COMMUNICATION LECTURETTE

Some specific changes that are creating a need for skills in communicating with diverse types of people are as follows.

Globalization of the Economy. The lowering of worldwide trade barriers has opened new markets and allowed worldwide access in product production, sales, and service. Organizations are servicing a more diverse customer base. To compete effectively, they must increase worker knowledge of cultural differences and similarities and look for new ways of meeting customer expectations.

Women in the Work Force. Because of their rapid entry into the workplace, women's traditional roles in society have shifted. Women as colleagues and consumers are changing the ways in which organizations conduct their business.

Demographic Shifts. Longer life expectancies and the decline of births in many countries have changed population profiles. There are more older people. In some areas, there is beginning to be an acute shortage of entry-level employees. Other demographic shifts include increases in the number of minorities and people with disabilities in the business environment. These people have diverse backgrounds, orientations, ways of relating and communicating, and needs.

Changing Legal Environment. In the U.S., a number of laws have been enacted in the past decades to guarantee equal treatment and opportunity to all, regardless of race, cultural background, age, gender, disability, or religion. Intentional or unintentional violations could lead to personal and organizational liability.

551. LINES: UNDERSTANDING GOALS AND PERFORMANCE FEEDBACK

Goals

- To demonstrate the characteristics of effective feedback and how it influences performance.

- To illustrate the differences in performance based on receiving no feedback, partial feedback, and full feedback.

Group Size

Twelve to fifteen participants, divided into three subgroups of four or five members each.

Time Required

One hour to one and one-half hours.

Materials

- A copy of the Lines Characteristics of Effective Feedback Sheet for each participant.

- A newsprint flip chart and felt-tipped markers for each subgroup.

- A blindfold for each subgroup.

- A yardstick for the manager of each subgroup.

- A copy of the Lines Recording Sheet and a pencil for the manager of each subgroup.

The 1996 Annual: Volume 1, Training.
Copyright © 1996 by Pfeiffer & Company, San Diego, CA.

- A clipboard or other portable writing surface for the manager of each subgroup.
- A copy of the Lines Observer Sheet and a pencil for each subordinate.
- A newsprint flip chart and felt-tipped marker for the facilitator.
- Masking tape for posting newsprint.

Physical Setting

A room large enough to accommodate the three groups, so that each group can work without disturbing the others.

Process

1. The facilitator explains that the participants will be working in groups and will need to quickly select three "managers" to lead three groups of "subordinates."

2. As soon as the managers are identified, they are asked to select four subordinates each. (Five minutes.)

3. The facilitator asks all subordinates to stay in their groups at one end of the room and to discuss what "good feedback" is. The facilitator takes the managers to another part of the room where they cannot be overheard by the subordinates.

4. The facilitator introduces the activity to the managers: "This activity is designed to help distinguish between different types of feedback and to identify the characteristics of effective performance feedback. The task of each subordinate, in turn, will be to draw five 24-inch (61 cm) lines, one at a time, while blindfolded."

5. The facilitator assigns each manager to give one of the three types of feedback, as follows:

   - *The "no feedback" manager* will measure and record each line and simply say "continue with the next line" or "that is the last one, thank you."

   - *The "partial feedback" manager* will measure and record each line and say only "too long" or "too short," depending on the actual length of the line.

   - *The "full feedback" manager* will measure and record each line and tell the subordinate exactly how long the line is. The manager will

encourage and compliment each subordinate as his or her lines get closer to the goal of 24 inches.
(Ten minutes.)

6. After providing each manager with a newsprint flip chart, felt-tipped markers, a blindfold, a yardstick, a Lines Recording Sheet, and a pencil, the facilitator assigns each manager and his or her "subordinates" to a specific area of the room. (Five minutes.)

7. Each subordinate is given a copy of the Lines Observer Sheet and a pencil.

8. The facilitator tells the managers to begin the activity. Each manager takes the following actions:

- Invites one subordinate at a time to come to the flip chart.

- Explains to the subordinate that the goal is to draw five lines, each 24 inches (61 cm) long.

- Shows the subordinate the newsprint flip chart, gives the subordinate a felt-tipped marker, blindfolds the subordinate, and tells the subordinate to begin by drawing his or her first line.

- Measures and records each line as it is drawn and records it on the Lines Recording Sheet.

- Provides the assigned type of feedback.

(Five minutes.)

9. Each manager continues the process until all subordinates have completed five lines each. (Ten to twenty minutes.)

10. The total group is reassembled. The facilitator reviews the goals of the activity and states how each group differed in the nature of its feedback. The facilitator totals the number of "successful" (i.e., 23-25 inches long) lines for each group, lists the results on newsprint, and discusses the results. The following chart may be created:

Condition	Results	Comments
No Feedback		
Partial Feedback		
Full Feedback		

(Five minutes.)

11. The facilitator begins a discussion by asking the subordinates to report on what they observed. As key feelings and ideas are identified, the facilitator writes them next to the appropriate group's graphed results. The facilitator then asks the following questions:

- *The no feedback group.* How did you feel about your performance? How did you feel about your manager? What similar feelings have you experienced on the job? What are some examples?

- *The partial feedback group.* How did you feel about your performance? How did you feel about your manager? What similar feelings have you experienced on the job? What are some examples?

- *The full feedback group.* How did you feel about your performance? How did you feel about your manager? What similar feelings have you experienced on the job? What are some examples?

(Fifteen to twenty minutes.)

12. The facilitator leads a discussion of the characteristics of effective feedback and lists them on newsprint as each is identified. (The Lines Characteristics of Effective Feedback Sheet may be distributed to the participants at the end of the discussion.) (Ten minutes.)

13. The facilitator asks the following questions:

- What ramifications do you see in setting goals without providing feedback on goal progress?

- How would you vary the kind and amount of feedback under different conditions, for example, with a new employee or one who is learning a new task or with an experienced, motivated employee?

- What implications does this activity have for managers? What implications does this activity have in other roles you play?

- How and to whom could you improve your feedback? What, specifically, will you do to start? How will you ensure that you will follow through in providing effective feedback?

(Ten to fifteen minutes.)

Variations

- Allow the full feedback manager to provide ongoing coaching to his or her subordinates (e.g., as the subordinate draws a line, the manager says "a little longer...stop!").

- Diameters of circles or sides of squares, rectangles, or triangles can be drawn instead of lines.

- Participants can create action plans for improving their feedback with specific individuals. They may share their plans with partners.

Submitted by Michael R. Larsen.

Michael R. Larsen *is a manager of organizational development at TRW Safety Systems in Mesa, Arizona. He has developed and conducted management training programs on a variety of subjects in the Middle East, Europe, and the United States. Mr. Larsen is a faculty member with the University of Phoenix.*

LINES RECORDING SHEET

Subordinate 1	Subordinate 2	Subordinate 3	Subordinate 4
1.	1.	1.	1.
2.	2.	2.	2.
3.	3.	3.	3.
4.	4.	4.	4.
5.	5.	5.	5.

LINES OBSERVER SHEET

Please make notes on the following information as you watch the other subordinates in your group attempt to complete the task.

1. How would you describe the feedback given by your manager?

2. How did subordinates in your group respond to the feedback? What emotions did you detect?

3. How did the feedback seem to affect performance?

4. If you were the manager, how would you give feedback differently?

LINES CHARACTERISTICS OF EFFECTIVE FEEDBACK SHEET

Effective feedback is

1. **Specific.** It is explicit, free from ambiguity, and quantitative, whenever possible.

2. **Behavioral.** It is descriptive of what has been seen or heard or of results that have been evaluated thoroughly.

3. **Timely.** It is delivered soon after the performance.

4. **Frequent.** Regular feedback helps the performer to reach the desired standard of performance more quickly. It builds accountability.

5. **Balanced.** We need feedback both when performance is desirable (to help us sustain the effort) and when it is undesirable (so that we can take appropriate corrective actions).

6. **Constructive.** Feedback, particularly on undesirable performance, should be delivered in a supportive manner.

7. **Relevant.** Not all of a person's work is equally important. Most feedback should be reserved for more critical accountabilities. Its focus should be on end results or, at least, on progress toward results, not on the means of achieving them. Discussion of other issues should be avoided; it dilutes the primary feedback.

8. **Accurate.** A manager's evaluation of a subordinate's performance must be relatively precise. An accurate assessment of performance builds mutual trust and the manager's credibility.

The 1996 Annual: Volume 1, Training.
Copyright © 1996 by Pfeiffer & Company, San Diego, CA.

552. BEAN COUNTERS: ANALYZING PRODUCTION ERRORS

Goals

- To demonstrate one cause of quality variation in a production process.

- To demonstrate a situation in which a team's output problems have systemic causes.

- To stimulate group thinking about data collection to better understand process and error.

- To construct simple graphics to highlight random variations in individual or group production.

Group Size

Up to six subgroups of two to four participants each.

Time Required

One hour and forty minutes to two hours.

Materials

- A tub or deep tray filled with two types of dried beans of contrasting color and size, well mixed (e.g., lentils and black beans), in a ratio of approximately 80 percent and 20 percent.

- One scoop for each subgroup (all scoops should be the same size).

- One copy of Bean Counters Inspection Report for each subgroup.

- One copy of Bean Counters Data Sheet for each subgroup.

The 1996 Annual: Volume 1, Training.
Copyright © 1996 by Pfeiffer & Company, San Diego, CA.

- One pencil for each subgroup.
- One pocket calculator for each subgroup.
- A newsprint flip chart and a felt-tipped marker.
- Masking tape for posting newsprint.

Physical Setting

A room large enough for subgroups to work without disturbing one another.

Process

1. The participants are asked to form subgroups of two to four members each. *[Note to the facilitator: It is important not to reveal the goals of the activity at this time.]* (Five minutes.)

2. Each subgroup is given a scoop, a copy of the Bean Counters Inspection Report, a pencil, and a pocket calculator. (Five minutes.)

3. The facilitator sets the tub of dried beans in the center of the room and explains that a scoop of beans represents the end result of a production process. *[Note to the facilitator: Depending on the audience, the beans can be considered to be input, output, raw materials, etc.]* Most of the beans are acceptable products; however, some of the beans are defective products. *[Note to the facilitator: Show the types of beans that are acceptable and not acceptable products.]* He or she explains that the subgroups will be collecting data about the effectiveness of this particular production process, which is called "scooping." (Five minutes.)

4. Each subgroup is asked to designate an "inspector" and a "scooper." The scooper will retrieve a scoop of beans from the bean tub, after which the inspector will count, verify, and record the defects on the Bean Counters Inspection Report. Team members are free to collaborate and offer suggestions to one another. The facilitator answers any questions about the instructions, and the subgroups are instructed to begin. (Five minutes.)

5. Each subgroup sends its scooper to the tub for the first round of production. When he or she brings the scoopful back to the subgroup, the inspector counts the number of both types of beans and records them on the Bean Counters Inspection Report. Once counted, the inspectors return the beans to the tub. (Five to ten minutes.)

6. The facilitator polls the inspectors, asking each to record his or her subgroup's number of defects. The facilitator records the results on the newsprint flip chart and calls for a round of applause for the subgroup with the lowest number of defects. He or she then stirs the tub of beans in preparation for the next round of production. (Five minutes.)

7. Steps 5 and 6 are repeated four times, rotating the tasks of inspector and scooper among the subgroup members. (Forty to fifty minutes.)

8. The facilitator debriefs the activity by asking questions similar to the following:

   ▪ What did you notice happening during the activity? What was your reaction to that?

   ▪ What lessons about quality variation can you draw from the experience? What lessons about causes of variation in quality?

   ▪ How might you analyze the variation of results obtained for the purpose of reducing variation?

   (Ten to fifteen minutes.)

9. The facilitator gives each subgroup a copy of the Bean Counters Data Sheet and reviews the instructions. Subgroups are asked to complete the handout. (Five to ten minutes.)

10. The facilitator polls each subgroup for its results, recording the responses on newsprint. He or she leads a discussion of the variation in the results based on the following questions:

    ▪ What would you estimate to be the proportion of defects in the original supply? [*Note:* The facilitator reveals the actual answer (20 percent) after participants have made their estimates.]

    ▪ What does this suggest about the "supplier" or input quality of this production process?

    ▪ What influence did your individual efforts have on the variation in the recorded results?

    ▪ What does this suggest about the benefits of collaboration about reducing variation?

    (Ten to fifteen minutes.)

11. The facilitator then reviews the goals of the activity:

- To demonstrate one cause of quality variation in a production process.

- To demonstrate a situation in which a team's output problems have systemic causes.

- To stimulate group thinking about data collection to better understand process and error.

- To construct simple graphics to highlight random variations in individual or group production.

(Five minutes.)

Variations

- The number of rounds of production may be reduced to three if time is limited.

- Subgroups may combine their results together into various aggregate figures, such as total production, total defects, and percentage of total defects.

- Inspectors may rotate from subgroup to subgroup to ensure impartiality during the inspections.

- Other small, available materials (paper clips and safety pins, two types of candy, etc.) may be used instead of beans.

- A pillowcase may be used instead of a tub, forcing scoopers to draw a sample of beans without being able to see the supply.

References

Aguayo, R. (1990). *Dr. Deming: The American who taught the Japanese about quality.* New York: Simon & Schuster.

Walton, M. (1986). *The Deming management method.* New York: Putnam.

Submitted by W. Norman Gustafson.

W. Norman Gustafson, M.S., is a trainer, educator, and consultant. He serves as an adjunct faculty member for Fresno City College and the University of California, Davis Extension. Mr. Gustafson consults and trains in the service sector on Total Quality Management. His interests include competitive analysis, customer surveys, and systems theory for organizational change. In addition, he does research in the content analysis of competition and participates in Lakewood Research's annual survey of trainers.

BEAN COUNTERS INSPECTION REPORT

Instructions: For each round, record the number of acceptable beans and the number of defective beans in the appropriate columns.

ROUND	# of acceptable products	# of defective products
1		
2		
3		
4		
5		

BEAN COUNTERS DATA SHEET

Instructions: For each round, calculate the percentage of defective products. This calculation is the result of adding together the number of acceptable products and the number of defective products to get a total. The number of defective products is divided by the total in order to determine the percentage of defective products. After calculating this figure for all five rounds, graph the percentage of defective products on the graph at the bottom of the page.

ROUND	(A) #of acceptable products	(B) # of defective products	(C) total # of products (A + B)	(D) % of defective products (B/D)
Example:	35	4	39	10%
1				
2				
3				
4				
5				

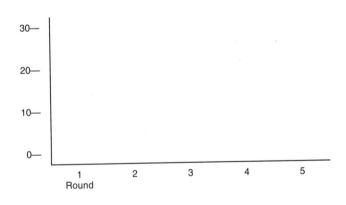

% of
defective
products

553. Bugs: Improving Customer Service

Goals

- To help the participants to identify universal problems in customer service.
- To enhance the participants' awareness of their own responses to customer service issues.
- To offer the participants the opportunity to share ideas about dealing with customer service problems.

Group Size

Twelve to twenty participants in subgroups of four or five members each.

Time Required

One hour and one-half hours to two hours.

Materials

- One pad of Post-it™ Notes for each participant.
- A pencil for each participant.
- Several sheets of newsprint and a felt-tipped marker for each subgroup.
- A newsprint flip chart and a felt-tipped marker for the facilitator's use.
- Masking tape for posting newsprint.

The 1996 Annual: Volume 1, Training.
Copyright © 1996 by Pfeiffer & Company, San Diego, CA.

Physical Setting

Any room in which the group can work comfortably and which has ample space for posting newsprint. Movable chairs should be provided.

Process

1. The facilitator introduces the goals of the activity and distributes a pad of Post-it™ Notes and a pencil to each participant. He or she gives the following instructions:

   "Think about times in the past when you have been annoyed by poor customer service. These can be very specific instances, or general annoyances, such as unfriendly clerks. Write each customer service 'bug' or annoyance on a separate Post-it™ Note sheet. You will have five minutes to complete this portion of the activity."

   (Five minutes.)

2. After five minutes, the facilitator calls time and reconvenes the total group. He or she goes around the group, asking each person in turn to come to the flip chart, name annoyances that they have experienced, and attach their Post-it™ Notes to the flip chart page. If more than one participant has written the same annoyance, their Post-it™ Notes can be pasted on top of each other. The facilitator provides new flip chart pages as needed, posting the filled sheets around the room. (Twenty to thirty minutes.)

3. When all of the Post-it™ Notes have been collected, the facilitator leads the participants in clustering and naming the clusters. He or she posts clean flip chart pages for the clusters (e.g., the ones that deal with waiting, the ones about product knowledge, etc.) and moves the Post-it™ Notes to the appropriate page. (Ten to fifteen minutes.)

4. When all of the annoyances have been grouped, the participants are asked to form subgroups of four or five members each. Each subgroup chooses to work with one of the clusters of annoyances. (Five minutes.)

5. Each subgroup is given the appropriate cluster of Post-it™ Notes, several sheets of newsprint, and a felt-tipped marker. The facilitator instructs the subgroups to accomplish two goals:

   ■ Draw a service "bug," an animal that represents that particular annoyance. This service "bug" should be given a name (e.g., Slowmotionitis or Idunno bug) and a description of its characteristics should be listed on the newsprint. If desired, the Post-it™ Notes may be used as part of the composition of the drawing.

- Brainstorm solutions to combat this type of service "bug" in your organizations and list these on another sheet of newsprint.

(Twenty minutes.)

6. The facilitator reconvenes the total group. Each subgroup posts its "bug" creation, describes its characteristics, and presents ideas for how to prevent it. (Fifteen to twenty minutes.)

7. The facilitator leads a concluding discussion based on the following questions:

- What similarities did you identify in these "bugs?" What differences did you notice? How do you account for the differences?

- Which of the approaches to satisfying customers appeal to you as a customer? Which do not? What are some reasons for the differences in your reactions?

- What is the most important thing you have learned about customer service?

- What new thoughts do you want to adopt? What new behaviors do you want to try in dealing with customers?

(Fifteen minutes.)

Variations

- Subgroups could name the bugs without drawing them.

- Participants could name and post their annoyances one at a time, with those already posted not being repeated.

- If extra time is allotted, subgroups could decide on the solution they think best from the brainstorming and develop a plan to implement the solution.

Submitted by James W. Kinneer.

James W. Kinneer, M.A., is a support services supervisor at Indiana Hospital, Indiana, Pennsylvania. He has developed and presented numerous human resource development activities specific to the needs of the healthcare and hospitality industries. Presently he serves as chair of the

Certifying Board for Dietary Managers. He frequently contributes to national publications on the topics of managing skills, quality improvement, team building, and customer service.

554: THE PROPERTY GAME: EXPLORING MOTIVATION TO WORK

Goal

- To explore the effects of various incentives and dis-incentives to work.

Group Size

Optimum group size is twenty participants.

Time Required

One hour to one hour and forty-five minutes.

Materials

- One copy of The Property Game Instruction Sheet for each participant.

- A different Property Game Deed Card and Property Game Worker Card for each participant.

- One poster-sized copy of The Property Game Map of the Town, pre-pared in advance. (See Instruction Sheet for map.)

- One poster-sized copy of The Property Game Tally Sheet, prepared in advance.

- One calculator.

- A newsprint flip chart and felt-tipped markers.

- Masking tape.

The 1996 Annual: Volume 1, Training.
Copyright © 1996 by Pfeiffer & Company, San Diego, CA.

Physical Setting

A room large enough for participants to walk quickly around the room in a repeated pattern. The "lane" for walking (wide enough for several participants) should be marked with masking tape prior to the activity.

Process

1. The facilitator introduces the activity, but does not state the goal. Each participant is given a copy of The Property Game Instruction Sheet, a Property Game Deed Card, and a Property Game Worker Card, and is instructed to read the handouts. (Five minutes.)

2. While the participants are reading their handouts, the facilitator posts The Property Game Map of the Town, prepared in advance.

3. To begin Stage 1, the facilitator announces the following: "Each participant has been allocated a plot of land with specific fertility and each participant has been assigned a certain working ability. In order to simulate production of the land, each participant must walk quickly (not run) around the perimeter of the room, following the route indicated by masking tape. However, you may not earn more money per circuit than whichever is the lower amount of your fertility and working ability. For example, if your land fertility is $10, and your working ability is $20, you may not earn more than $10 per circuit— the lower of the two amounts. You will have one minute to try to produce as much as possible as quickly as possible." (Five minutes.)

4. The participants are lined up at the Map of the Town, and each begins to walk around the room to simulate production.

5. At the end of one minute, the facilitator announces that the work period, symbolizing a year, is over. Each participant announces his or her total production (circuits made), which the facilitator records on The Property Game Tally Sheet. (Five minutes.)

6. The total productivity of all workers—the gross national product (GNP)—is calculated, announced, and divided evenly among the participants, regardless of fertility and/or work accomplished. Each participant's bank account is credited with the calculated amount. (Five to ten minutes.)

7. Steps 4 through 6 are repeated twice. (Although there is no incentive to work hard, it will take time before most participants realize the absence of incentives. Eventually, no one will work very hard, because

the redistribution of GNP is mandated and the participants' pay is unrelated to work effort.) (Ten to twenty minutes.)

8. To begin Stage II, the facilitator posts the following notice: "The settlement has switched to a capitalist economy—pay for production." The facilitator announces that this means that, from now on, each participant can keep what he or she earns.

9. Two more rounds of the circuit activity are conducted. Tallies are recorded, and payoffs are made according to the new rules. (As participants perceive that they now have the opportunity to accumulate wealth, there is an incentive to produce, and the total GNP usually rises.) (Ten to twenty minutes.)

10. To begin Stage III, the facilitator posts the following: "To increase your wealth, the settlement has decided that you may now transfer your plots. Find someone to trade with, exchange deeds, and use the money credited in your bank account, if necessary. If you need more money, the settlement will provide interest-free loans." (It is expected that trading of deeds will take place in order to match land fertility and working ability.) (Ten to fifteen minutes.)

11. Two more rounds of the circuit activity, tally, and payoff are conducted. (Ten to twenty minutes.)

12. The facilitator leads a total-group discussion of the activity, beginning by stating its goal. The following may be included:

■ How did you feel about the distribution of wealth in the first rounds of the activity? Were you motivated to work or demotivated? Why?

■ How did you feel when capitalism was introduced and you could keep your earnings? Did your attitude or behavior change? How and why?

■ How did you feel about the opportunity to trade plots? What did you do about it? How was your interaction with others? How did all this affect your motivation to work? How can you identify with this in your work place?

■ What did you learn about the effect of property and the distribution of wealth on motivation to work?

■ What implications does this have for how you can motivate others?

The facilitator may refer to the tally sheet to note production trends, etc., during the discussion. (Fifteen to twenty minutes.)

Variations

- The activity can be conducted with more than twenty participants by using two-person teams: one person walking (a "worker") and the other recording the production (a "manager"). This also adds a competitive dynamic, matching teams against one another.

- If the activity is to be conducted with fewer than twenty participants, the following table can be used to determine which plots of land should be abandoned:

18 participants = omit Plots 15 and 20.
16 participants = omit Plots 9, 14, 15, and 20.
14 participants = omit Plots 5, 8, 9, 14, 15, and 20.
12 participants = omit Plots 1, 4, 5, 8, 9, 14, 15, and 20.
10 participants = omit Plots 1, 2, 3, 4, 5, 8, 9, 14, 15, and 20.

- Other variations can be introduced, such as zoning ordinances that allow trading in one-half of the town and prohibit it in the other half, income taxes, a limit on the amount of loans, and so on.

Submitted by Tom G. Geurts and Austin J. Jaffe.[1]

Tom G. Geurts is a doctoral student in the Department of Insurance and Real Estate at The Pennsylvania State University, University Park, Pennsylvania. He has master's degrees in economics and political science from the University of Amsterdam, The Netherlands. Mr. Geurts has teaching experience and is the author of five academic publications.

Austin J. Jaffe, Ph.D., is the Philip H. Sieg Professor of Business Administration and the research director of the Institute for Real Estate Studies of the Smeal College of Business Administration, The Pennsylvania State University, University Park, Pennsylvania. He also is the president of JS & Associates, a real estate software firm. Dr. Jaffe has held faculty appointments at three international universities, has been invited to present papers at more than seventy-five institutions in twenty-five countries, and has served as a consultant to The World Bank, the Federal Home Loan Bank Board, and other institutions. He is the author or coauthor of nine books in the areas of real estate and economics.

---

[1] An article explaining the use of an expanded version of this activity in real-estate, business, and economics training can be found in Tom G. Geurts and Austin J. Jaffe (1995, November), "The Property Rights Game: Discovering the Meaning of Private Property," *Journal of Real Estate Finance and Economics, 11.*

THE PROPERTY GAME INSTRUCTION SHEET

This activity takes you back to the year 1621. A year ago, the first settlers, brought by the "Mayflower," landed in the New World. You belong to the second group of settlers, aboard the "Juneflower," and you are determined to start a new and prosperous life. The leaders of the settlement have decided the following:

■ The land in the settlement will be divided into twenty-one plots. On plot 0, the Town Hall will be built. The remaining plots will be allocated to participants.

Map of the Town

Plot 1	Plot 2	Town Hall		Plot 3	Plot 4
Plot 5	Plot 6	(Plot 0)		Plot 7	Plot 8
Plot 9	Plot 10	Plot 11	Plot 12	Plot 13	Plot 14
Plot 15	Plot 16	Plot 17	Plot 18	Plot 19	Plot 20

■ You will receive a Deed, which is proof of ownership of your plot of land. The Deed also shows the level of fertility of your land. In addition, you will receive a Worker Card that indicates your working ability.

■ In order to prosper in this New World, you need to produce something using the land. Working is simulated by walking around a circuit in the room. You will have one minute to earn as much as possible, based on your production.

■ However, your production will be the lower number of your land fertility and working ability. For example, for Plot 1, the land fertility equals $1, and the working ability equals $10. Thus, for every circuit completed, the production value is $1.

■ It is expected that all participants will report their number of circuits honestly.

PROPERTY GAME DEED CARD

Plot 1 is assigned to you. This is your deed of ownership.
The fertility of your land is assessed at $1.

PROPERTY GAME WORKER CARD

#1: Your working ability is $10 per circuit.

PROPERTY GAME DEED CARD

Plot 2 is assigned to you. This is your deed of ownership.
The fertility of your land is assessed at $10.

PROPERTY GAME WORKER CARD

#2: Your working ability is $20 per circuit.

PROPERTY GAME DEED CARD

Plot 3 is assigned to you. This is your deed of ownership.
The fertility of your land is assessed at $20.

PROPERTY GAME WORKER CARD

#3: Your working ability is $10 per circuit.

PROPERTY GAME DEED CARD

Plot 4 is assigned to you. This is your deed of ownership.
The fertility of your land is assessed at $10.

PROPERTY GAME WORKER CARD

#4: Your working ability is $1 per circuit.

PROPERTY GAME DEED CARD

Plot 5 is assigned to you. This is your deed of ownership.
The fertility of your land is assessed at $5.

PROPERTY GAME WORKER CARD

#5: Your working ability is $20 per circuit.

PROPERTY GAME DEED CARD

Plot 6 is assigned to you. This is your deed of ownership.
The fertility of your land is assessed at $5.

PROPERTY GAME WORKER CARD

#6: Your working ability is $20 per circuit.

Property Game Deed Card

Plot 7 is assigned to you. This is your deed of ownership.
The fertility of your land is assessed at $20.

Property Game Worker Card

#7: Your working ability is $5 per circuit.

Property Game Deed Card

Plot 8 is assigned to you. This is your deed of ownership.
The fertility of your land is assessed at $20.

Property Game Worker Card

#8: Your working ability is $5 per circuit.

PROPERTY GAME DEED CARD

Plot 9 is assigned to you. This is your deed of ownership.
The fertility of your land is assessed at $1.

PROPERTY GAME WORKER CARD

#9: Your working ability is $10 per circuit.

PROPERTY GAME DEED CARD

Plot 10 is assigned to you. This is your deed of ownership.
The fertility of your land is assessed at $1.

PROPERTY GAME WORKER CARD

#10: Your working ability is $10 per circuit.

PROPERTY GAME DEED CARD

Plot 11 is assigned to you. This is your deed of ownership.
The fertility of your land is assessed at $10.

PROPERTY GAME WORKER CARD

#11: Your working ability is $20 per circuit.

PROPERTY GAME DEED CARD

Plot 12 is assigned to you. This is your deed of ownership.
The fertility of your land is assessed at $10.

PROPERTY GAME WORKER CARD

#12: Your working ability is $1 per circuit.

PROPERTY GAME DEED CARD

Plot 13 is assigned to you. This is your deed of ownership. The fertility of your land is assessed at $20.

PROPERTY GAME WORKER CARD

#13: Your working ability is $10 per circuit.

PROPERTY GAME DEED CARD

Plot 14 is assigned to you. This is your deed of ownership. The fertility of your land is assessed at $10.

PROPERTY GAME WORKER CARD

#14: Your working ability is $1 per circuit.

PROPERTY GAME DEED CARD

Plot 15 is assigned to you. This is your deed of ownership.
The fertility of your land is assessed at $10.

The 1996 Annual: Volume 1, Training.
Copyright © 1996 by Pfeiffer & Company, San Diego, CA.

PROPERTY GAME WORKER CARD

#15: Your working ability is $20 per circuit.

The 1996 Annual: Volume 1, Training.
Copyright © 1996 by Pfeiffer & Company, San Diego, CA.

PROPERTY GAME DEED CARD

Plot 16 is assigned to you. This is your deed of ownership.
The fertility of your land is assessed at $5.

The 1996 Annual: Volume 1, Training.
Copyright © 1996 by Pfeiffer & Company, San Diego, CA.

PROPERTY GAME WORKER CARD

#16: Your working ability is $20 per circuit.

The 1996 Annual: Volume 1, Training.
Copyright © 1996 by Pfeiffer & Company, San Diego, CA.

Property Game Deed Card

Plot 17 is assigned to you. This is your deed of ownership.
The fertility of your land is assessed at $20.

Property Game Worker Card

#17: Your working ability is $5 per circuit.

Property Game Deed Card

Plot 18 is assigned to you. This is your deed of ownership.
The fertility of your land is assessed at $1.

Property Game Worker Card

#18: Your working ability is $10 per circuit.

PROPERTY GAME DEED CARD

Plot 19 is assigned to you. This is your deed of ownership.
The fertility of your land is assessed at $10.

PROPERTY GAME WORKER CARD

#19: Your working ability is $1 per circuit.

PROPERTY GAME DEED CARD

Plot 20 is assigned to you. This is your deed of ownership.
The fertility of your land is assessed at $20.

PROPERTY GAME WORKER CARD

#20: Your working ability is $10 per circuit.

THE PROPERTY GAME TALLY SHEET

Plot and $	Circuits Per Round						
Plot 1: $1							
Plot 2: $10							
Plot 3: $10							
Plot 4: $1							
Plot 5: $5							
Plot 6: $5							
Plot 7: $5							
Plot 8: $5							
Plot 9: $1							
Plot 10: $1							
Plot 11: $10							
Plot 12: $1							
Plot 13: $10							
Plot 14: $1							
Plot 15: $10							
Plot 16: $5							
Plot 17: $5							
Plot 18: $1							
Plot 19: $1							
Plot 20: $10							

The 1996 Annual: Volume 1, Training.
Copyright © 1996 by Pfeiffer & Company, San Diego, CA.

555. THE RIVER OF CHANGE: EXPLORING COPING SKILLS

Goals

- To review changes experienced by the participants during the past year.

- To introduce Bridges' view of the change process.

- To explore the process of individual change by identifying change events, accompanying emotions, and typical patterns of coping.

- To anticipate changes the participants may experience in the next year and how they may better cope with them.

Group Size

Twelve to fifteen participants.

Time Required

One and one-half to two and one-half hours.

Materials

- A copy of the River of Change Lecturette for each participant and the facilitator.

- A sheet of newsprint flip-chart paper for each participant.

- Several felt-tipped markers of different colors for each participant.

- A newsprint flip chart and felt-tipped markers for the facilitator.

- Masking tape for posting newsprint.

The 1996 Annual: Volume 1, Training.
Copyright © 1996 by Pfeiffer & Company, San Diego, CA.

Physical Setting

Table space and a chair for each participant. Enough wall space to post the pictures created by the participants.

Process

1. The facilitator states that the activity will explore the process of change and is divided into two parts: in the first part, individuals will work on their own; in the second part, they will work in pairs or trios.

2. Each participant receives a sheet of newsprint flip-chart paper and several felt-tipped markers. The facilitator asks that each participant draw a river depicting the changes he or she has experienced in the past year, with a major focus on the change that was most significant or most impacted the participant. The change may be in the participant's personal or work life. Participants are instructed to recall the emotions involved and how they coped with their changes. The facilitator encourages the participants to be creative. Incidents or emotions in their rivers may be depicted as rocks, waterfalls, whirlpools, dams, storms, etc. (Fifteen to twenty minutes.)

3. The facilitator calls time. All pictures are posted on the wall in a gallery format. The facilitator asks for a volunteer to share his or her picture with the rest of the group, describing his or her major change, emotions, and coping mechanisms. Each participant is asked to share in the same manner. (Fifteen to forty-five minutes.)

4. As individuals share their changes, the facilitator records on the flip chart the changes, emotions, and coping mechanisms that have been mentioned. If a change, emotion, or coping mechanism is mentioned more than once, a check mark is put next to it each additional time it is mentioned. The flip chart may be set up as shown on the next page.

5. The facilitator leads the total group in discussing the activity. The following questions may be used:

   ▪ How did it feel to recall the changes you have experienced?

   ▪ Which changes happened to the most people?

   ▪ What emotions did most people experience?

   ▪ What techniques did most people use to cope with the changes?

   (Ten minutes.)

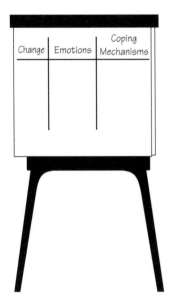

Change	Emotions	Coping Mechanisms

6. The facilitator distributes a copy of the River of Change Lecturette to each participant and delivers it orally. (Five minutes.)

7. The facilitator solicits the participants' responses to the River of Change Lecturette and Bridges' view of change in light of what participants have reported about emotions and coping mechanisms. (Five to ten minutes.)

8. Participants are directed to form pairs or trios. The facilitator tells them to discuss the following (and posts the list on newsprint where all can see it):

- What patterns they see in their rivers in terms of how they coped with their changes;

- How they feel about those patterns;

- What they would like to change about those patterns; and

- How each of them can cope more effectively with an upcoming change.

(Fifteen minutes.)

9. The total group is reassembled, and the partners/triads report their common patterns and what they would change about those patterns. The facilitator records this information on the flip chart, as follows:

Coping Mechanisms	Common Patterns	Intended Changes

(Ten to fifteen minutes.)

10. The facilitator leads a discussion of the second half of the activity. The following questions may be used:

- What seems to be the most common pattern in coping with change? Which patterns seem to be unique? What does that suggest to you?

- What changes in coping mechanisms were suggested by most people? How do you react to that?

- What did you learn about yourself in this activity?

- What did you learn about change in this activity?

- Which coping mechanism do you predict will be the most helpful to you in the next year? How can you support yourself in using it?

(Fifteen minutes.)

Variations

- With intact work groups or with people who work in the same part of an organization, the entire activity can be completed in small groups. Only work-related changes are used.

- As a final step, each participant can create a written action plan for how to cope with an anticipated change.

- As a final step, the participants may choose others who will be experiencing similar changes and contract to provide support and encouragement to one another. (Ten to fifteen minutes.)

- Participants can use the metaphor of a bridge instead of a river to focus on how best to make the transition to change. They can be asked to draw the "ending" as one end of the bridge, the "beginning" as the other end of the bridge, the river as the emotions experienced in the change, and the bridge span as the coping mechanism.

Submitted by Mary Sue Barry.

Mary Sue Barry is the owner of Full-Circle Training and Consulting in St. Petersburg, Florida. The firm specializes in service industries. Ms. Barry has over fifteen years' experience as an internal consultant, designing and facilitating management and leadership-development programs and OD interventions. She specializes in negotiating skills, interviewing skills, and quality action teams. She is an active member of the American Society for Training and Development (ASTD).

River of Change Lecturette

When people are faced with adjusting to change, a crisis often develops. For some individuals, change is a challenge; for others, it is a threat. Even changes we choose, such as marriage, having children, returning to school, and taking a new job, require some adaptation. One set of circumstances is ending while another set is beginning.

The Chinese language has no one symbol for change. It requires two characters: one is the symbol for opportunity, the other is the symbol for danger or risk. All change, personal or organizational, carries both opportunity and risk.

The change cycle, as described by William Bridges[1], begins with endings. Endings are followed by a transition period, which can be a difficult time. We must let go of the past, as it no longer exists, and the future is uncertain. The final stage of change is the new beginning. We are energized by the future and move forward with anticipation of positive outcomes.

As people progress through the cycle of change, they experience the emotions associated with the grieving process. Denial, disbelief, anger, anxiety, confusion, and bargaining lead to fear, uncertainty, and feeling lost and unattached, which turn into enthusiasm, hope, interest, assimilation, energy, and a sense of belonging.

No one change happens in a vacuum; as we are asked to change at work, there are changes happening in our personal lives. Most of us can deal with a few minor changes at the same time, but as the number of changes we face builds up, our tolerance and ability to adapt gives out. It is much like a house of cards. Things are going along fine until a card is placed on top and the structure collapses.

We may think that others are better or worse at coping with change in general. It is important to remember that each of us has our own frame of reference—how we view the world, how we make judgements, and how we place value on things. The challenge is to find coping mechanisms that can help us perceive and deal with the changes in our lives. One way of doing that is to look at past changes and examine how we perceived them and how we coped with them. A pattern will surface as we examine several past changes in our lives. By examining our patterns and discussing them with others, we can take the first step in improving our ability to deal with change.

---

[1] Based on William W. Bridges (1991), *Managing Transitions: Making the Most of Change.* Reading, MA: Addison-Wesley.

556. FEEDBACK LETTERS: ACHIEVING CLOSURE

Goals

- To offer group members an opportunity at the conclusion of their group experience to share feedback about the role(s) that each member assumed.

- To offer a forum for resolving and providing closure to any unfinished business in the group.

- To ease the members' transition out of the group.

- To provide the members with an opportunity to practice giving and receiving feedback.

Group Size

All members (maximum fifteen) of a group that is about to disband (for example, a task force, a project team, or a reengineering team that has completed its assignment). The group needs to have had basic training in group dynamics and communication skills.

Time Required

Thirty-five minutes to one hour and fifteen minutes (excluding prework), depending on the size of the group.

Materials

- A copy of the Feedback Letters Template for each group member.

The 1996 Annual: Volume 1, Training.
Copyright © 1996 by Pfeiffer & Company, San Diego, CA.

- Each group member's completed letters to all group members.
- A pad of paper and a pencil for each group member.

Physical Setting

A room large enough to accommodate a number of two-person conversations simultaneously in such a way that each pair is afforded a degree of privacy. Or the facilitator may have the group members meet in a new and very different setting for the feedback session, for example, in a park.

Process

1. At least a week before the feedback session, the facilitator assembles the group members, describes the activity and its goals, gives each member a copy of the Feedback Letters Template, and reviews the template content. Questions are elicited and answered. The facilitator emphasizes that each member should write honest feedback for every member, including himself or herself, using the template content as a guide. The group members also are encouraged to be creative and include any comments they wish in addition to completing the sentence stems. Each member is instructed to bring all of the completed letters, including the one to himself or herself, to the feedback session.

2. At the beginning of the feedback session, the facilitator asks the members to distribute the letters they have written to others, to read the ones they receive, and to seek out the authors for clarification/discussion at their own discretion. Each member is given a pad of paper and a pencil for making notes as desired. The members are encouraged to ask for clarification of any points of confusion and to resolve any unresolved feelings. The facilitator states that he or she will be available for help with any part of this feedback process. (Ten to forty-five minutes.)

3. The facilitator asks the members to reread the letters they wrote to themselves and to compare the content of these letters with the feedback received from others. (Ten minutes.)

4. The facilitator leads a discussion about the activity by asking the following questions:
   - How did it feel to write the letters to others? How did it feel to write feedback to yourself?

- What are your reactions to the feedback you received from others?

- What similarities and differences are there between your view of yourself (as shown in the letter you wrote yourself) and the feedback you received from others?

- What did you learn about yourself and your roles during your discussions with your fellow group members? What did you learn about your fellow members? What did you learn about giving and receiving feedback?

- What are your feelings now about leaving the group? What would you like to say to your fellow members now?

- How will you apply what you have learned about yourself in future group experiences?

(Fifteen to twenty minutes.)

Variations

- The facilitator may change the sentence stems on the Feedback Letters Template to reflect the situations, conditions, or events in the particular group.

- The group may design its own feedback letter.

- Each group member may be asked to include a letter to the facilitator.

- Step 2 may be made more structured by having each member talk with every other member about the feedback letters.

Submitted by Gary Wagenheim and Gary Gemmill.

Gary Wagenheim is an associate professor of organizational leadership at Purdue University. He teaches courses in applied leadership, entrepreneurship, and human relations. Prior to his academic appointment he founded a seven-store retail-clothing chain, operated it for thirteen years, and subsequently sold it to employees. He has worked as an organizational consultant in the areas of team management, leadership, and strategic planning. Professor Wagenheim has also received numerous teaching awards and has published articles in The Journal of Management Education, *Pfeiffer & Company's* Annual *Series,* The Teaching Professor, *and* The Facilitator. *In addition, he presents workshops on teaching at a number of international conferences.*

Gary Gemmill, Ph.D., *is a professor emeritus of organizational behavior in the School of Management at Syracuse University, where he has taught applied group dynamics and interpersonal skills for the past twenty-eight years. Currently he consults with the top-management groups of diverse organizations in the area of team dynamics and leads workshops in personal growth. He has published many professional articles on the psychodynamics of groups and human growth in* Human Relations, Consultation, Group & Organization Studies, *and* Small Group Research.

Additional information about the use of this activity may be found in "Feedback Exchange: Managing Group Closure" by G. Wagenheim and G. Gemmill, 1994, *Journal of Management Education, 18*(2), 265-269.

FEEDBACK LETTERS TEMPLATE

[Date]

Dear [Name],

The way I experienced your behavior in the group is...

What I personally think that you contributed to the group is...

The role that I think you played in the group is...

Something that you might do in future groups to improve your effectiveness as a member would be...

A symbolic gift that I would like to give you for use in future groups is...

[Other comments]

Sincerely,
[Your name, address, and phone number]

Introduction
to the Inventories, Questionnaires, and Surveys Section

Inventories, questionnaires, and surveys are feedback tools that help respondents to understand how a particular theory applies to their own lives. Understanding the theories involved in the dynamics of their own group situations increases respondents' involvement. Instruments allow the facilitator of a small group to focus the energies and time of the respondents on the most appropriate material and also to direct, to some extent, the matters that are dealt with in a session. In this way, the facilitator can ensure that the issues worked on are crucial, existing ones, rather than the less important ones that the members may introduce to avoid grappling with the more uncomfortable issues.

The contents of the Inventories, Questionnaires, and Surveys section are provided for training and development purposes. These instruments are not intended for in-depth personal growth, psychodiagnostic, or therapeutic work. Instead, they are intended for use in training groups; for demonstration purposes; to generate data for training or organization development sessions; and for other group applications in which the trainer, consultant, or facilitator helps respondents to use the data generated by an instrument for achieving some form of progress.

Each instrument includes the theory necessary for understanding, presenting, and using it. All interpretive information, scales or inventory forms, and scoring sheets are also provided for each instrument. In addition, Pfeiffer & Company publishes all of the reliability and validity data contributed by the authors of instruments; if readers want additional information on reliability and validity, they are encouraged to contact instrument authors directly. (Authors' addresses and telephone numbers appear in the Contributors list that follows the Presentation and Discussion Resources section.)

Other assessment tools that address certain goals (and experiential learning activities and presentation/discussion resources to accompany them) can be located by using our comprehensive *Reference Guide to Handbooks and Annuals*. This book, which is updated regularly, indexes all of the *Annuals* and all of the *Handbooks of Structured Experiences* that we have published to date. With each revision, the *Reference Guide* becomes a complete, up-to-date, and easy-to-use resource for selecting appropriate materials from *all* of the *Annuals* and *Handbooks*.

The 1996 Annual: Volume 1, Training includes three assessment tools in the following categories:

Individual Development

The Career-Dimension Survey: Asking the Right Career-Development Questions, by Caela Farren and Beverly Kaye (page 123)

Consulting and Facilitating

Instructional Styles Diagnosis Inventory: Increasing Style Awareness and Flexibility, by Greg Cripple (page 139)

The Big Five Locator: A Quick Assessment Tool for Consultants and Trainers, by Pierce J. Howard, Phyllis L. Medina, and Jane Mitchell Howard (page 107)

THE BIG FIVE LOCATOR: A QUICK ASSESSMENT TOOL FOR CONSULTANTS AND TRAINERS

Pierce J. Howard, Phyllis L. Medina, and Jane Mitchell Howard

Abstract: Instruments based on individual trait theory tend to be cumbersome and to take a long time to complete and score. The Big Five Locator is a quick and easy-to-use instrument designed to be used by a consultant or trainer with a willing client who desires a quick assessment of his or her individual traits. It also can be used to assess team traits.

The instrument is based on the traditional five-factor model (FFM). The bipolar factors measured are negative emotionality (resilient, responsive, reactive); extraversion (introvert, ambivert, extravert); openness (preserver, moderate, explorer); agreeableness (challenger, negotiator, adapter); and conscientiousness (flexible, balanced, focused). The scoring is simple, and the validity and reliability are sufficient to warrant use of the instrument in a training or consulting context.

$$T$$he organization development (OD) consultant and professional development trainer have a common need: occasionally they would like to have a quick means to assess the personality of a client. However, most instruments take twenty minutes or longer to complete, and to pull one out in the middle of an interview or training session would be awkward. Therefore, one needs a tool that takes only two or three minutes to complete, that is valid and reliable, and that can be scored quickly and on the spot. The Big Five Locator fills this need.

FUNDAMENTAL THEORY

Over the past decade, trait theory has regained the interest of personality researchers. One model in particular, the five-factor model (FFM), has received the most attention because of its ability to withstand every kind of statistical analysis using modern, high-speed computers (Goldberg, 1993; Barrick & Mount, 1991; Digman, 1990).

The FFM—popularly referred to as the Big Five—is founded in the tradition of the lexical hypothesis (Galton, 1884), which postulates that single terms are encoded and used in all languages to describe the most important individual differences. Pioneering researchers, stimulated by the lexical hypothesis, conducted exhaustive searches through English dictionaries in attempts to glean from them personality-descriptive terms (see John, Angleitner, & Ostendorf, 1988, for a historical review of the model). Through these efforts, it was found that people describe themselves and others in terms of five fundamental dimensions of individual difference. These dimensions are:

Negative Emotionality: adjustment versus emotional instability, an individual's resilience in the face of unpleasant and disturbing emotions, reliance on rational processes, resistance to excessive cravings or urges, and use of constructive coping responses. (Note: In the research literature, this dimension has been referred to as neuroticism, but, in the process of adapting the model from academic and clinical uses to those of the business world, we prefer this less clinical term.

Extraversion: preference for social interaction and lively activity, one's need for stimulation and capacity for joy.

Openness: one's receptiveness to, or tolerance of, new ideas, experiences, and approaches; proactive seeking and appreciation of experience for its own sake.

Pfeiffer & Company

Agreeableness: the quality of one's interpersonal orientation along a continuum from compassion to antagonism in thoughts, feelings, and actions.

Conscientiousness: an individual's degree of organization, persistence, and motivation in goal-directed behavior; contrasts dependable, fastidious people with those who are spontaneous and unorganized.

DESCRIPTION OF THE INSTRUMENT

Format

It has been shown that the five dimensions of the FFM—negative emotionality, extraversion, openness, agreeableness, and conscientiousness—are normally distributed among the population (Costa & McCrae, 1992; McCrae & Costa, 1990). That is, the five dimensions identify domains that vary from person to person rather than define all-or-nothing categories into which some people fall and others do not. For this reason, a bipolar, adjective-pair format was selected for use in the Big Five Locator. The format utilizes adjective pairs that represent opposite poles of a single continuum. A five-point scale is presented between the adjectives, and the respondent is instructed to mark the spot on the continuum that is most descriptive of him or her.

Validity

The adjective pairs selected for the Big Five Locator were obtained through an extensive review of the literature. Because of the academic and clinical orientation of the literature, care was taken to select personality-descriptive adjectives that are found in typical business communications. The instrument developers field tested a large pool of items and selected those items that make the greatest contribution to validity and reliability.

The *NEO PI-R* currently is the best measure of the FFM's five dimensions of personality (McCrae & Costa, 1990), and provides the reference by which to establish the construct validity of the desired subset. After several revisions, the current form of the Locator was determined. It contains twenty-five pairs of bipolar adjectives or phrases that correlate with the five NEO factors at .40.

Reliability

Test-retest was utilized to establish the reliability of the Big Five Locator. Thirty adults, ranging in age from twenty-two to forty-six, completed the Big Five Locator form twice, one week apart. The coefficients of reliability resulting from the test-retest sample indicate that the Big Five Locator is sufficiently reliable ($r \geq .728$) for its intended purpose. Coefficient alpha, a measure of internal consistency, was as follows: N = .63, E = .77, O = .69, A = .74, and C = .75 (n = 110).

SUGGESTED USES

Personality-test scores have become useful adjuncts to the information that OD consultants and trainers garner during interviews and other forms of data collection. The Big Five Locator allows comprehensive assessment of normal adult personality. In providing a quick, general look at the "whole person," the Big Five Locator can be used to facilitate training and consulting and to provide a means of quick intervention during communication problems that stem from identifiable individual differences. Use of the Big Five Locator is ideal for consultants and trainers who are proficient in applying the FFM but do not have the time or financial resources to conduct more extensive evaluation of clients' personalities. Some situations in which such knowledge would be helpful include the following:

- A consultant is confronted with two clients who do not understand their source of conflict or who do not acknowledge each others' opinions or perspectives.

- Over lunch during a training program, a trainee asks for insight into his or her behavior or personality.

- Team members request an evaluation that will aid their understanding of personality differences within the team.

- A consultant or trainer is asked to work with a nonprofit group that cannot afford to use a commercial instrument.

Because of its effectiveness and ease of use, the Big Five Locator provides a quick solution to unexpected or resource-limited situations in which proper identification of individual differences would prove to be beneficial.

LIMITATIONS

Despite the fact that the Big Five Locator provides a brief, comprehensive measure of the five dimensions of personality, care must be taken in using it. Limitations do exist. For instance, the instrument does not provide the validity and reliability obtained by other personality inventories (e.g., the *NEO PI-R* or *NEO-FFI*). Additionally, there are situations in which a more detailed personality evaluation is appropriate (e.g., career counseling). The five dimensions measured by the Big Five Locator are broad personality descriptions and, thus, do not provide the depth attainable by using measures that account for the specific individual differences underlying each dimension. Therefore, the Big Five Locator should be used by professionals who are familiar with the FFM and who already utilize the *NEO PI-R* or *NEO-FFI*. Ideally, use of the Big Five Locator would be followed by use of the *NEO PI-R*.

ADMINISTRATION

Both the administration and scoring of the Big Five Locator are straightforward and do not require special training. The Big Five Locator may be administered to individuals alone or in groups. In some circumstances, a consultant or trainer may choose to have someone who knows another individual well complete the instrument *about* the other person in order to obtain an "other" score. There is no time limit for completing the Big Five Locator; most respondents, however, will complete the inventory in less than two minutes.

SCORING

Calculating Dimension Scores

In order to calculate raw scores for the five dimensions (i.e., the individual scores for each dimension), the administrator should sum the following item sequences, tallying the scores circled by the respondent:

Dimensions Item (= Row) Numbers to be Summed
1. Negative Emotionality: 1, 6, 11, 16, 21
2. Extraversion: 2, 7, 12, 17, 22
3. Openness: 3, 8, 13, 18, 23
4. Agreeableness: 4, 9, 14, 19, 24
5. Conscientiousness: 5, 10, 15, 20, 25

Enter the sums of these sequences in the spaces provided on the bottom of the inventory.

Missing Responses

If any item has been left blank on any one dimension scale, the blank item should be scored as neutral (i.e., 3). If more than one item on any dimension scale has been left blank, the inventory should be considered invalid and should not be scored.

Profiling Scores

Profile areas are provided on the Score Conversion Sheet. Locate the row labeled "Negative Emotionality" and within this row place an "X" over the number that corresponds to the respondent's negative emotionality dimension raw score. Use a similar procedure for all the respondent's raw scores. Connect the Xs with a line after all the respondent's scores have been marked to produce a graph.

Preparing to Provide Feedback

The Big Five Locator Interpretation Sheet was designed to provide feedback to the respondent after scoring and profiling the results of the Big Five Locator have been completed. Examine the respondent's T score (the top row of the Big Five Locator Score Conversion Sheet) for negative emotionality. Locate the row labeled "Negative Emotionality" on the Big Five Locator Interpretation Sheet. Within this row, place an "X" over the number that corresponds to the respondent's negative emotionality T score. Use a similar procedure to complete the remainder of the sheet.

INTERPRETATION

In order to interpret the results of the Big Five Locator effectively, one must be familiar with the basics of psychological testing, know what the scales measure, and be able to integrate the information provided by the scale scores into a meaningful profile. The following provides basic information regarding the constructs measured by the Big Five Locator and suggests guidelines for interpreting profiles.

The Meaning of Scale Scores

The Big Five Locator's scales measure traits that approximate normal distributions. Most respondents will score near the average for each scale, with a small percentage at either end of the continuum. Thus, professionals should avoid "typing" any individual when interpreting scores. For instance, because most individuals can best be described as "ambiverts" who show a combination of introverted and extraverted tendencies, it is unfair to think or speak strictly in terms of "introverts" and "extraverts" (Costa & McCrae, 1992).

Expanded Definitions of the Five Domains

Negative Emotionality

The negative emotionality trait is about an individual's resilience in response to stressful situations. At one extreme is the "reactive," who experiences more negative emotions than most people and who reports less satisfaction with life than most people. This is not meant to place a value judgment on reactives; the susceptibility to negative emotions and discontent with life provides the basis for several roles in our society, such as social scientists and customer-oriented workers. At higher intellectual and academic levels, however, extreme reactivity (high negative emotionality) interferes with performance.

On the other extreme are the "resilients," who tend to experience life on a more rational level than most people and who appear impervious to what is going on around them. Such people seem unflappable. This extreme is the foundation for many valuable social roles, from air-traffic controllers and airline pilots to military snipers, finance managers, and engineers.

Along the continuum from resilient to reactive is the vast middle range of "responsives," who are a mixture of qualities characteristic of resilients and reactives. Responsives are more able to turn behaviors from both extremes on and off, calling on what seems appropriate to the situation. A responsive typically is not able to maintain the calmness of a resilient for as long a period of time, nor is a responsive typically able to maintain the nervous edge of alertness of a reactive.

Extraversion

The extraversion trait is about the degree of one's preference for being actively engaged with other people. On the one hand, the "extravert" tends to exert more leadership, to be more physically and verbally active, and to be more friendly and outgoing around others than most people tend to be. The extraverted profile is the foundation of many social roles, including sales, politics, the arts, and the social sciences.

At the other extreme, the "introvert" tends to be more independent, reserved, steady, and more comfortable with being alone than are most people. The introverted profile is the basis of such varied social roles as production managers and the physical and natural sciences.

In between these two extremes are the "ambiverts," who are able to move comfortably from outgoing social situations to the isolation of working alone. The stereotypical ambivert is the player-coach, who moves on demand from the leadership demands of coach to the personal-production demands of player.

Openness

The openness trait is about the degree to which one is curious about one's inner and outer worlds. On the one hand, the "explorer" has broader interests, has a fascination with novelty and innovation, would generally be perceived as liberal, and reports more introspection and reflection than most people. Explorers are not unprincipled but tend to be open to considering new approaches. The explorer profile forms the basis for such social roles as entrepreneurs, architects, change agents, artists, and theoretical scientists (social and physical).

On the other hand, the "preserver" has narrower interests, is perceived as more conventional, and is more comfortable with the familiar. Preservers are perceived as more conservative but not necessarily as more authoritarian. The preserver profile is the basis for such social roles as financial managers, performers, project managers, and applied scientists.

In the middle of the continuum lies the "moderate." The moderate can explore the unusual with interest when necessary but would find too much exploration to be tiresome; on the other hand, the moderate can focus on the familiar for extended periods of time but eventually would develop a hunger for novelty. This trait is not an indicator of intelligence, as explorers and preservers both score well on traditional measures of intelligence. It does tend to be a measure of creativity, as openness to new experience is an important ingredient of creativity.

Agreeableness

The agreeableness trait is a measure of altruism versus egocentrism. At one end of the continuum, the "adapter" is prone to subordinate personal needs to those of the group, to accept the group's norms rather

114

than insisting on his or her personal norms. Harmony is more important to the adapter than, for example, broadcasting his or her personal notion of truth. Galileo, in recanting his Copernican views before the Roman Inquisition, behaved as an adapter. The adapter profile is the core of such social roles as teaching, social work, and psychology.

At the other end of the continuum, the "challenger" is more focused on his or her personal norms and needs rather than on those of the group. The challenger is more concerned with acquiring and exercising power. Challengers follow the beat of their own drums, rather than falling in step with the group. The challenger profile is the foundation of such social roles as advertising, managing, and military leadership.

In the middle of the continuum is the "negotiator," who is able to move from leadership to followership as the situation demands. Karen Horney (1945) describes the two extremes of this trait as "moving toward people" (adapter) and "moving against people" (challenger). The former, known as the tender-minded, in the extreme becomes a dependent personality who has lost his or her sense of self. The latter, known as the tough-minded, in the extreme becomes narcissistic, antisocial, authoritarian, or paranoid—a person who has lost his or her sense of fellow-feeling. In one sense, this trait is about the dependence (altruism) of the adapter, the independence (egocentrism) of the challenger, and the interdependence (situationalism) of the negotiator.

Conscientiousness

The conscientiousness trait is about self-control in the service of one's will to achieve. At one extreme, the "focused" profile portrays high self-control, resulting in consistent focus on personal and occupational goals. In a normal state, the focused person is characterized by academic and career achievement, but when focus turns extreme, it results in workaholism. The focused person is difficult to distract. Such a profile is the basis for such social roles as leaders, executives, and high achievers in general.

At the other extreme, "flexible" person is more easily distracted, is less focused on goals, is more hedonistic, and is generally more lax with respect to goals. The flexible is easily seduced from the task at hand by a passing idea, activity, or person; he or she has weak control over his or her impulses. Flexibles do not necessarily work less than focused people, but less of their total work effort is goal-directed. Flexibleness facilitates creativity, inasmuch as it remains open to possibilities longer without feeling driven to closure and moving on. This profile is the core of such social roles as researchers, detectives, and consultants.

Toward the middle of this continuum is the "balanced" person, who finds it easier to move from focus to laxity, from production to research. A balanced person would make an ideal manager of either a group of flexibles or a group of focuseds, providing just enough of both qualities to keep flexibles reasonably on target without alienating them and to keep focused people sufficiently spontaneous to prevent them from missing important opportunities.

SAMPLE PROFILES

An Individual Profile: The Burned-Out Producer

Negative Emotionality	= 76	(Very High)
Extraversion	= 67	(Very High)
Openness	= 42	(Low)
Agreeableness	= 51	(Medium)
Conscientiousness	= 72	(Very High)

Situation: Henry is a freelance television sports producer who is rich and miserable. He has plenty of work but he is worn out. At 11:00 p.m., after wrapping up his evening's work broadcasting a professional basketball game, he finds that he cannot get to sleep until five or six in the morning, and then it is time to get up. Each game frazzles his nerves, and it takes him a long time to calm down. He is good at his job and he loves sports. He does not know what is wrong with him but knows that the quality of his life must change.

Analysis: The key here is Henry's high N. His scores on the other four dimensions are a perfect fit for his job, but live, on-the-air sports production is no place for a reactive personality. The behind-the-scenes producer needs to be relatively sedate, calmly monitoring all the cameras and coolly giving instructions to guide the show's progress. Henry's high reactivity in a stressful environment with no margin for error is an unhealthy combination. He would probably be more comfortable in a job doing sports documentaries, where he could edit without the stress of real time.

A Team Profile: A Human-Service-Agency Team

Negative Emotionality	= 3 low, 5 medium, 8 high
Extraversion	= 2 low, 1 medium, 13 high
Openness	= 3 low, 4 medium, 9 high
Agreeableness	= 4 low, 2 medium, 10 high
Conscientiousness	= 2 low, 2 medium, 12 high

Situation: In this team of sixteen members, meetings are loud and competitive, with little real listening. Side conversations continually crop up. Team members love to brainstorm but often lose track of many of their good ideas. Some tend to feel arrogant with respect to the rest of the agency, particularly to what they perceive as sluggish upper management. Most of them, however, are uncomfortable with conflict and dread the meetings, which frequently erupt into accusation, blaming, and intimidation.

Analysis: The fact that thirteen of the sixteen team members are moderate or higher in N suggests that the problems simply will not go away. The abundance of extraverts calls for strict norms regarding how to conduct meetings. The abundance of explorers (high O) calls for detailed minutes with follow-up to evaluate suggestions, establish priorities, and assign responsibility for implementation. The high number of adapters (high A) accounts for the discomfort with conflict and the need to agree to turn every complaint into a plan of action ("fix it or accept it"). The large number of focused (high C) team members accounts for the perception of others as sluggish. Members need to learn to ask for and accept time lines for decisions from top management.

References

Barrick, M.R., & Mount, M.K. (1991). The big five personality dimensions and job performance: A meta-analysis. *Personnel Psychology, 44,* 1-26.

Costa, P.T., Jr., & McCrae, R.R. (1992). *NEO PI-R: Professional manual.* Odessa, FL: Psychological Assessment Resources.

Digman, J.M. (1989). Five robust trait dimensions: Development, stability, and utility. *Journal of Personality, 57*(2), 195-214.

Digman, J.M. (1990). Personality structure: Emergence of the five-factor model. *Annual Review of Psychology, 41,* 417-440.

Galton, F. (1884). Measurement of character. *Fortnightly Review, 36,* 179-185.

Goldberg, L.R. (1993, January). The structure of phenotypic personality traits. *American Psychologist, 48*(1), 26-34.

Horney, K. (1945). *Our inner conflicts.* New York: Norton.

Howard, P.J., & Howard, J.M. (1993). *The big five workbook: A roadmap for individual and team interpretation of scores on the five-factor model of personality.* Charlotte, NC: Center for Applied Cognitive Studies.

John, O.P., Angleitner, A., & Ostendorf, F. (1988). The lexical approach to personality: A historical review of trait taxonomic research. *European Journal of Personality, 2,* 171-203.

McCrae, R.R. (Ed.). (1992, June). The five-factor model: Issues and applications. *Journal of Personality* (special issue), *60*(2).

McCrae, R.R., & Costa, P.T. (1989). Reinterpreting the Myers-Briggs Type Indicator from the perspective of the five-factor model of personality. *Journal of Personality, 57*(1), 17-40.

McCrae, R.R., & Costa, P.T. (1990). *Personality in adulthood.* New York: Guilford.

Norman, W.T. (1963). Toward an adequate taxonomy of personality attributes: Replicated factor structure in peer nomination personality ratings. *Journal of Abnormal and Social Psychology, 66,* 574-583.

Peabody, D. (1987). Personality dimensions through trait inferences. *Journal of Personality and Social Psychology, 52,* 59-71.

Pierce J. Howard, Ph.D., is the director of research at the Center for Applied Cognitive Studies in Charlotte, North Carolina. He has twenty-five years of experience in the field of organization development consulting. Dr. Howard has authored two books, one with Jane Mitchell Howard. He also has served as a board member for the Charlotte Area Chapter of ASTD, from which he received the Excellence in Service to the Profession Award for 1992. Dr. Howard is a member of the American Psychological Association and the International Society for the Study of Individual Differences.

Phyllis L. Medina, Ph.D., is an independent researcher and consultant for a variety of organizations in the fields of cognitive research, outplacement, and executive search. These activities have led to her involvement in several research projects including continued work focusing on the FFM of personality and a study concerning the impact of leader social power bases on subordinate creativity. Dr. Medina also specializes in corporate research and is the former director of research and job development for a prominent outplacement firm in Oklahoma.

Jane Mitchell Howard, M.B.A., is the director of programs at the Center for Applied Cognitive Studies in Charlotte, North Carolina. She specializes in the areas of team building, leadership/management/supervisory training, and interpersonal communication skills. She has coauthored (with Pierce Howard) a book and a forthcoming article. Mrs. Howard is a past president and current member of the Charlotte Area Chapter of ASTD, from which she has received the Member Excellence Award and the Excellence in Service to the Community Award. She is also a member of the Organization Development Network.

THE BIG FIVE LOCATOR

Pierce J. Howard, Phyllis L. Medina, and Jane M. Howard

Name:_____

Instructions: On each numerical scale that follows, indicate which point is generally more descriptive of you. If the two terms are equally descriptive, mark the midpoint.

1.	Eager	5 4 3 2 1	Calm
2. Prefer Being with Other People		5 4 3 2 1	Prefer Being Alone
3.	A Dreamer	5 4 3 2 1	No-Nonsense
4.	Courteous	5 4 3 2 1	Abrupt
5.	Neat	5 4 3 2 1	Messy
6.	Cautious	5 4 3 2 1	Confident
7.	Optimistic	5 4 3 2 1	Pessimistic
8.	Theoretical	5 4 3 2 1	Practical
9.	Generous	5 4 3 2 1	Selfish
10.	Decisive	5 4 3 2 1	Open-Ended
11.	Discouraged	5 4 3 2 1	Upbeat
12.	Exhibitionist	5 4 3 2 1	Private
13.	Follow Imagination	5 4 3 2 1	Follow Authority
14.	Warm	5 4 3 2 1	Cold
15.	Stay Focused	5 4 3 2 1	Easily Distracted
16.	Easily Embarrassed	5 4 3 2 1	Don't Give a Darn
17.	Outgoing	5 4 3 2 1	Cool
18.	Seek Novelty	5 4 3 2 1	Seek Routine
19.	Team Player	5 4 3 2 1	Independent
20.	A Preference for Order	5 4 3 2 1	Comfortable with Chaos
21.	Distractible	5 4 3 2 1	Unflappable
22.	Conversational	5 4 3 2 1	Thoughtful
23.	Comfortable with Ambiguity	5 4 3 2 1	Prefer Things Clear-Cut
24.	Trusting	5 4 3 2 1	Skeptical
25.	On Time	5 4 3 2 1	Procrastinate

N=_____ E=_____ O=_____ A=_____ C=_____

The 1996 Annual: Volume 1, Training.
Copyright © 1996 by Pfeiffer & Company, San Diego, CA.

THE BIG FIVE LOCATOR SCORING SHEET

Instructions:

1. Find the sum of the circled numbers on the *first* row of each of the five-line groupings (Row 1 + Row 6 + Row 11 + Row 16 + Row 21 = _____). This is your raw score for "negative emotionality." Circle the number in the NEGAT EMOT: column of the Score Conversion Sheet that corresponds to this raw score.

2. Find the sum of the circled numbers on the *second* row of each of the five-line groupings (Row 2 + Row 7 + Row 12 + Row 17 + Row 22 = _____). This is your raw score for "extraversion." Circle the number in the EXTRA: column of the Score Conversion Sheet that corresponds to this raw score.

3. Find the sum of the circled numbers on the *third* row of each of the five-line groupings (Row 3 + Row 8 + Row 13 + Row 18 + Row 23 = _____). This is your raw score for "openness." Circle the number in the OPEN: column of the Score Conversion Sheet that corresponds to this raw score.

4. Find the sum of the circled numbers on the *fourth* row of each of the five-line groupings (Row 4 + Row 9 + Row 14 + Row 19 + Row 24 = _____). This is your raw score for "agreeableness." Circle the number in the AGREE: column of the Score Conversion Sheet that corresponds to this raw score.

5. Find the sum of the circled numbers on the *fifth* row of each of the five-line groupings (Row 5 + Row 10 + Row 15 + Row 20 + Row 25 = _____). This is your raw score for "conscientiousness." Circle the number in the CONSC: column of the Score Conversion Sheet that corresponds to this raw score.

6. Find the number in the far right or far left column that is parallel to your circled raw score. Enter this norm score in the box at the bottom of the appropriate column.

7. Transfer your norm score to the appropriate scale on the Big Five Locator Interpretation Sheet.

The 1996 Annual: Volume 1, Training.
Copyright © 1996 by Pfeiffer & Company, San Diego, CA.

BIG FIVE LOCATOR SCORE CONVERSION SHEET

NORM SCORE:	NEGAT. EMOT:	EXTRA:	OPEN:	AGREE:	CONSC:	NORM SCORE:
80			25			80
78	22					78
76			24			76
74	21		23			74
72		25	22	25		72
70	20	24			25	70
68		23	21	24		68
66	19				24	66
64		22	20	23	23	64
62	18	21	19	22	22	62
60		20	18	21	21	60
58	17	19			20	58
56			17			56
54	16	18	16	20	19	54
52	15	17		19	18	52
50		16	15	18	17	50
48	14	15	14	17	16	48
46		14	13		15	46
44	13			16	14	44
42		13	12	15	13	42
40	12	12	11	14	12	40
38		11	10			38
36	11					36
34	10	10	9	13	11	34
32		9	8	12	10	32
30	9	8		11	9	30
28		7	7	10	8	28
26	8	6	6		7	26
24				9	6	24
22	7	5	5		5	22
20				8		20
ENTER NORM SCORES HERE:	N =	E =	O =	A =	C =	

(Norms based on a sample of 161 forms completed in 1993-94.)

THE BIG FIVE LOCATOR INTERPRETATION SHEET

Name:_____

LOW NEG. EMOTIONALITY: secure, unflappable, rational, unresponsive, guilt free	Resilient Responsive Reactive 35 45 55 65	HIGH NEG. EMOTIONALITY: excitable, worrying, reactive, high strung, alert
LOW EXTRAVERSION: private, independent, works alone, reserved, hard to read	Introvert Ambivert Extravert 35 45 55 65	HIGH EXTRAVERSION: assertive, sociable, warm, optimistic, talkative
LOW OPENNESS: practical, conservative, depth of knowledge, efficient, expert	Preserver Moderate Explorer 35 45 55 65	HIGH OPENNESS: broad interests, curious, liberal, impractical, likes novelty
LOW AGREEABLENESS: skeptical, questioning, tough, aggressive, self-interest	Challenger Negotiator Adapter 35 45 55 65	HIGH AGREEABLENESS: trusting, humble, altruistic, team player, conflict averse, frank
LOW CONSCIENTIOUSNESS: spontaneous, fun loving, experimental, unorganized	Flexible Balanced Focused 35 45 55 65	HIGH CONSCIENTIOUSNESS: dependable, organized, disciplined, cautious, stubborn

The Big Five Locator is intended for use only as a quick assessment to be used with a consultant and a willing client. Care should be taken to follow up this profile with a more reliable instrument, such as the *NEO PI-R* or the *NEO-FFI* (Costa & McCrae, 1992).

Pfeiffer & Company

THE CAREER-DIMENSION SURVEY: ASKING THE RIGHT CAREER-DEVELOPMENT QUESTIONS

Caela Farren and Beverly Kaye

Abstract: Organizations are aware of the fact that career-development issues have a strong impact on motivation, satisfaction, productivity, and the competitive edge. Employees' career goals should be aligned with organizational goals. An organization that is examining its career-development systems can use the Career-Dimension Survey to discover what key areas need to be improved. The five key areas identified are future perspective, organizational systems and practices, work design, managerial support, and individual career-management concerns.

The 1996 Annual: Volume 1, Training.
Copyright © 1996 by Pfeiffer & Company, San Diego, CA.

In today's rapidly changing workplace, people are concerned and often confused about their careers. An effective career-development system unites employees' aspirations with the strategic direction of the organization. It helps to ensure that the work force possesses the competence necessary for the organization to fulfill its mission. This article identifies five key factors that help to pinpoint the critical career-development issues in an organization.

1. FUTURE PERSPECTIVE

The view of the future held by the people who work in an organization plays a significant role in determining their actions. People who understand the strategic direction of the organization and see the prospect of a desirable future for themselves will commit themselves to making that future a reality. The following are indicators of the future perspective of a work force.

Organizational Mission and Strategy

Employees need to understand and endorse the fundamental purpose of the organization. Without a clear strategic direction, employees can only surmise which of their actions are mere routine and which are vital for the future. People will go to extraordinary lengths to produce strategically important results, but first they must understand the relationship between present action and future opportunity.

Future Prospects

People need to believe that the organization has a future that holds a place for them. If an organization is retrenching, or the industry is shrinking, employees may be unwilling to exert themselves on behalf of dim future prospects. People who doubt whether their organization's future holds a place for them reserve their commitment and make defensive, shortsighted decisions.

Support for Long-Range Planning and Results

When organizations initiate career-development programs, the hoped-for benefit is usually partnership, with employees linking their personal aspirations to the organization's strategic goals. This form of partnership can occur only in an organizational culture that values long-term results.

Core Processes and Competences

Every organization has core processes without which it could not accomplish its fundamental purpose. Each of these processes requires the efforts of people with special competences. People in an organization must recognize its core processes and know which competences are essential for achieving the organization's mission, both now and in the future.

Preparedness for Technological Change

Falling behind the technological curve can have drastic consequences for organizations and individuals alike. The organization must identify the new technologies it must master to meet the changing expectations of its customers. It must tell employees when their current skills are in danger of becoming obsolete and help them prepare for the transition to a new way of working.

Preparedness for Organizational Change

People cannot plan intelligently for the future if the shape of the playing field continually is being changed without notice. The result of repeated reorganizations can be confusion, resistance, and a perceived loss of control over the direction of one's work life. Employees need to understand why the organization is introducing structural changes. They should have an opportunity to contribute to or comment on planned changes before they are implemented.

2. ORGANIZATIONAL SYSTEMS AND PRACTICES

Career-development programs cannot succeed in a vacuum. They must be integrated with the organization's other human resource practices. One need not map out all the connections among these systems before introducing a career-development program, but it is important to review them as part of the planning process. The practices that follow are likely to either reinforce or undercut an organization's career-development "message."

Job Posting

People in an organization need to believe that the job-posting system is relevant to the way in which people actually are hired. In many organizations the prevailing assumption is that most positions are "wired" for preselected individuals and are posted only to forestall grievances. In the same vein, job postings are sometimes criticized because the listings do not accurately describe the competences necessary for the positions. If job postings are seen as incomplete, employees will not take them seriously as career-development resources.

Career Information

People in an organization should know where and how to get information about career opportunities within the organization. This is an area in which organizations can take the initiative by preparing easy-to-use informational resources. Unfortunately, information of this type often is relegated to a dusty back shelf in a supervisor's office, leaving most employees unaware of its existence.

Mentoring

Good mentors are scarce. Few senior-level people possess both the time and inclination to groom potential successors. For this reason, some organizations have initiated formal mentoring programs that pair junior or intermediate-level employees with more experienced colleagues. Other organizations have had success with group mentoring programs, in which a senior's savvy can be dispensed to two or three junior people rather than just one. People in an organization should know how to locate a mentor. The organization should know who the best mentors are and how to prepare others for that role.

Compensation

Compensation can take many forms, the most prominent of which is money. Other types of compensation that affect career decisions include flexible scheduling, opportunities to attend professional conferences, and personal recognition of one's efforts. People want to consider themselves fairly compensated for their work. Employees should be rewarded equitably for accepting temporary assignments and for expanding their contributions to the organization even if they stay in the same positions.

Training and Development

People in an organization want to have access to the continuing education and training they need to maintain or upgrade their marketable skills. Organizations can offer developmental activities such as apprenticeships, on-the-job training, and professional-development sabbaticals. Managers can recommend training courses as well as different forms of hands-on work experience.

Developmental Assignments

People in an organization can be assigned to special projects or to other units of the organization in order to help them develop new competences. This powerful learning method is often underutilized because no one wants to undertake the necessary negotiations and paperwork. It is a good sign when people in an organization feel free to request developmental assignments.

3. WORK DESIGN

A third career-development factor to consider is the nature of people's work. We are all affected by the inherent characteristics of the work we do. Most people will tolerate difficult working conditions if they find their own work satisfying. However, if people consider their work unrewarding, the organization can offer few inducements that will sustain a high degree of motivated effort. Redesigning work to incorporate the following factors can have a substantial effect on people's career plans.

Participation

People in an organization want to be consulted about changes that directly affect their work. They want to participate in making decisions as well as implementing them. Work that affords ample scope for participation is generally regarded as more attractive. There is also evidence that suggests that people are more productive when they believe that their views regarding the best way to get a job done are valued.

Empowerment

People like to be encouraged to make necessary decisions about their work on their own initiative. Most people can determine their own work procedures within the standards of responsible practice. Not everybody craves autonomy, but for many people the chance to call their own shots is the pivotal difference between satisfying work or career dissatisfaction.

Meaning

People want to believe that their work is worthwhile. Work can be a cornerstone of personal growth and identity. Its rewards range from the gradual development of mastery in a craft to the satisfactions of accomplishment and service. When one's work seems trivial and dull, it can be a wearisome burden. People who experience little pride or meaning in their work give it correspondingly little commitment.

Teamwork

Effective teams can produce results that exceed the previous levels of performance of their individual members. Of course, some people work better as individual contributors rather than as members of a team. But work structured by and for teams has widespread appeal for employees who prefer not to labor in isolation. Participation in self-directed work teams is an increasingly popular career move in many organizations and is well-suited to fast-paced business conditions.

Feedback from Customers

People like to see the results of their work. In complex organizations, actions too often are divorced from their eventual consequences. People in these organizations may not receive reliable information about whether their daily efforts make any difference. Built-in feedback from internal and external customers enables people to gauge the effectiveness of their work. This practice pays off in improved service quality and better customer relations as well as increased career satisfaction.

4. MANAGERIAL SUPPORT

Discussions between managers and employees are natural forums for career planning. Managers are ideally situated to communicate the direction of the organization to employees and to convey the career interests of employees to the larger organization. Managers' boundary-spanning role enables them to open doors for employees in the wider organization. Aspects of managerial support that affect career development include the following.

Feedback and Career Discussions

Effective career management is directly related to the frequency and quality of career discussions. The manager is in a position to suggest steps that will enable the employee to bring himself or herself in line with desired goals. Managers should hold frequent career-oriented discussions with the people in their work units.

Visibility Opportunities

One practical form of managerial support consists of assigning people to tasks or projects that take them outside their customary work areas. These special assignments are opportunities for them to make their abilities and potential known in the organization at large. Wise managers help employees develop their own reputations for excellent performance; both the manager and the employee benefit from the impression of strength added to strength.

Stretch Assignments

Adults learn most effectively through direct experience. Assignments that require people to acquire and use new abilities to produce actual results are invaluable. At the same time, these assignments build up the "bench strength" of the work unit, with experienced employees helping to develop their successors in order to increase their own career mobility.

Advice on Career Options

Managers, by virtue of their positions, usually have a broader perspective of the organization than is available to the people in their work units.

This enables them to offer advice on career options, the roles within the organization that are suited to a particular individual's abilities and aspirations, and what that person needs to do to be considered a candidate. This advice comes from a thorough knowledge of both the present realities and the strategic aims of the organization.

Rewards for Developing People

Managers should be held accountable for developing the people who work with them. The organization's best "people developers" should be recognized and rewarded for this contribution. There should be consequences if a manger fails to develop people or holds people back. Managers who are vying to earn reputations as terrific career coaches benefit everyone: the organization, the employees, and themselves.

5. INDIVIDUAL CAREER-MANAGEMENT CONCERNS

An important career-development issue is the extent to which people can identify and move among various career options in their organization. Limitations on such movement serve as barriers to setting or attaining personal goals. For the organization, their presence may indicate larger structural deficiencies.

Career-management concerns are as diverse as the situations and perceptions of individuals. Those that follow are among the most significant for planning purposes.

Control

Some organizations expect people to build their own futures or bide their time. Those who consider themselves the principal architects of their own careers actively seek out or create opportunities to achieve their goals. Those who believe that other people control their careers tend to adopt more passive or apathetic attitudes.

Plateauing

Many people feel trapped in their present roles. For some individuals this feeling occurs because they do not see where else in the organization they can go from their present jobs. For others, this concern results from a lack of stimulation in their current roles. People who believe that they are in dead-end jobs are likely to leave the organization, either in fact or in spirit, unless they can be shown how to invent fresh career opportunities.

Mobility

Mobility means that people can move easily from one part of the organization to another. In small organizations this is less of an issue, because everyone must step in wherever a need arises. Large organizations, which must track the movement of masses of people, sometimes impose unintended barriers to career mobility in their zeal for order. In "flatter" organizations, fewer people can expect to move up through a multitiered management hierarchy. A increase in the degree of lateral movement is important to prevent people from feeling stuck.

Variety of Options

Some organizations offer many different career options; some offer just a few. People want to know how to find out what options are available to them. Job enrichment can be a career-development option. Temporary assignments to special projects or other business units are career options that do not require formal job changes. It is important that people view the career-development possibilities in an organization as open and expandable rather than as cramped and restricted.

Career Progression

People need to understand how careers are built in an organization and what one must do to become a serious candidate for a desired opportunity. They need to know which competences will help them achieve their goals and whether it is more beneficial to have a wide range of experiences or to become an expert in a specialized discipline. They need to know whether certain positions or work experiences are necessary prerequisites to increased levels of responsibility.

CAREER-DEVELOPMENT SYSTEMS

Career-development systems address the common ground between the individual and the organization. Both have resources to offer and aims to achieve. Accurate needs assessment, careful targeting of pilot groups for intervention, and clear objectives are essential for a successful career-development system. Otherwise the limited resources available for this purpose may be misapplied. When one asks the right questions, the appropriate starting point will become evident.

The new career paradigm is that of an alliance or partnership, with the organization positioned as a community of compatible interests being realized through a common purpose. Paying attention to the key career-development factors can help an organization to assure that this community of interests remains strong and creative.

THE CAREER-DIMENSION SURVEY

Introduction

The Career-Dimension Survey is meant to be a quick way to draw attention to the fact that if career development is to be done well, five critical arenas have to be considered. The survey is designed to assist organizations that are beginning to look at their development cultures. Although many organizations approach the subject of career development from a purely educational point of view, some recognize that education alone will not do. They are motivated to bring lasting change and realize that if a development intervention is to work, one must look at a variety of interrelated systems.

The Career-Dimension Survey is the culmination of over twenty years of research in the areas that truly affect a development effort. It should be utilized to build interest on the part of colleagues and/or senior line managers.

The Career-Dimension Survey is adapted from a larger survey containing 125 questions. Twenty items have been pulled from the original instrument; the four items under each of the five topical areas are those that the authors believe are most indicative of the subsystem under study.

The answers are meant to stimulate discussion, capture insights, and begin a frank conversation about the place of career development within the organization.

How to Administer the Survey

The survey contains twenty items that are to be rated on a scale of one (not true) to five (very true). Respondents are told to rate the twenty items according to how they perceive their organization (or division) responding to their personal career needs. Respondents are instructed to mark their answers directly on the answer sheet provided.

The survey should take no longer than ten minutes to complete.

Presentation of Theory

The theory of the survey suggests that there are five distinct factors that enable an organization to build a successful career-development process. Each of these factors is essential to the design. The five areas are described in brief on the survey form and as follows:

Future Perspective: Understanding and communicating future trends and their implications for the work force.

Organizational Systems and Practices: Other management and human resource initiatives that interact and support the career-management system.

Work Design: The degree to which individuals find their work satisfying and motivating.

Managerial Support: The ability of managers to support the development of their staffs and teams.

Individual Concerns: The ability of the individual to self-manage his or her career.

Prediction of Scores

The facilitator can engage participants in a variety of ways. Depending on the size and scope of the group, the facilitator may want to ask any or all of the following questions:

1. Where do you think this group will score higher or lower?
2. Where will the composite scores of this group fall?
3. Which of the five areas will have the higher scores? Lower scores?
4. How will the five scores fall in each of the major divisions? Which will come out higher? Lower? Why?
5. Which professional group might score higher or lower in these areas? (The facilitator should be more specific, and can list the different professional groups on flip chart paper and ask the group to predict the scores and discuss their predictions.)

Scoring

All respondents should be directed use the Scoring and Interpretation Sheet to score their responses simultaneously. Instructions for scoring appear on the sheet, and respondents merely need to transpose their scores and total their subscores.

Interpretation

The Scoring and Interpretation Sheet provides a scoring key, indicates high and low scores, and provides a brief interpretation of scores.

Posting

All scores can be posted. The quality of the discussion is based on whether respondents are willing to discuss the divergence or convergence of their scores. They can converse about the areas in which their organization (or division) is stronger or weaker.

Caela Farren, Ph.D., *is an organization development consultant with more than twenty-five years of experience, specializing in strategic business management, organization design, and career and management development. Her clients have included AT&T, Merrill Lynch, Ethicon, Marriott, Bell Labs, Glaxo, Warner Lambert, BASF, CIA, and the Department of Commerce. She is currently CEO of Farren Associates and a principal in Career Systems, Inc., as well as serving as a visiting professor at The American University. Dr. Farren is the author of numerous articles and a book, entitled* Designing Career Development Systems.

Beverly L. Kaye, Ph.D., *is an organization consultant based in Sherman Oaks, California. Her specialty lies in career development, management training, and human resource planning. For the past twenty years, Dr. Kaye has been designing and conducting a variety of management and career-development programs for business and industry. She is the author of* Up Is Not the Only Way *and* Designing Career Development Systems. *In addition to her activities with Beverly Kaye & Associates, Inc., Dr. Kaye is vice president of Career Systems, Inc., a career-development publishing company based in Scranton, Pennsylvania.*

THE CAREER-DIMENSION SURVEY

Caela Farren and Beverly Kaye

Instructions: Respond to the items below by rating each from one (not true) to five (very true) for your organization (or division).

1	2	3	4	5
Not True		Somewhat True		Very True

1. This organization expects me to take the lead in managing my own career. _____

2. I coordinate my professional-development plans with the organization's strategic plan. _____

3. I am free to choose what tasks I will work on from day to day, as long as I deliver the expected final results. _____

4. My manager encourages me to develop skills that will qualify me for other jobs in my career field. _____

5. My organization/division uses succession planning to identify and prepare candidates for key positions. _____

6. Information moves easily between my division and the senior management of the organization. _____

7. My manager advises me on my career options and alternatives. _____

8. My job allows me to decide how I am going to do my work, as long as I meet certain recognized standards. _____

9. My manager discusses with me the probable impact of new technology on our work unit. _____

10. This division's expected work force requirements for the next two or more years have been explained to me. _____

1	2	3	4	5
Not True		Somewhat True		Very True

11. The final results of my work depend more on an effective team effort than on my individual contribution. _____

12. I have been told of my standing in the succession plan for key positions in my division. _____

13. A variety of desirable career options are available to me in this organization. _____

14. This organization assists me to prepare myself for technological changes in my field. _____

15. I initiate career discussions with my coworkers. _____

16. My manager has told me his or her personal assessment of my current competence and ability in the past three months. _____

17. In my work I am involved with many different tasks and/or projects. _____

18. Special projects or rotational assignments are available to me for career-development purposes. _____

19. I am not sure exactly what my career field or discipline is. _____

20. This organization's long-term plans will result in the availability of more career options in my field. _____

Pfeiffer & Company

CAREER-DIMENSION SURVEY SCORING AND INTERPRETATION SHEET

Instructions: Refer to the survey form and locate your score for each item. Fill in your score next to the item number below. Next, add up your scores and fill in the "total" box. Refer to the scoring key to assess your perceptions in each of the dimensions.

2. 10. 14. 20. **TOTAL**	_____ _____ _____ _____ [ ]	These questions assess the *Future Perspective* in your organization. A low score in this section could indicate a need to work at communicating the future needs of your organization. It is important for employees to see where they fit in and how new competences will improve their marketability in the future.
3. 8. 11. 17. **TOTAL**	_____ _____ _____ _____ [ ]	These questions assess *Work Design* in your organization. A low score in this section could indicate a need to restructure jobs and foster employee involvement. It is important to realize that the nature of the work people do is one of the most influential elements in people's assessment of their career satisfaction and contribution.
5. 6. 12. 18. **TOTAL**	_____ _____ _____ _____ [ ]	These questions assess *Organizational Systems and Practices* in your organization. A low score in this section could indicate a need to eliminate conflicting messages between what is said and what is done. It is important to realize that an organization either supports its employees or it does not; people are seldom fooled for long.
4. 7. 9. 16. **TOTAL**	_____ _____ _____ _____ [ ]	These questions assess *Managerial Support* in your organization. A low score in this section could indicate a need to help managers increase their effectiveness. It is important to realize that managers' attitudes and behaviors exert a powerful influence on the productivity and professional development of employees.
1. 13. 15. 19. **TOTAL**	_____ _____ _____ _____ [ ]	These questions assess *Individual Concerns* in your organization. A low score in this section could indicate a need to encourage employees to take responsibility for their own career development. It is important to realize that if employees fail to acquire new skills, they will not keep your organization ahead of the competition.

SCORING KEY

1-7: Need to take action immediately.

8-13: Need to consider further evaluation.

14-20: Need to reexamine from time to time.

INSTRUCTIONAL STYLES DIAGNOSIS INVENTORY: INCREASING STYLE AWARENESS AND FLEXIBILITY

Greg Cripple

Abstract: The Instructional Styles Diagnosis Inventory (ISDI) has the potential to provide feedback from multiple sources on a trainer's instructional style. Style is measured on two dimensions: who and what. The "who" dimension indicates the degree to which the trainer gives greater attention to trainer delivery or to learner receptivity. The "what" dimension indicates the degree to which the trainer's attention is on the content/subject matter or on the actual learning/skill development taking place.

For each of the two dimensions (who and what), twenty behavioral variables are identified, and for each variable there are two neutrally worded statements, one representing each extreme in focus of attention.

The pure styles described are "the seller," "the professor," "the entertainer," and "the coach." The ISDI Interpretation Sheet allows trainers to see how close they are to each of these pure styles and to explore the possibility of increasing their behavioral flexibility in terms of training styles.

The 1996 Annual: Volume 1, Training.
Copyright © 1996 by Pfeiffer & Company, San Diego, CA.

Instructing others often can be a frustrating undertaking. In addition, the rapid changes in our society; the accelerated production of new knowledge; the escalating requirements that employers have of employees; the increasing expectations of learners; and the steady movement to lifelong learning, multiple career changes, and learning organizations have added difficult new challenges to the instructional process.

To meet these challenges, trainers today need to be able to balance simultaneous demands. This places a premium on frequent, accurate feedback about the impact of the trainer's efforts on the many stakeholders in the learning process.

Most traditional trainer-feedback forms result in a single-source appraisal of trainer performance. Because of their predominantly evaluative nature, such forms tend to be perceived by trainers as threatening. Thus, these forms are more likely to produce defensive reactions than productive behavioral change. The focus of the Instructional Styles Diagnosis Inventory (ISDI) is on style rather than performance assessment and may offer a more attractive alternative to trainers.

INTRODUCTION TO THE ISDI

The ISDI serves as a catalyst to open participants' minds to the potential benefits of various instructional approaches.

The ISDI is similar in intent to the Employee Training Development Grid (Blake & Mouton, 1976), the Training Style Inventory (Bostrom, 1979), the Educational Orientation Questionnaire (Hadley, 1975), the Principles of Adult Learning Scale (Conti, 1982), the Student-Content Teaching Inventory (Spier, 1974), the Canfield Instructional Styles Inventory (Canfield & Canfield, 1975) and the Instructional Skills Assessment (Training House, 1982). Each of these yield unique insights into training styles. The ISDI is more similar in content to the Styles of Training Index (Michalak, 1974), the Jacobs-Fuhrmann Learning Style Inventory: Trainer Version (Jacobs & Fuhrmann, 1984), and the Trainer Type Inventory (Wheeler & Marshall, 1986). In deciding on the most appropriate instrument for a specific purpose, the trainer is encouraged to examine all these instruments before making a decision.

Pfeiffer & Company

Instructional Style

Most trainers have a preferred set of training philosophies, methods, and behaviors that form a predictable "instructional style." Each instructional style has a different impact on different types of learners.

The training and development literature presents variety of definitions of instructional style. Mann, Arnold, Binder, Cytrunbaum, Newman, Ringwald, and Rosenwein (1970) propose that an instructor's style is a combination of six primary styles:

- Expert/giving information,
- Formal authority/directing and controlling,
- Socializing agent/developing professionals,
- Facilitator/enabler,
- Ego ideal/inspirational model, and
- Person/caring co-learner.

Baird (1973) also describes instructor style as being a combination of six dimensions; these include:

- Didactic approach,
- Generalist approach,
- Researcher approach,
- Degree of direct student-teacher contact,
- Clarity/ambiguity of teacher demands, and
- Degree of affective rewards given to students.

Dobson & Dobson (1974) suggest that style is a synthesis of instructors' efforts to establish congruence between their beliefs and practices. Bostrom (1979) sees style defined by degree of disposition toward the behavioralist, structuralist, functionalist, or humanist approaches. Spier (1974) proposes that style is the outgrowth of an attempt to balance beliefs about student attitudes toward learning with beliefs about content emphasis. Bergquist and Phillips (1975) relate style to the type of learning environment the instructor creates (teacher-oriented, automated, interaction-oriented, or experience-oriented). Jacobs & Fuhrmann (1984) base style distinctions on Hersey and Blanchard's Situational Leadership® Model (directive, collaborative, or delegative). Wheeler and Marshall (1986) relate "trainer type" to the trainer's effectiveness in training students who are operating in one of Kolb's (1976) four learning-style categories (concrete experiencer, active experimenter, abstract conceptualizer, or reflective observer).

In contrast, the ISDI suggests that instructional styles are determined by dichotomies between "who" and "what" are the focus of the trainer's attention. The "who" dimension indicates the degree to which the trainer gives greater attention to trainer delivery or to learner receptivity. The "what" dimension indicates the degree to which the trainer's attention is on the content/subject matter or on the actual learning/skill development taking place. Several years after the ISDI was developed, the author discovered that Michalak (1974) had used this idea in his Styles of Training Index. However, Michalak's scales are not dichotomous, and he defines them differently.

PURPOSE AND FORMAT OF THE ISDI

It is not the intention of the ISDI to promote an "ideal" style. There is a great deal of debate in instructional style research about whether there is such a thing as an ideal style and, if so, what determines it (e.g., student learning style, instructional objectives, nature of subject matter, situational variables). As early as 1969, Flanders, in his research on high- and low-achieving instructors, suggested that ideal style be viewed as the trainer's ability to use a wide range of styles as his or her reading of situational variables demands. Reddin (1970) referred to this as "style flexibility." Entwhistle (1982) concluded, "The existence of widely different learning styles prevents there being any possibility of there being any single correct way to teach.... Versatility in teaching is essential.... No extreme style of teaching can be expected to be suitable for the majority of students."

The purpose of the ISDI is to provide "style awareness," defined as the accuracy of one's perception of his or her preferred instructional behavior.

To achieve this, for each of the two dimensions (who and what), twenty behavioral variables are identified. For each variable, two neutrally worded statements are presented, one representing each extreme in focus of attention. (The final part of the ISDI Interpretation Sheet contains a complete listing of paired statements by dimension.) The statements are distributed among twenty groups of four statements representing each of the four possible extremes of instructor behavior along the two dimensions. No statement is in the same group with the statement representing its contrasting extreme. This approach was chosen to reduce the "fakability" of results and to simulate the simultaneous decisions on aspects of the learning experience that trainers must make.

Completing the ISDI requires the respondent to rank each statement in a group of four from most descriptive (4) to least descriptive (1) of the trainer's instructional behavior.

ADMINISTRATION OF THE ISDI WITH TRAINERS

1. The ISDI is distributed to participants, with instructions to complete it using their most recent training assignments as frames of reference. They are reminded that they are evaluating themselves as trainers just as future respondents will be evaluating them.

2. (Optional) Before scoring and interpreting the ISDI, each participant is asked to prepare a three-to-five-minute "mini-class" on a simple task such as making a paper airplane or tying a square knot. The classes are then videotaped as they are presented to other participants.

3. The ISDI Scoring Sheets are distributed, and participants begin by transferring their responses from the ISDI to the Scoring Sheet. They then complete six more steps, as directed on the Scoring Sheet, totaling their response scores for each extreme of each dimension, and plotting their final two dimension scores on the ISDI Scoring Sheet.

4. The ISDI Interpretation Sheets are distributed, and time is provided for participants to review their profiles in light of the information on the Interpretation Sheet. The facilitator answers any questions.

5. (Optional) The videos of participants' "mini-classes" are replayed. Participants are instructed to compare their ISDI scores with what they observe of themselves on video. After hearing comments of others in their group, participants share their results and reactions with the group.

6. Participants are asked to review the figure of the ISDI Quick Reference Guide on the Interpretation Sheet and to contrast the behaviors that characterize the four basic styles.

7. Participants are asked to volunteer situations in which they can use the ISDI with others to receive feedback on their instructional styles.

Suggested Discussion Questions

The following items are suggested for use in a general discussion.

1. General reactions/comments/questions.
2. Do you think that the inventory was accurate? Did it assess or describe you as you think you are?
3. As you completed the inventory, were you ranking the statements in terms of how you think you are or how you would like to be seen?
4. What concerns other than "who" and "what" would be key influences on your instructional style?

The following items are suggested for use after replay of the mini-classes video.

1. Do the results of the inventory and what you saw of yourself on the video match?
2. What are the discrepancies, if any?
3. Why do you believe you have the particular instructional style you now have? What have been the key influences on your style?
4. Which of these styles have you noticed most frequently in other trainers to whom you have been exposed recently? Were they appropriate and/or effective in the particular situations?
5. Which instructional style do you respond to best as a learner? Why?
6. Which style is most appropriate to your specific instructional situations? Why?
7. What changes do you think you need to make to become a more effective instructor?

RECOMMENDED USES OF THE ISDI

Feedback from only a single source no longer is adequate if we expect continuous improvement in trainers and instructional processes. Self-assessment is beneficial to a point, but research has shown that it typically suffers from a leniency effect. Feedback from multiple sources has proven to be a much more valuable indicator of performance.

The ISDI can be useful as a multi-source, nonevaluative perform-ance-development tool for trainers. It provides learners, peers, supervisors, and other stakeholders an objective means to provide behaviorally based feedback. The knowledge of how their actions are actually perceived (style awareness) should lead to an increase in trainers' behavioral repertoires (style flexibility) and, ultimately, to continuous improvement of the learning process.

References and Bibliography

Baird, L.I. (1973). Teaching styles: An exploratory study of dimensions and effects. *Journal of Experimental Psychology, 64,* 15-21.

Bergquist, W.H., & Phillips, S.R. (1975). *A handbook for faculty development.* Washington, DC: Council for the Advancement of Small Colleges.

Blake, R., & Mouton, J.S. (1976). *The employee training & development grid.* Austin, TX: Scientific Methods.

Bostrom, R. (1979). Training style inventory (TSI). In J.E. Jones & J.W. Pfeiffer (Eds.), *The 1979 annual handbook for group facilitators.* San Diego, CA: Pfeiffer & Company.

Canfield, A.A., & Canfield, J.S. (1975). *Instructional styles inventory.* Ann Arbor, MI: Humanics Media.

Conti, G.J. (1982, Spring). The principles of adult learning scale. *Adult Literacy and Basic Education.*

Dobson, R.L., and Dobson, J.E. (1974). Teacher beliefs-practices congruency. *Journal of the Student Personnel Association for Higher Education, 12,* 157-164.

Entwhistle, N. (1982). *Styles of learning and teaching.* New York: John Wiley.

Flanagan, D. (1983, January). Check out your training personality. *Training,* pp. 26-27.

Flanders, N.A. (1969). Teaching effectiveness. In Robert L. Ebel (Ed.), *Encyclopedia of Educational Research* (4th ed.). New York: Macmillan.

Hadley, H.N. (1975). *Development of an instrument to determine adult educators' orientation: Andragogical or pedagogical.* Unpublished thesis, Boston University School of Education, Boston, MA.

Jacobs, R.T., & Fuhrmann, B.S. (1984). The concept of learning style. In J.E. Jones & J.W. Pfeiffer (Eds.), *The 1984 annual: Developing human resources.* San Diego, CA: Pfeiffer & Company.

Kolb, D.A. (1976). *Learning style inventory: Technical manual.* Boston: McBer.

Lefton, R.E., & Buzzota, V.R. (1980, November). Trainers, learners and training results. *Training & Development Journal,* pp. 12-18.

Mann, R.D., Arnold, S.M., Binder, J., Cytrunbaum, S., Newman, B.M., Ringwald, J., & Rosenwein, R. (1970). *The college classroom: Conflict, change, and learning.* New York: John Wiley.

Michalak, D. (1974). *Styles of training index.* Tucson, AZ: Michalak Training Associates.

Newstrom, J.W. (1987, September). HRD and the rule of four. *Training,* pp. 61-65.

Parry, S. (1982). *Instructional skills assessment.* Princeton, NJ: Training House.

Pickren, B., & Blitzer, R.J. (1992, March). How to escape your training horrors. *Training*, pp. 32-35.

Reddin, W.J. (1970). *Managerial effectiveness*. New York: McGraw-Hill.

Spier, M.S. (1974). S-C (student content) teaching inventory. In J.E. Jones & J.W. Pfeiffer (Eds.), *The 1974 annual handbook for group facilitators*. San Diego, CA: Pfeiffer & Company.

Tindal, C.R., & Doyle, P. (1977, May). Trainers or trainees—Who dominates? *Training & Development Journal*, pp. 64-71.

Wheeler, M., & Marshall, J. (1986). The trainer type inventory (TTI): Identifying training style preferences. In J.E. Jones & J.W. Pfeiffer (Eds.), *The 1986 annual: Developing human resources*. San Diego, CA: Pfeiffer & Company.

Yeager, D.A. (1981, December). Understanding—and adapting—your instructional style. *Training*, pp. 44, 48.

Greg Cripple *is the manager of HR planning and development at John Deere Credit Company in Moline, Illinois, where he has worked for twenty-one years. He received his master's degree in social studies education from the University of Iowa. He coauthored the article, "How to Prepare Your People," which appeared in* Training & Development Journal *and* Training and Development Sourcebook. *Mr. Cripple would welcome collaboration with academics who want to validate this instrument.*

INSTRUCTIONAL STYLES DIAGNOSIS INVENTORY

Greg Cripple

Instructions: Think of your most recent learning experience with the trainer who is being evaluated. Each of the twenty items that follows contains four statements about what instructors can do or ways in which they can act.

Rank each set of statements to reflect the degree to which each statement in the set describes the trainer's instructional style. Assign a ranking of four (4) to the statement most characteristic or descriptive of the trainer; assign a three (3) to the next most descriptive statement; a two (2) to the next most descriptive statement; and a one (1) to the statement that is least descriptive of the trainer. Record your response for each statement in the blank next to it.

For some items, you may think that all statements are very descriptive or that none fit very well. To give the most accurate feedback, force yourself to rank the statements as best you can.

"WHEN INSTRUCTING ADULTS, THIS PERSON WOULD BE MOST LIKELY TO..."

1.____ a. Allow extended practice or discussion in areas of particular interest to learners.

____ b. Judge trainer's effectiveness by how well the prepared materials are covered.

____ c. Sit down with learners while instructing them.

____ d. Set trainer up as a role model and encourage learners to emulate trainer.

2.____ a. End a training session by summarizing the key subject matter and recommending that learners find ways to apply it on the job.

____ b. Arrange the room so as to provide for better discipline and control.

____ c. Use specific course objectives to inform learners as to what they should expect to be able to do.

____ d. Focus learners' attention more on themselves and their own performance than on trainer.

The 1996 Annual: Volume 1, Training.
Copyright © 1996 by Pfeiffer & Company, San Diego, CA.

3. _____ a. Gain supervisors' involvement by providing ideas on how to support learners' attempts to apply new skills.

_____ b. Let the group "handle" difficult learners or privately explore reasons for problems.

_____ c. Evaluate learners by giving examinations to test their retention of presented materials.

_____ d. Carefully lead and control any group discussions.

4. _____ a. Put his or her primary focus on giving a technically polished presentation.

_____ b. Avoid reducing impact by not disclosing any course materials prior to the program.

_____ c. Show willingness to learn from learners by admitting errors or lack of knowledge when appropriate.

_____ d. Collect background information and adjust the level of content material for each particular group.

5. _____ a. Involve learners in activities designed to stimulate critical or reflective thought.

_____ b. Communicate positive expectations to slower learners through feedback and encouragement, in order to help them improve.

_____ c. Motivate learners with enthusiastic talks, humorous stories, and entertaining or inspirational videos.

_____ d. Maintain punctuality of published program schedules.

6. _____ a. Make occasional use of media tools to support other primary learning activities.

_____ b. Present materials in the most logical order.

_____ c. Allow learners to influence or prioritize course content and objectives.

_____ d. Ensure that learners perform and apply newly learned skills as instructed.

7. ____ a. Thoroughly cover all subject-matter areas in the scheduled time allotted.

____ b. Change course materials or training methods based on feedback about learners' performance changes after training.

____ c. Maintain a consistent pace of presentation throughout the program.

____ d. Express concern for and interest in individual learners and their problems.

8. ____ a. Judge trainer's effectiveness based on learners' "liking" of trainer.

____ b. Allow learners to make mistakes and learn from session experiences.

____ c. Expose learners to traditionally accepted subject matter and correct procedures.

____ d. Ask learners questions designed to guide them to self-discovery of key points.

9. ____ a. Frequently assess learners' body language and emotional states and adjust activities or schedule appropriately.

____ b. Explore content-related controversial issues as potential learning experiences.

____ c. Plan and structure course materials in considerable detail.

____ d. Begin program by informing learners of trainer's experience or qualifications and trainer's goals for the program.

10. ____ a. Cite a bibliography of resources concerning materials discussed for further learner self-development.

____ b. Use position as instructor to quickly resolve "difficult learner" problems (e.g., monopolizers, side conversations, sharpshooters, etc.).

____ c. Encourage casual or comfortable dress to increase the informality of the learning environment.

____ d. Avoid potentially time-wasting tangents by dealing with learners' questions quickly and moving on.

11.____ a. Direct learners' attention primarily to trainer and to what is being said or demonstrated.

____ b. Frequently redirect learners' questions to other learners to be answered.

____ c. Send out self-study "prework" materials to spark learner interest and formation of course expectations.

____ d. Consistently cover the same material with each group.

12.____ a. Arrange the room so as to promote group activities and discussions.

____ b. Always stand in front of the class while instructing.

____ c. Send learners' bosses an overview of course subject matter.

____ d. Judge trainer's effectiveness based on how proficient learners are in performing new skills or applying new concepts on the job.

13.____ a. Project a professional image by maintaining a separation between trainer and learners.

____ b. Help learners motivate themselves by developing new skills through involvement and participation.

____ c. Closely direct learners' activities.

____ d. Allow learners to analyze materials and draw their own conclusions.

14.____ a. End a training session by helping learners create action plans to apply course content to real-world problems.

____ b. Criticize slow learners to help them improve.

____ c. Avoid controversy as a potential distraction or turnoff.

____ d. Coach learners as they practice new skills.

15.____ a. Encourage detailed note taking by learners.

____ b. Encourage learners to challenge outdated course materials or concepts of questionable value on the job.

____ c. Sequence activities so as to stimulate and hold learner interest.

____ d. Use media (video, slides, overheads, etc.) extensively to increase the professionalism of the presentation.

16.____ a. Use an introductory overview to inform learners of the subject matter to be covered.

____ b. Judge trainer's effectiveness based on learners' increase in confidence and self-esteem.

____ c. Maintain a formal dress code to establish a more serious atmosphere.

____ d. Encourage creativity in the performance and application of course concepts.

17.____ a. Change course materials or training methods based on update of expertise in the subject matter.

____ b. Begin a program by having learners introduce themselves to one another and communicate to trainer what their expectations are.

____ c. Adjust time schedules during the program in response to learners' interests and concerns.

____ d. Enhance credibility with learners by answering all questions quickly and accurately.

18.____ a. Avoid potentially embarrassing questions and protect material by keeping content resources confidential.

____ b. Highlight key points in detail, speaking from carefully prepared notes.

____ c. Vary pace of the program to adjust to natural daily highs and lows in learners' energy levels.

____ d. Evaluate learners based on their abilities to perform specific objectives.

19. ____ a. Defend trainer's expertise and credibility when challenged by a learner on a content issue.

____ b. Emphasize establishing open, two-way communication.

____ c. Leave the structure of the program loose to respond to the specific needs of the group.

____ d. Aim the level of sophistication of course material at the "average" learner.

20. ____ a. Listen attentively and observe group discussion of content issues or problem applications.

____ b. Ensure that learners reach the right conclusions and accept the key points or concepts presented.

____ c. Explore reasons that learners ask questions, to bring out individual concerns and hidden agendas.

____ d. Project confidence and assurance by using effective gestures, posture, and vocal dynamics while instructing.

INSTRUCTIONAL STYLES DIAGNOSIS INVENTORY SCORING SHEET
(To be completed by trainer)

Step 1. *Instructions:* Transfer the rankings from the ISDI to the Scoring Chart below. Note that the letter items in each set are **not** in alphabetical order.

Scoring Chart

	A	B	C	D
1	d	a	c	b
2	b	c	d	a
3	d	a	b	c
4	a	d	c	b
5	c	a	b	d
6	b	c	a	d
7	c	b	d	a
8	a	b	d	c
9	d	b	a	c
10	b	a	c	d
11	a	c	b	d
12	b	d	a	c
13	a	d	b	c
14	b	a	d	c
15	d	b	c	a
16	c	d	b	a
17	d	c	b	a
18	b	d	c	a
19	a	c	b	d
20	d	c	a	b
Total				

Step 2. Determine the sum of the rankings in each column and record them at the bottom of that column.

Step 3. Subtract the lower of the Column A or C totals from the higher.

The 1996 Annual: Volume 1, Training.
Copyright © 1996 by Pfeiffer & Company, San Diego, CA.

Step 4. Subtract the lower of the Column B and D totals from the higher.

Step 5. Plot the result from Step 3 on the vertical scale of the graph that follows. If the "A" total is higher, plot the result below the midpoint "O." If the "C" total is higher, plot the result above this point.

Step 6. Plot the result from Step 4 on the horizontal scale. If the "B" total is higher, plot the result to the right of the midpoint "O." If the "D" total is higher, plot the result to the left of this point.

Step 7. Extend lines from the plotted points on each scale to the point where the two lines intersect.

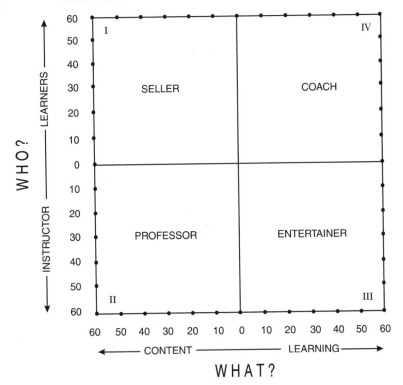

INSTRUCTIONAL STYLES DIAGNOSTIC INVENTORY INTERPRETATION SHEET
(For the trainer)

COMPONENTS OF INSTRUCTIONAL STYLES

The styles that trainers use in developing and presenting learning experiences are based on their personal beliefs about what the purposes of instruction are and how they can best contribute to achieving those purposes.

The ISDI attempts to determine training style as the interactive product of two dimensions: *what* the trainer's attention is focused on and *who* is the focus of attention while the trainer is instructing. Each dimension is a function of two sets of concerns.

The *what* dimension (the horizontal scale) represents the tradeoff between:

1. Concern for content quality and thoroughness of presentation coverage (represented by the Column D total); and

2. Concern for the actual learning that takes place with learners who are working with the content (represented by the Column B total).

The *who* dimension (the vertical scale) represents the tradeoff between:

1. Concern for the trainer and how polished, impressive, or entertaining his or her delivery is (represented by the Column A total); and

2. Concern for the learners and how effectively or positively they are receiving, practicing, considering, discussing, or applying new skills (represented by the Column C total).

No model of this type is perfect. For instance, you may be able to think of trainers who are able to balance a high concern for content with a high concern for the learning that the content produces. However, for most instructors, it is realistic to expect that balancing the two involves influencing one at the expense of the other. The same may be said for the who dimension.

INTERPRETING YOUR SCORES

The point on the graph at which the scores of these two dimensions intersect represents your overall training style.

To interpret your results, you must consider three things:

1. The comparative strengths of the four individual column totals,
2. The position of each of the two dimension scores, and
3. The direction and distance from the center of the point where the two dimension scores intersect.

For instance, were the four column totals high and low or were they close to one another? This indicates whether you tend to balance each aspect of training style equally or whether some aspects differ greatly to you in degree of importance. This directly effects the position of the dimension scores, which is the next consideration. If a dimension score is far toward one extreme or the other, this indicates a higher degree of tradeoff between the two sets of concerns involved. Dimension scores more near the middle represent a balanced degree of tradeoff, regardless of individual emphasis.

The intersection of the two dimension scores represents your overall training style, the product of your attempt to achieve balance among concerns for content, learning, delivery, and reception. The further this point is from the center of the graph, the more extreme your training style tends to be. The closer to the center this point is, the more "balanced" it tends to be.

DESCRIPTIONS OF STYLES

Following are short descriptions of the types of behaviors, attitudes, tendencies, and preferences that characterize each of the four styles.

 ## I. "The Seller"

A person who has the "seller" instructional style is primarily concerned with the content and how positively it is received and understood. Learning is the participant's responsibility, and it may or may not happen as a result. Because getting the message across and creating a good attitude toward it are the primary goals, "seller" instructors tend to focus their attention on the learners and the learners' receptivity to the message.

They build a receptive atmosphere by creating a comfortable learning environment, encouraging learners, answering questions, varying the pace of the program, and so on. They tend to use lectures or prepared media presentation methods, interspersed with discussion to hold interest and attention. Note taking is encouraged to aid retention of material.

Homework, prework, and course-summary materials are used extensively to communicate or reinforce the content. Pass/fail or non-graded examinations are preferred to assess retention without turning the learners off.

The "seller" style is common in public schools and is probably more appropriate for building general educational backgrounds than for developing specific skills. It may also be appropriate for situations in which the selling of a technique, concept, or product is more important than the learners' becoming proficient in it. It is not as appropriate when learners are expected to perform better or differently as a result of the training.

II. "The Professor"

Instructors who have a high concern for both content and delivery probably see themselves primarily as presenters. The "professor" types tend to be highly concerned about such things as their image, their technique and smoothness of speaking, and creating a proper impression. They prefer to have the spotlight on themselves, because this focuses the learners' attention on them. The atmosphere in their sessions tends to be formal, and the separation between the presenter and the audience is emphasized.

"Professor" types are, at the same time, concerned with the adequacy of what they are presenting. Their presentations are usually well-researched, often impressively footnoted and referenced, planned and organized in detail, and well-rehearsed. Time is important because it reflects on their images as presenters (i.e., punctuality is impressive) and on their ability to cover all important content.

Their preferred teaching method is to lecture, as this allows them to focus attention on themselves, to control time, and to cover the content they believe is important. There is a tendency to overuse or inappropriately use media such as video, slides, or overheads because of their perceived ability to impress, entertain, and present large amounts of information in short time spans.

Typical situations where the "professor" style would be appropriate are: making a speech, delivering an after-dinner talk, communicating a report, and presenting or selling ideas to decision makers. This style usually is not as effective where actual skill development or behavioral change is expected from the learners. It may be appropriate for attitude change purposes; however, change produced by this method typically is short-lived unless constantly reinforced.

 ## III. "The Entertainer"

Instructors who use the "entertainer" style focus on the results of training but also feel that people will learn best from instructors they like, respect, or admire. They have many of the same personal-image concerns as "professors." They are very concerned with their credibility and whether the learners have confidence in their expertise.

"Entertainers" are concerned about involvement in the learning process, but more with their own than with the learners'. Thus, methods such as watching a role model (the instructor) demonstrate proper technique are preferred over self-discovery or group learning activities. When more participatory methods are used, these instructors tend to exercise close control and make themselves an integral part of the learning process.

Because these instructors generally believe that learners need to be "inspired" if they are going to perform differently, sessions often are designed to be highly motivational or entertaining. This can be effective but has the potential limitation of making what is learned instructor-dependent. When this occurs, learners can suffer drops in motivation when attempting to apply new skills on the job because the dynamic instructor is not there.

The fact that they are personally influencing learners is often more important to these instructors than the specific change that take place or the input that cause it. Thus, specific content is not an important issue.

This style probably is most appropriate for personal growth seminars, sales meetings, and programs that are meant to "recharge learners' batteries."

In its worst case, the "entertainer" style could be likened to a medicine-show huckster who dazzles you and takes your money before you have a chance to judge the value of his product.

 ## IV. "The Coach"

Instructors who are oriented both to learning and to the learners tend to have the spotlight reversed so that the learners' attention is focused on themselves most of the time. These trainers see their role more as facilitators of learning experiences than as presenters of information. They see value in course content only insofar as it enables learners to perform in new ways.

The focus of most coaching activities is on skill development, confidence building, and application, rather than on retention of information. Learners are evaluated, but mostly through observation of performance or behavioral change rather than through written tests. Grades usually are ignored, because most instruction is aimed at upgrading everyone's skills to a minimum or improved level rather than on determining who is most proficient.

There is less concern for polished delivery because "coach" instructors spend much less time "delivering." Also, because of the informal atmosphere created, there is less pressure on the instructor to perform, motivate, or entertain. Use of a high ratio of self-discovery and group-learning activities allows the learners to motivate and entertain themselves. The responsibility to perform is, in effect, shifted from the instructor to them.

Separation between the instructor and the learners is deemphasized. The prevailing philosophy typically is that the best instructor is the one who sets high expectations, guides and coaches the learners, and then gets out of the way so they can perform.

The instructor has a message, but the message is determined more by specific learner needs and less by what the instructor thinks might be good for the learners. Rather than forcing learners to understand and accept new ideas, "coaches" use questions, discussions, self-study, group work, and other involving techniques to lead learners to conclusions, but they allow the learners to make the commitments on their own.

The "coach" style tends to be most effective in bona fide training situations where skill building and behavioral change are the primary concerns. Potential problems with this style are tendencies to ignore time constraints, skip over important content issues, lose control of the class, turn off learners who are used to more traditional instructional styles, or be overly influenced by learners' perceptions of their own needs.

A QUICK REFERENCE SHEET

The following figure provides an overview of the instructional styles measured by the Instructional Styles Diagnostic Instrument.

SELLER	COACH
Sellers are: Task oriented	Coaches are: Learner oriented
They see themselves as: Taskmasters/persuaders	They see themselves as: Facilitators/guides
Sellers' main concern is: Product/content	Coaches' main concern is: Results/performance
They strive to be: Driving, aggressive, enthusiastic, convincing	They strive to be: Participative, accepting, empathic, supportive
Programs are structured to be: Informal but inflexible	Programs are structured to be: Informal and flexible
Leading to sessions that are: Informative, productive, efficient, complete, persuasive	Leading to sessions that are: Involving, encouraging, constructive, developmental
Learners are evaluated by: Objective testing	Learners are evaluated by: Comparing behaviors or performance objectives
PROFESSOR	**ENTERTAINER**
Professors are: Instructor oriented	Entertainers are: Relations oriented
They see themselves as: Presenters/experts	They see themselves as: Role models/stars
Professors' main concern is: Process/delivery	Entertainers' main concern is: Reactions/feelings
They strive to be: Impressive, polished, professional, aloof	They strive to be: Dynamic, animated, charismatic, outgoing, inspirational
Programs are structured to be: Formal and inflexible	Programs are structured to be: Formal but flexible
Leading to sessions that are: Scheduled, controlled, organized, disciplined	Leading to sessions that are: Motivated, lively, fun, entertaining
Learners are evaluated by: Subjective testing and instructor judgment	Learners are evaluated by: Assessment of their feelings and opinions

WHO?
LEARNERS — INSTRUCTOR

←——— CONTENT ——————— LEARNING ———→

WHAT?

ISDI Quick Reference Guide

SOURCES OF ANSWERS

Obviously, the preceding descriptions are those of the more extreme examples in each quadrant. The closer the intersection of the two scales to the center of the graph, the closer one would tend to be to a more "middle of the road" style with aspects of all four dimensions.

If you think that some respondents ranked you as more to the "ideal" than the "real," it would probably be worth your time to go back and rank the items yourself, being brutally honest, to get a more balanced picture of yourself.

The following shows the location of the polar statements for each item measured by the ISDI.

WHAT

Content ← → Learning

Application of Skills

L 16. d. Encourage creativity in the performance and application of course concepts.

C   6. d. Ensure that learners perform and apply newly learned skills as instructed.

Punctuality of Scheduling

L 17. c. Adjust time schedules during the program in response to learners' interests and concerns.

C   5. d. Maintain punctuality of published program schedules.

Currency and Applicability of Materials

L 15. b. Encourage learners to challenge outdated course materials or concepts of questionable value on the job.

C   8. c. Expose learners to traditionally accepted subject matter and correct procedures.

Degree of Program Structure

L 19. c. Leave the structure of the program loose to respond to the specific needs of the group.

C   9. c. Plan and structure course materials in considerable detail.

Evaluation of Learners

L 18. d. Evaluate learners based on their abilities to perform objectives.

C   3. c. Evaluate learners by giving examinations to test their retention of presented materials.

Direction of Activities

L   8. b. Allow learners to make mistakes and also learn from session experiences.

C 13. c. Closely direct learners' activities.

Handling of Controversy

L   9. b. Explore content-related controversial issues as potential learning experiences.

C 14. c. Avoid controversy as a potential distraction or turnoff.

Role of the Learner

L   5. a. Involve learners in activities designed to stimulate critical or reflective thought.

C 15. a. Encourage detailed note taking by learners.

Updating Methods or Materials

L   7. b. Change course materials or training methods based on feedback about learners' performance changes after training.

C 17. a. Change course materials or training methods based on update of expertise in the subject matter.

Probing Individual Concerns

L 20. c. Explore reasons that learners ask questions, to bring out individual concerns and hidden agendas.

C 10. d. Avoid potential time-wasting tangents by dealing with learners' questions quickly and moving on.

Determining Level of Material

L   4. d. Collect background information and adjust the level of content material for each particular group.

C 19. d. Aim the level of sophistication of course material at the "average" learner.

Sharing Resources

L 10. a. Cite a bibliography of resources concerning materials discussed for further learner self-development.

C 18. a. Avoid potentially embarrassing questions and protect material by keeping content resources confidential.

Controlling Learner Expectations

L 11. c. Send out self-study "prework" materials to spark learner interest and formation of course expectations.

C 4. b. Avoid reducing impact by not disclosing any course materials prior to the program.

Flexibility of Course Content

L 1. a. Allow extended practice or discussion in areas of particular interest to learners.

C 7. a. Thoroughly cover all subject-matter areas in the time allotted.

Instructor Evaluation

L 12. d. Judge trainer's effectiveness based on how proficient learners are in performing new skills or applying new concepts on the job.

C 1. b. Judge trainer's effectiveness by how well the prepared materials are covered.

Gaining Learner Commitment

L 13. d. Allow learners to analyze the materials and draw their own conclusions.

C 20. b. Ensure that learners reach the right conclusions and accept the key points or concepts presented.

Maintenance of Learned Behavior

L 14. a. End a training session by helping learners create action plans to apply course content to real-world problems.

C 2. a. End a training session by summarizing key subject matter and recommending that learners find ways to apply it on the job.

Communicating Course Intent

L 2. c. Use specific course objectives to inform learners as to what they should expect to be able to do.

C 16. a. Use an introductory overview to inform learners of the subject matter to be covered.

Involving Learners' Bosses

L 3. a. Gain supervisors' involvement by providing ideas on how to support learners' attempts to apply new skills.

C 12. c. Send learners' bosses an overview of course subject matter.

Responding to Learners' Needs

L 6. c. Allow learners to influence or prioritize course content and objectives.

C 11. d. Consistently cover the same material with each group.

WHO

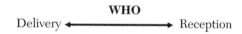

Delivery ←——————→ Reception

Communication of Expectations

I 9. d. Begin program by informing learners of trainer's experience or qualifications and trainer's goals for the program.

S 17. b. Begin a program by having learners introduce themselves to one another and communicate to trainer what their expectations are.

Dress/Atmosphere

I 16. c. Maintain a formal dress code to establish a more serious atmosphere for the learning environment.

S 10. c. Encourage casual or comfortable dress to increase the informality of the learning environment.

Motivation of Learners

I 5. c. Motivate learners with enthusiastic talks, humorous stories, and entertaining or inspirational videos.

S 13. b. Help learners motivate themselves by developing new skills through involvement and participation.

Improving Learner Performance

I 14. b. Criticize slow learners to help them improve.

S 5. b. Communicate positive expectations to slower learners through feedback and encouragement, in order to help them improve.

Establishing Program Pace

I 7. c. Maintain a consistent pace of presentation throughout the entire program.

S 18. c. Vary pace of the program to adjust to natural daily highs and lows in learners' energy levels.

Building Communication Patterns

I 4. a. Put primary focus on giving a technically polished presentation.

S 19. b. Emphasize establishing open, two-way communication.

Use of Media

I 15. d. Use media (video, slides, overheads, etc.) extensively to increase the professionalism of the presentation.

S 6. a. Make occasional use of media tools to support other primary learning activities.

Method of Presentation

I 18. b. Highlight key points, in detail, speaking from carefully prepared notes.

S 8. d. Ask learners questions designed to guide them to self-discovery of key points.

Building Instructor Credibility

I 19. a. Defend trainer's expertise and credibility when challenged by a learner on a content issue.

S 4. c. Show willingness to learn from learners by admitting errors or lack of knowledge when appropriate.

Guiding Learner Performance

I 1. d. Set trainer up as a role model and encourage learners to emulate trainer.

S 14. d. Coach learners as they practice new skills.

Sequencing Activities

I 6. b. Present materials in the most logical order.

S 15. c. Sequence activities so as to stimulate and hold learner interest.

Positioning the Instructor

I 12. b. Always stand in front of the class while instructing.

S 1. c. Sit down with learners while instructing them.

Evaluating Instructor Effectiveness

I 8. a. Judge trainer's effectiveness based on learners' "liking" of trainer.

S 16. b. Judge trainer's effectiveness based on learners' increase in confidence and self-esteem.

Use of Body Language

I 20. d. Project confidence and assurance by using effective gestures, posture, and vocal dynamics while instructing.

S 9. a. Frequently assess learners' body language and emotional states and adjust activities or schedule appropriately.

Arranging the Room

I 2. b. Arrange the room so as to provide for better discipline and control.

S 12. a. Arrange the room so as to promote group activities and group discussions.

Focusing Learners' Attention

I 11. a. Direct learners' attention primarily to trainer and to what is being said or demonstrated.

S 2. d. Focus learners' attention more on themselves and their own performance than on trainer.

Personal Concern for Learners

I 13. a. Project a professional image by maintaining a separation between trainer and learners.

S 7. d. Express concern for and interest in individual learners and their problems.

Controlling Activities

I 3. d. Carefully lead and control any group discussions.

S 20. a. Listen attentively and observe group discussion of content issues or problem applications.

Maintaining Discipline

I 10. b. Use position as instructor to quickly resolve "difficult learner" problems (e.g., monopolizers, side conversations, sharpshooters, etc.).

S 3. b. Let the group "handle" difficult learners or privately explore reasons for problems.

Handling Learners' Questions

I 17. d. Enhance credibility with learners by answering all questions quickly and accurately.

S 11. b. Frequently redirect learners' questions to other learners to be answered.

Introduction
to the Presentation and Discussion Resources Section

Every facilitator needs to develop a repertoire of theory and background that he or she can use in a variety of situations. Learning based on direct experience is not the only kind of learning appropriate to human-interaction training. A practical combination of theory and research with experiential learning generally enriches training and may be essential in many types of cognitive and skill development. Affective and cognitive data support, alter, validate, extend, and complement each other.

The 1996 Annual: Volume 1, Training includes ten articles, in the following categories:

Individual Development: Stress and Burnout

Stress Management for HRD Professionals: Taking Time to Practice What You Preach, by Herbert S. Kindler and Marilyn Ginsburg (page 201)

Communication: Coaching and Encouraging

Attribution Theory: Applications to the Managerial Coaching Process, by J. Craig VanHouten (page 189)

Communication: Communication in Organizations

From Vision to Action: Determining the Impact of a Mission Statement, by John Geirland and Eva Sonesh-Kedar (page 227)

Problem Solving: Change and Change Agents

Reigniting Spirit in the Work Place, by Laura Hauser (page 297)

Groups and Teams: Behavior and Roles in Groups

Diversity and Team Development, by Claire B. Halverson and Guillermo Cuéllar (page 235)

Consulting: Organizations: Their Characteristics and How They Function

Customer Value: The Strategic Advantage, by Howard E. Butz, Jr., and Leonard D. Goodstein (page 209)

Facilitating: Techniques and Strategies

How to Talk So Your Audience Will Listen: Three Ingredients for Killer Presentations, by Tom Henschel (page 171)

Leadership: Theories and Models

Leadership from the Gestalt Perspective, by Hank Karp (page 277)

Values-Based Leadership for the 21st Century, by Robert C. Preziosi (page 245)

Leadership: Top-Management Issues and Concerns

Getting Your Message Through: A Guide for CEOs, by Robert Hargrove (page 251)

As with previous *Annuals*, this volume covers a variety of topics; not every article will appeal to every reader. Yet the range of articles presented should encourage a good deal of thought-provoking, serious discussion about the present and the future of HRD. Other articles on specific subjects can be located by using our comprehensive *Reference Guide to Handbooks and Annuals*. This book, which is updated regularly, indexes all of the *Annuals* and all of the *Handbooks of Structured Experiences* that we have published to date. With each revision, the *Reference Guide* becomes a complete, up-to-date, and easy-to-use resource for selecting appropriate materials from *all* of the *Annuals* and *Handbooks*.

HOW TO TALK SO YOUR AUDIENCE WILL LISTEN: THREE INGREDIENTS FOR KILLER PRESENTATIONS

Tom Henschel

Abstract: For the purposes of this article, the definition of "presentation" is as follows: "An interchange between a trainer and one or more other people when the trainer has had the opportunity to prepare some of the communication." A presentation can be a phone call, a department meeting, or a keynote address. This article was written with the following three goals in mind:

- To convince trainers that removing barriers between themselves and the audience enhances credibility;

- To persuade trainers that their major task is to make sure the audience understands what they are saying; and

- To focus on ways that trainers can make presentations memorable.

The author presents helpful hints for reducing nervousness, a template for structuring easy-to-follow presentations, and suggestions for enhancing delivery style.

The 1996 Annual: Volume 1, Training.
Copyright © 1996 by Pfeiffer & Company, San Diego, CA.

Is there a doctor in the house?

Richard Dreyfuss was starring in a play in Los Angeles a few years ago. Just before the emotional climax of the first act, a woman in the second row of the audience had some kind of attack. The woman's companion, not wanting to disrupt the play, went for help as quietly as possible. However, those of us on stage were aware that this woman was in serious trouble. Within a minute, Richard descended into the audience and asked the question that, up until that moment in my life, had only existed in Warner Brothers cartoons: "Is there a doctor in the house?"

Collectively, the six of us on stage had well over one hundred years of theater experience, but none of us had ever before broken the golden rule of "The show must go on." Moustaches might slip or scenery collapse, but the show had always continued as if it were completely natural. Not so this night.

What did the theater-goers do when this award-winning actor asked for their help? Nothing. His plea was met with total silence. As if they were passive television watchers, they sat and stared, unwilling to believe he was talking to them. Finally, of course, he shook them back to reality, and the doctors in the house charged forward to give aid.

Fascinated by the audience's initial lack of response, I asked three members of the audience what they had experienced. Each had thought that the question was part of the play until the doctors actually ran down the aisle. Amazed, I said, "But it wouldn't have made any sense for Richard's character to do that as part of the play!" They answered, "It just seemed so natural we accepted it." This should not have been so amazing to me: Theater audiences are wonderfully willing to ignore any barrier that comes between them and the imaginary world being created on the stage.

ONE TOUGH ACT

Trainers do not have the same advantages. We stand in the harsh light of some meeting room without the aid of costumes, sets, or music. The only props we have are flip charts or handouts, meager tricks for making people forget their busy, complicated lives. In fact, trainers often end up talking about the very issues that remind people that their lives *are* busy and complicated!

Then again, trainers do not have the same goals as actors. In theater, the evening is a success if the audience is moved emotionally. In order to be moved, the audience must believe. They must believe that a canvas square can be a door of iron, that a pink liquid is a poison potion, or that one actress is another's mother. Everything artists do in the theater is done to protect the fragile bubble of belief; any barrier to believing must be removed.

Trainers, on the other hand, rarely think about being believable. But if the audience does not believe, the presenter cannot succeed. This article has three goals, each of which is meant to increase a trainer's believability:

- To convince trainers that removing barriers between themselves and the audience enhances credibility;

- To persuade trainers that their major task is to make sure the audience understands what they are saying; and

- To focus on ways to make presentations memorable.

Achieving these goals requires improvements in three areas: reducing nervousness, formulating a structure for the presentation, and enhancing delivery style.

REDUCING YOUR NERVES

I was recently in someone's home to listen to a presentation on certain legal issues. Twenty of us gathered comfortably in the high-ceilinged room. The presenter was well rehearsed: She delivered jokes with assurance, knew exactly when to change her transparencies, and spoke in a manner that showed she was confident. This woman does not sound particularly nervous, but let me add three other details: First, in this cozy room, she chose to speak into a hand-held microphone; second, she stated plainly and directly that she preferred for us to hold questions until she was finished speaking; and third, for most of her presentation, she focused on a spot on the back wall about eight inches above our hostess's head. Does this woman sound nervous now?

This woman did not suffer obvious symptoms of nervousness like knocking knees or a sweaty brow. Instead her credibility was undermined more subtly: She showed a confident exterior but erected barriers that prevented her from connecting with her audience. Her nervousness caused her to give the appearance of not caring whether I understood or remembered her material. Consequently, I found it impossible to pay attention to her.

This woman is not alone in being undermined by her nervousness. Everyone is nervous. Different people experience different symptoms for different reasons. Barbra Streisand's nervousness forced her off the stage for years. Marilyn Monroe was sick to her stomach before public performances. Even the world-acclaimed Sir Laurence Olivier once suffered such acute stage fright that he forbade other actors to look him in the eye.

But there is some good news: Nervousness can be controlled. Take, for example, the case of a very affable manager for one of the major automobile manufacturers named Kurt. His job, which he loved, consisted mainly of making highly technical presentations at automobile dealerships. Kurt wanted me to help him to control his nerves. I began by asking him when he experienced his nerves, and he replied, "Only when the owners of the dealerships drop in on my presentations."

Because he had identified his trigger so specifically, I felt certain we could reprogram his nerves. I asked when his nerves first made themselves felt. Although Kurt contended that they did not occur at all unless the owner actually walked into the presentation room, I was sure that was not the case. After further discussion, he admitted he sometimes worried about the owners before he even arrived to set up for the sessions.

Kurt's dread increased his fear. It is like a child who fears getting an injection even before getting to the doctor's office. When the time arrives to roll up his or her sleeve, the fear makes the muscles tense, which makes the needle harder to push and makes the shot hurt all the more. Worrying makes the worst-case scenario come true.

If Kurt was willing to focus on his fear in its earliest stages, while it was still manageable, I knew he would be able to reduce his nervousness. He was skeptical but said he would give it a try. I assured him the process was as easy as "A B C":

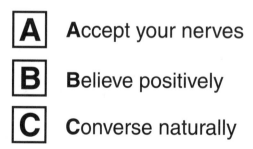

A	Accept your nerves
B	Believe positively
C	Converse naturally

Accept Your Nerves

Kurt did not like feeling nervous. He felt that as an intelligent man he should be able to suppress his nerves. But like most people, he was afraid that if he accepted his nerves they would rage out of control and consume him like a wildfire. He did not understand that nervousness feeds on resistance; stop fearing your nerves and they immediately decrease.

Although you must accept that you will feel nervous, you must also be active in trying to reprogram the thoughts that cause your nervousness. In Kurt's case I urged him to change his thoughts the very moment he felt his dread begin. I offered these new thoughts as an alternative: "The owner might come to my presentation today. That probably will make me nervous. But I still will do fine." Although this is not a huge shift in thinking, it allowed him to stop tensing against the fear. By beginning to accept his nerves he began to reprogram himself.

Believe Positively

The next step in reducing your nerves is to believe positively about whatever is triggering your anxiety. In Kurt's case, perhaps the owners frightened him because they represented authority or power. Included with issues of power and authority is a negative belief about how that power might be used against us. That negative belief needs to be uncovered and reversed.

I asked Kurt why the dealership owners would care to drop in on his presentations if the information were so technical. He answered, "Oh, I don't think they want to understand it; they just want to be in on everything." I then asked if there would be any benefit if the owners did understand his information. He protested that they would never understand it—and he was right. As long as Kurt believed that the owners would not understand, they wouldn't. Like the woman who used a hand-held microphone in a small room, Kurt had erected unconscious barriers between himself and the owners.

The good news here was that Kurt really did want to affect a change. He was willing to listen to himself. He heard how negatively he spoke about the owners and began to see that his negative beliefs had no positive benefits. Finally, he began to see that his beliefs were just beliefs; they were not facts, and he could change them if he wanted.

Picture Kurt now. He says to himself, "The owner might come to my presentation today. That'll probably make me nervous. But I'll still do fine. Besides, I really would like him to hear about the digital system. If he could get the mechanics invested in those, it would be great." Kurt began to accept his nerves and believe positively about the owners. And guess what? His nerves began to decrease.

Converse Naturally

Now we arrive at the letter C of the ABC formula: Converse naturally. This last change is what finally broke the back of Kurt's vulnerability. I asked him if he ever conversed with the owners individually. He said he did. "And are you nervous then?" I asked. "No," he said. "Usually I enjoy talking with them." "Then the next time an owner pops in, stop making a presentation and try conversing with him." Kurt's response to this was a look of such puzzlement that I had to smile.

Most people are pretty comfortable sitting across a desk and explaining an idea in a give-and-take manner. However, as soon as they imagine themselves speaking those same ideas in front of a group of people, they become fearful. What triggers this response? One contributing factor is the feeling that they are solely responsible for all the communication in the room.

Conversing naturally requires a casual, confident delivery style, just like a good one-on-one meeting. To be able to converse naturally you must first believe positively about your listeners. They are friendly people, not nameless shapes critically judging you. These people have needs and wants that you may be able to fulfill. They will listen to you because your ideas are valuable.

Once you believe positively about your audience and your presentation, avoid lecturing. Do not "present" and do not "deliver." Instead, converse naturally. Talk to the audience as if you were talking across a desk with someone you enjoy. Look them in the eyes. If you fix your gaze on a flip chart, your notes, or a spot in mid-air, you erect a barrier to understanding and retention. Your watchers lose the visual connection to your message and struggle to stay tuned in.

Conversing naturally also means you can actually talk to them. Ask them directly if they understand what you are saying, or comment on what you see in their eyes. Remind them often of where you are within your presentation's structure. Be willing to depart from your script and respond to them in the moment. This is not hard to do if you picture yourself as having a conversation.

Eye contact quickly will tell you who understands and who does not understand. Be sure the people you address are following you when you move to your next point. There is no point in rushing through your third and fourth points and finishing on time if the audience is still confused about something you said back at point two.

The point of conversing naturally is to keep everyone together and involved: They are watching you in order to understand, and you are watching them to be sure they do understand. This can work in large auditoriums or under the pressure of time. You cannot afford not to converse naturally: Your presentation has no value if no one is listening.

The wonderful by-product of this shift in attitude, aside from creating more positive connections with your audience by removing barriers, is that your nerves will decrease. Remember our ABC formula:

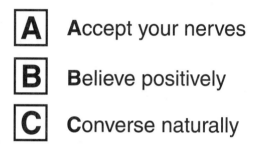

A Accept your nerves

B Believe positively

C Converse naturally

The steps that lead up to the ABCs are as follows:

1. Define the specific triggers that make you nervous;

2. Find the earliest moment that your nerves make themselves felt; and

3. Examine the thoughts that occur when your nerves first appear.

Now that you have the tools to keep your nerves under control, let's look at ways to make every presentation easy to understand.

STRUCTURING FOR SUCCESS

Your presentation is a journey. You must guide people through a landscape that you know better than anyone else. Guiding these people puts one very serious responsibility on you: You must keep everyone together. To do this you have to know where you are going and how you are going to get there. If the group is not all together when you reach the destination, you have not done your job. This is no easy task, but there is a template you can use for any type of presentation you ever have to give. This template will help you to create a map so your tour will be understandable, memorable, and easy to follow.

Before you actually set out with people in tow, you have to gather some information. What are you going to show on your tour? Is it going to be a broad overview of the entire City of Angels, or will it focus tightly on the narrow alleys of Chinatown?

Another piece of information to know is who you will be leading. You logically would show different things to children from Nairobi than you would to architects who specialize in Art Deco re-creations. What does your group already know and what do they think they want to know?

A final piece of information to know is whether your presentation is going to be informative or persuasive. Informative presentations primarily dispense data and their purpose is to educate. Persuasive presentations also dispense data but their primary purpose is to change how people think and to motivate them to action. Every advertisement in every medium is an attempt at a persuasive presentation.

You Need a Headline

Once you have answered these three questions, you will need to formulate a headline, such as "Inside Russian Nesting Dolls" or "The Cosmos: A Walking Tour." A headline answers the question "What are you going to talk about?" The headline may or may not become the actual title you use for your presentation. It has no details, just a broad umbrella of an idea.

After the headline, the next step in creating your map is a brainstorming exercise. Write down everything you can think of that you might ever want these people to know. Once you have exhausted your ideas, get a blank sheet of paper and divide it into four squares. Looking at your list, see which items naturally relate to which others. Put the first set of related items together in one box on the new page. In the second and third boxes, put other items that form natural groups. Box number four is the catch-all bin for miscellaneous, unrelated items.

Next, consider each box by itself. Do the grouped details in a box suggest a topic? Keep thinking until you can name the three boxes. When you are finished, you will have assembled a page of information that looks like the table on the next page.

Boxes one, two, and three are the building blocks you will use to fill in the template. The ideas in box number four, however, will have to wait until another time. Why? It is a proven fact that things in threes are easier to remember. Look at this article: it has three sections (Nerves, Structure, Delivery). Section one even had three subsections (ABCs). Threes work. Listeners will not retain more than three topics; with fewer than three topics, you risk giving them the sense that the information is inconsequential.

Topic Title #1	**Topic Title #2**
Detail Detail Detail	Detail Detail Detail
Topic Title #3	**Misc.**
Detail Detail Detail	Detail Detail Detail

Headline

The first thing to fill in on the template is the headline. In order to give you a sense of different ways the template can work, what follows are some brief transcripts from real presentations. Because the words were meant to be spoken and heard, reading them out loud will help you more than reading with your eyes only.

First, some sample headlines, the very first words these presenters spoke:

"Today I'm going to demonstrate how to create successful presentations."

"I'd like to share some success stories about peer education on our college campuses."

"I want to talk about the training tracks available to our employees."

Each of these headlines is successful. It is a simple, declarative sentence that announces what will come next without details. It is the beginning of a map.

Announce Three Topic Titles

Next you will use the details from the three boxes. However, do not just launch into the details in box one. First, lay out a map so that people know where you are taking them. Two of the following examples are complete successes; one is not as good as it could be.

> "Today I'm going to demonstrate how to create successful presentations. There are three important components I'm going to show you. Each one contributes to a successful presentation. First is being able to control your nerves; second is giving your presentation a solid structure; and third is being able to monitor your delivery style."

> "I'd like to share some success stories about peer education on our college campuses. There are three different phases of the process that I'm going to focus on: 1) the selection process; 2) the training process; and 3) monitoring the peers' performance."

> "I want to talk about the training tracks available to our employees because our company really supports employee education and has set up a lot of different tracks people can participate in. One track is continuing education, which does not contribute toward any degree. It's just there if people want to better themselves. There are also equivalency courses that are just what the name says: courses to help people work toward a high school diploma. Then there are degree courses, which have many different components and can be rather confusing. I will get to those in a few minutes."

The third example clearly is different than the other two. It is not as effective because the headline was a long, compound sentence. The presenter did choose three topics to discuss, but did not announce that fact. He said there were "a lot of tracks," which could mean two or fourteen. He also gave details and definitions before introducing all of the topics. As a listener, I cannot distinguish topics from headlines from details. When I hear them all at once, I feel lost. In addition, the presenter failed to give numerical listings. Using the format "Number one is..., number two is..., and number three is..." is one of the easiest, most powerful mapping tools in existence.

When announcing your topic titles, use the following rules:

1. Tell your listeners that you are about to list three items;

2. Introduce the items by using the same ordinal/numeric words (for example, "the first is..., the second is..., and the third is...."):

3. Use titles that are short, declarative statements; save the details for later.

Following these rules, presenter number three would change the introduction to be more like the following:

"I want to talk about the training tracks available to our employees. Our company supports employee education and has set up three different educational tracks people can participate in. The first track is Continuing Education. The second track is an Equivalency Course. And the third track is a Degree track. I'm going to start with number one, the Continuing Education track."

This describes a clean map that anyone can follow and remember. So far the template has two items:

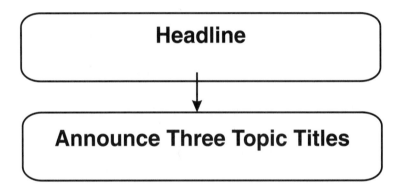

Transition Statements

In the presenter's last sentence, he said "I'm going to start with number one, the Continuing Education track." This is called a "transition statement." In this case, the statement guided the audience from the list of topic titles into the actual details of the first topic. Transition statements are to presentations what surveyor's levels are to map making: You can muddle through without them but the end product will not be first rate. Transition statements help people know how far they have come and how far they still have to go. Using them makes the comfort level in the room soar.

Later in her speech, the second presenter used two great transition statements, as well as creating a list that promoted understanding and memorability.

> "...Now I'm going to move on to number three: 'Monitoring the peers' performance.' We've found there are four ways to successfully monitor the performance of the peer counselors. One is to have participants fill out evaluations immediately after a session; another is to have the counselor fill out self-assessment forms about every six weeks; a third way is to record the sessions on tape; and a final option is to sit in on the sessions. I'd like to discuss the pros and the cons of each of these options and hand out some sample forms. First, let's look at number one: the participant's evaluation form."

This presenter's listeners are following right along. The transition statements (first and last sentences) guarantee that everyone knows that they are about to hear about topic three, "Monitoring Performance"; they then are poised to hear about detail number one.

This presenter's four details were announced and numbered in the same way as headlines and topic titles. When introducing details, it is important not to spew data. Giving details is similar to introducing topics, as follows:

1. Announce how many details you are going to discuss;

2. Give titles first, actual facts later; and

3. End with a transition statement that clearly indicates where you are leading next.

It might seem that the entire presentation becomes nothing but transition statements and announcements. This is not the case. These sentences take mere seconds to interject, and including them helps your listeners understand and remember what you are telling them. You can use this structure for persuasive or informative presentations, sales calls, or departmental reports. The complete template for memorable, understandable structure is shown in Figure 1.

ENHANCING YOUR DELIVERY STYLE

An actress I worked with while filming a television movie needed to cry during a certain scene. Crying on cue can be difficult. However, before crying, she also had to get a prop and return to a new spot that was marked on the floor. She could not look at the new mark and if she missed it, the shot would be no good.

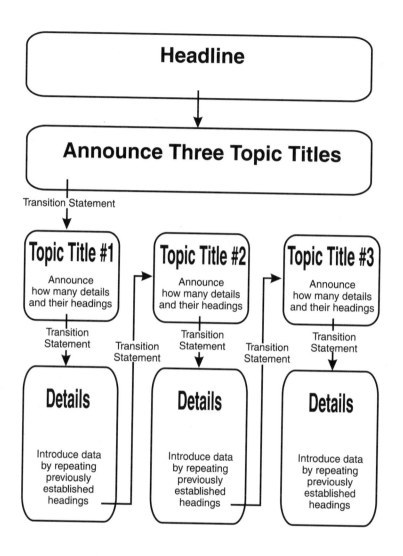

Figure 1. Successful Structure Template[1]

---

[1] This diagram is adapted from material developed by Communication Development Associates, Inc.

How was she able to create the **tears while also hitting her** marks? The kind of emotional thoughts that **generate tears** would seem to cancel out the technical awareness needed **to hit a precise mark.** Yet if they do cancel each other out, you cannot be an actor. In order to succeed in even the simplest scene, you must be able to do two things at once: 1) consciously choose your behavior, and 2) consciously repeat it or change it.

Improving delivery style requires the same two abilities. Do you choose to talk while you write on the flip chart or is it just a habit? Do you choose to pepper your speech with "um," "ah," or "you know," or does it seem out of your control? Do you **choose** to jingle the coins in your pocket or are you simply unaware that **you are** doing it? If you choose to improve your diction or eliminate nervous gestures, can you repeat the new behavior when you are standing in front of a tough audience?

The good news about these hard questions is that everyone can improve their delivery skills. The best speakers understand that this process is without end; they work on improving their skills every time they open their mouths. Because they acknowledge that there is no perfect delivery, they are not threatened by the thought that there is room for improvement. Everyone's arena for improvement is highly personal. Even when two **people happen** to need attention in similar areas, the tools that will **help them break** free of old habits often are vastly different.

Consequently, this article cannot be a standard prescription that will turn every reader into a fabulous delivery machine. However, I can prescribe certain tools that you can use to turn yourself into that fabulous delivery machine.

Taking Your Temperature

Most of us can take our own pulses, but it is almost impossible to accurately assess our inner body temperature. This is why thermometers were invented: to help us gain accurate, specific knowledge that can be vital to our health. Similarly, although most of us may be able to change our delivery habits over time, it is almost impossible to accurately assess what we are doing at the moment we are doing it. Without some sort of thermometer, this inability to assess ourselves means we may never become aware of the barriers we erect between our audiences and ourselves. Three such thermometers come under the headline of "Feedback." One has been around since at least ancient Greece. The other two are much more modern.

The oldest form of feedback is that that comes from another person. Just as every winning team has a coach and every Oscar-winning performance has a director, every presenter, no matter how good, needs the benefit of an outside eye. If you are ready to begin working on your delivery skills, there are many ways you can enlist other people in your development. Adult education centers offer professional development classes that help with awareness of yourself as a presenter. Many private companies offer group presentation courses, and personal coaches are available to work with you privately.

Another way to get feedback is to enlist friends or coworkers. Because the person you choose will probably not be trained as a coach, you both will benefit if you take control of the situation. First, decide as specifically as possible what you want to work on. Then let your coach know your area of focus by saying something like "I'm trying to improve my delivery skills. Specifically, I'm trying to change the habit I have of holding my hands behind my back. If you see me do that, would you help me be aware of it? Thanks."

> Every presenter needs the benefit of an outside eye.

Even with this kind of guidance, your friend's initial instinct will most likely be to tell you everything you do that is "wrong." This can be hard to hear. To help you keep the feedback in balance, I advocate "one-for-one" coaching. Each time your coach tells you something that needs improvement, he or she must also point out something that is working for you. This is a good rule for balanced feedback in general.

But how can you know what habits need changing? If you knew these habits were distracting, wouldn't you have changed them by now? This is where the other two, more modern thermometers come into play: audiotape and videotape.

I never have met a person who loves himself or herself on tape. People who make their living putting themselves on tape learn to accept recorded feedback, but they rarely look forward to examining the final product. I know several very successful actors who never watch themselves on film. To use these powerful tools effectively, you must be willing to accept whatever discomfort you might feel during playback.

Using an audiotape recorder gives you a partial picture of yourself that can be enlightening. Hit the "record" button when dialing or answering your phone, then listen to your end of the conversation. Focus on the words you chose. Were you direct? Did you load your speech with qualifiers such as "sort of," "kind of," "maybe," and "I guess"? Did you say what you meant? Does the tape reveal that you often repeated yourself?

Listen to your voice. Is there variety in your inflections? Do questions stand out clearly, ending with rising intonations? Does it sound as though you are smiling as you talk? Why not? Are there different rhythms to your speech, or is it all one speed? And is half of the tape silent while you are listening to the other person? It should be.

Suppose you are aware that you have trouble keeping your audience's attention. Is a repetitive gesture distracting them? If people are tuning out during a question-and-answer period, how can you know that you bounce nervously on your toes whenever you are asked a question? How can you take your temperature for these things that are completely unconscious? The answer is the greatest of all feedback tools: videotape.

No coach could ever be as impartial or convincing as video. Granted, many lenses make us look like ghoulish versions of our worst selves, but that is a discomfort that must be accepted. The truths that video reveal are indisputable and profound.

One way to use video is to watch your presentation on fast forward. Do you seem to be dancing around the screen as if infected with a medieval disorder? Or perhaps your silhouette never moves at all except for an occasional flick of a hand. In either case, the tape is saying you need to work toward integrating your energy and body movement.

Video reveals other barriers we erect between ourselves and our listeners, such as eye contact. For years I faced audiences thinking that I was not nervous. I talked to them, entertained them, taught them, and I loved doing it. If someone had asked me what barriers I erected between my audiences and myself, I would have said "None!" Videotape showed me that, of course, I did have barriers. I was, I can now confess, a darter.

A darter is someone who makes direct eye contact but darts his or her eyes to the next person just before establishing a real connection. To this day I continue to work on slowing down my darting. Thanks to videotape, I now strive for a full five seconds of eye contact before moving to the next person.

Play back the videotape of your presentation and try to concentrate on it 100 percent. This is especially difficult because our minds race ahead of our words. People commonly feel they speak too fast, but that usually is not the case. The human brain can process almost 500 spoken words per minute. The average rate of American speech is about 125 words per minute. Listen to your pace on the tape. Are you engaging the audience with your energy? The odds are you can pick up your pace without losing them.

These three feedback tools are ways you can increase your awareness of yourself as a presenter. Engaging other people in your development is an interactive, energized way to take your temperature.

Audiotape and videotape feedback are other thermometers that, as Hamlet said, "hold the mirror up to nature." Whichever ones you work with, remember that you are striving consciously to choose your behavior, then consciously to repeat or change it.

CONCLUSION

This article has taken the form of a persuasive presentation. Its goal was to persuade you that removing barriers between your audience and yourself is not only possible, it is critical for your success. Additionally, there was an attempt to persuade you that presentations can be seen as something other than fearsome ordeals.

Remember the story about Richard Dreyfuss asking for a doctor in the middle of a play? The audience did nothing because they refused to stop believing in him. If fifteen hundred people can accept an actor walking into the audience asking for a doctor as natural, you can persuade your listeners that everything you do is part of your grand plan. Such willing, trusting people surely must be your friends. So remove the barriers. Look people in the eye and tell them all the valuable things you have prepared.

Tom Henschel, founder of Essential Communications, trained as a classical actor at the Juilliard School at Lincoln Center in New York City. He has been working in television and theater for more than twenty years. Stage productions under his direction have received eighteen critics awards, including five for Best Director. Based on his deep conviction that direct communication between people increases success, Mr. Henschel designs and delivers courses ranging from "Killer Presentations" to "Effective Communication for Managers." In addition, he coaches small groups and individuals on presentation skills and communication issues, and is frequently seen on prime-time television.

ATTRIBUTION THEORY: APPLICATIONS TO THE MANAGERIAL COACHING PROCESS

J. Craig VanHouten

Abstract: Bernard Weiner's (1986) attributional theory of motivation and emotion is rich in potential applications to the human resource development (HRD) field. This article outlines its major premises and its possible applications to the managerial coaching process.

Success and failure usually are attributed to causes, such as ability, effort, luck, and task difficulty. There are three dimensions of achievement-related attribution: locus (internal/external), stability (stable/unstable), and controllability (controllable/uncontrollable). Some attributions are more advantageous than others because they increase the expectation of success at similar tasks in the future. Other attributions are disadvantageous because they increase the expectation of failure at similar tasks in the future.

Managers and employees give cues about their attributions and the effects that these have on their motivations and emotions (i.e., by demonstrating pride, anger, pity, guilt, or shame). Managers who learn to recognize such cues can improve their own attributions and those of their employees and, thus, can more effectively coach employees to improved performance.

The 1996 Annual: Volume 1, Training.
Copyright © 1996 by Pfeiffer & Company, San Diego, CA.

Y ou have just walked out of a meeting with your organization's executives in which you presented a proposal for a major training program. You prepared more for this presentation than ever before because you think this training is greatly needed at this time. However, not only did the executives say no, they seemed totally unimpressed with the training proposed, which means a long delay before it can be proposed again. Whether you are aware of it or not, you are about to ask yourself, "Why did I fail?" Again, whether you are aware of it or not, how you answer that question may have a tremendous impact on your future success.

Success comes easily at times, but for most of us, successfully reaching our most important goals requires motivation, confidence, and persistence. These are particularly important when the challenge is great or when we fail initially. When we succeed or fail in an attempt to accomplish something important to us, we will usually ask ourselves, "Why did I succeed?" or "Why did I fail?" The answer will determine, to a large extent, our future success at achieving this objective and other related objectives because the answer helps to shape our perceptions of our ability. These perceptions then affect what we attempt and how we react if we attempt something and either succeed or fail. How the "Why?" question is answered is part of what allows some people to be successful while others fail again or even fail to try.

> *Reaching our most important goals requires motivation, confidence, and persistence.*

To return to the example at the beginning of this article, the answer may be: "These people only care about this quarter's profits; they will never spend a dime to invest in our employees." Although this may be accurate, it is not an effective answer to "Why?" because it means that one would probably not attempt to implement this kind of training program in the future, perceiving it as an impossible task. Even attributing the failure to bad luck would be preferable. At least luck can change, leaving open the potential for future success.

Unfortunately, in such a situation a person might say, "I just cannot communicate with these people" or, even worse, "I am just not able to present a proposal effectively." By attributing failure to a lack of ability, the person may undermine whatever confidence he or she had in his or her ability to accomplish similar objectives.

On the other hand, a different person might say, "I didn't prepare enough information about the financial benefits of this training" or "I should have found out what their most immediate concerns are and focused the presentation on training solutions." This person is attributing failure to a lack of effort or to the use of an ineffective strategy. This is a much more effective answer because it leaves the person with the opportunity and confidence to persist in attempting to accomplish the objective.

ATTRIBUTIONS AND MOTIVATION

According to Bernard Weiner (1986), an attribution is an answer to the question "Why?," which we ask ourselves in order to make sense of events that happen to us and to others. In many ways, attributions are attempts to learn about ourselves and our environment. Of course, our perceptions of ourselves and our environment may differ from the perceptions of others; even our own perceptions are subject to change. Weiner's attribution theory is first concerned with *when* we ask the question; second, it is concerned with the answer to the question and how it affects our subsequent thoughts and behaviors.

In achievement-related activities such as work, we usually ask "Why did I succeed?" or "Why did I fail?" when we succeed or fail to complete a task or achieve an objective. We most often ask "Why?" when we fail or when an outcome is other than expected. This may be because we have an answer for the expected.

Causal Explanations: Ability, Effort, Luck, and Task Difficulty

Although there are an almost infinite number of causal explanations, in achievement-related activities, ability, effort, luck, and task difficulty are the most common. Among these, ability (how competent we are) and effort (how hard we try) are most frequently used as explanations of our successes and failures. Because achievement is so important in many cultures, the search for the answer to "Why did I succeed?" or "Why did I fail?" is a common practice.

Dimensions of Attributions

There are three generally agreed-on dimensions of attributions: locus, stability, and controllability. Causal attributions may be classified according to where they appear along a continuum between the extremes of each dimension.

- For locus, the extreme points are internal and external.
- For stability, the extreme points are stable and unstable.
- For controllability, the extreme points are controllable and uncontrollable.

There are no absolutes here because the relative locus, stability, or controllability of any particular attribution is a function of the attributor's perceptions. However, the predominant attributions in achievement-related activities (ability, effort, luck, and task difficulty) can be classified within generally accepted ranges within the three dimensions (Figure 1).

Ability is most often considered to be internal, relatively stable, and relatively uncontrollable, particularly when it is thought of as aptitude. Ability also may be thought of as a combination of genetically inherited characteristics (e.g., aptitude) and learning, which makes it more controllable and less stable.

Effort is internal, controllable, and often considered to be unstable in the case of failure and stable in the case of success. For example, in the event of failure, one can choose to try harder and, in the event of success, one may think of oneself as a hard worker—a characteristic that is relatively stable. This makes effort a particularly effective attribution for either success or failure. Effort may be internal yet uncontrollable if, for example, it is a result of tiredness rather than choice. Effort may be external and uncontrollable if, for example, it is referring to the effort of a manager as perceived by a subordinate.

Luck is external, uncontrollable, and generally considered unstable. However, if we think of someone as being a lucky person we may perceive luck, in this case, as stable.

Task difficulty is external, stable, and uncontrollable. However, our perceptions of the difficulty of a task are influenced by our perceptions of our ability and expenditure of effort in relation to the task. Because our ability and effort may change, the relative stability and controllability of a task is also subject to individual interpretation.

Just as there are an unlimited number of possible attributions for success or failure, there are an unlimited number of perceptions of the locus and relative stability and controllability of any particular attribution. However, those listed previously are generally agreed on.

Advantageous and Disadvantageous Attributions

Some attributions are more advantageous than others because they increase one's expectation of success, which increases one's motivation

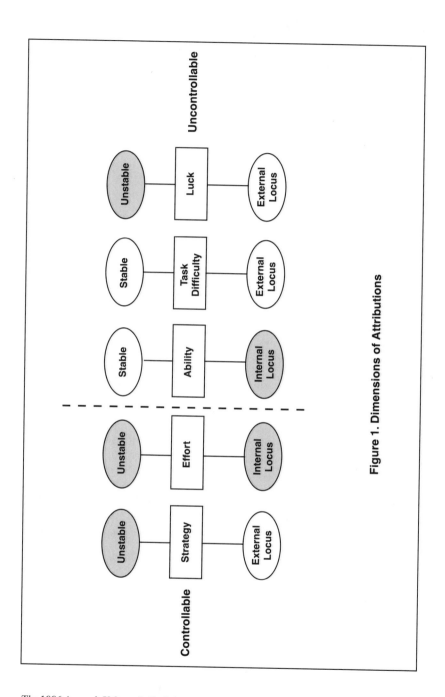

Figure 1. Dimensions of Attributions

and persistence. According to Weiner, attributing success to more stable causes and attributing failure to less stable causes generally increases persistence. Therefore, when one is successful, it is more advantageous to attribute the success to ability and effort (effort often being considered a stable attribution in cases of success). By doing this, the person increases his or her confidence in his or her ability to be successful in future attempts at similar tasks. If one attributes success to luck—an unstable attribution—one will not increase his or her expectation of success. In addition, attributing success to luck may indicate a lack of confidence in one's ability. Even though a person has succeeded, he or she may not persist if he or she fails in future attempts at the task. Success does not necessarily follow success.

> *Explaining failure as the use of an ineffective strategy is often correct as well as advantageous.*

After failure, it is more advantageous to attribute the failure to unstable causes such as a lack of effort or the use of an ineffective strategy. Although strategy is not one of the commonly used attributions, it can be particularly effective if the failure was preceded by a large expenditure of effort. This is because there is a perceived inverse or compensatory relationship between effort and ability.

For example, if a person is working hard to accomplish the same level of success as another person who appears to be expending little effort, the first person probably will assume that he or she has less ability than the other person. This is particularly critical in cases of failure. If a person works as hard or harder than others and still fails while the others are succeeding, the person often will be left with no other explanation than lack of ability. Thus, the person probably will not persist in an attempt to accomplish the task. However, by attributing failure to the use of an ineffective strategy, the person is more likely to persist.

There usually are many different ways to accomplish a task. Therefore, explaining failure as the use of an ineffective strategy is often correct as well as advantageous. Both explanations—lack of effort and the use of an ineffective strategy—will preserve a person's perception of his or her ability and provide the person with the option of either putting forth more effort or finding and using a different strategy in the next attempt. Both attributions will increase persistence.

Applications to the Managerial Coaching Process

Even when subordinates' objectives are clearly defined and subordinates are committed to achieving them, they may not persist in their attempts to accomplish those objectives. In many cases, it is not the subordinates' lack of commitment but their lack of confidence in their abilities in relation to the objective that determines whether they will initially attempt it and, if they fail, whether they will persist and make future attempts.

From a coaching perspective, it is important to accurately assess the abilities and efforts (including past effort as reflected in knowledge, skills, and experience) of subordinates and, when they fail or fail to try, to guide them toward additional training, effort, or strategies in order to help them persist in achieving their objectives.

Some subordinates may tend to explain their successes or failures in disadvantageous ways. A potentially effective motivational strategy would be to identify the subordinates' explanations for successes or failures and to suggest more advantageous causes. It has been demonstrated that simply suggesting more appropriate and advantageous attributions for failure will increase individuals' persistence and performance (Weiner, 1986).

When success is observed, managers should be alert to unstable attributions and suggest stable ones. The following is an example:

> Subordinate: "I was just lucky" (luck).
>
> Manager: "No, you have good communication skills" (ability) or "No, you did your research" (effort).

When failure is observed, managers should be alert to stable attributions and suggest unstable ones. The following are examples:

> Subordinate: "I can't motivate my team" (lack of ability).
>
> Manager: "Yes you can, but you will need to complete your training in order to learn how" (effort, in this case, prerequisite learning).
>
> Subordinate: "It is impossible to get this team to work cooperatively" (task difficulty).
>
> Manager: "No it isn't, but you may need to try another approach" (strategy).

If a manager attributes a subordinate's failure to lack of ability rather than to lack of effort, lack of prerequisite knowledge, or use of an ineffective strategy, the manager may not persist in helping the subordinate to succeed by providing encouragement and/or additional training. A manager also may attribute failure to a stable "trait" (e.g., laziness), which will reduce the expectations of change and affect the way in which the manager interacts with the subordinate. It is much better to think in terms of less stable "states" (e.g., "He has not been working as hard this quarter"). Again, the less stable attribution for failure leaves open the opportunity for change.

As has been suggested, managers may communicate their perceptions of the causes of subordinates' successes and failures and, therefore, communicate their perceptions of subordinates' relative abilities. These communications can have a tremendous effect on subordinates' perceptions of their own abilities. Because of this, managers should be mindful of their own attributions as well as the attributions of their subordinates.

ATTRIBUTIONS AND EMOTIONS

Just as there is a powerful connection between attributions and expectations, there is a powerful connection between attributions and emotions. How we think influences how we feel and what we do. Our attributions and the perceived dimensions (locus, stability, and controllability) of those attributions influence our emotions. Because the relationships between some emotions and attributions are understood, emotions may provide cues about our attributions (Weiner, 1986). Although there is a wide range of emotional responses, for our purposes the emotions of pride, anger, pity, guilt, and shame are most relevant.

Pride reflects self-esteem. In order to experience pride, we must attribute success to internal causes (ability, effort, or personality) as opposed to external causes (ease of task or luck). Many of us have a self-serving bias that encourages us to take credit for success by attributing the success to internal causes (ability and effort) and to deny responsibility for failure by attributing the failure to external causes (task difficulty or bad luck). This allows us to enhance our self-esteem when we succeed and protect it when we fail.

The emotions of anger, pity, guilt, and shame are linked to the perceived controllability of the cause of an event. These associations are understood by children and appear to span cultures as well (Weiner, 1986).

Anger is elicited when failure of others is perceived to be caused by a controllable factor, such as lack of effort. Lack of effort accompanied by high ability elicits even greater anger. If one observes someone else failing and believes that failure is due to a lack of effort, one will most likely feel anger. If one thinks the other person is very capable, one may be even more angry.

Pity (sympathy) is elicited when failure of others is perceived as being due to uncontrollable causes, such as lack of ability. Pity also is associated with perceived fundamental differences. Because of this, expressing pity or sympathy when someone fails may communicate a perceived difference or deficiency. Thus, sometimes being caring and understanding sends the wrong message.

Guilt is elicited when someone perceives his or her own failure to be attributable to controllable causes, such as lack of effort. For example, we demonstrate feelings of guilt when we fail to produce reports on time because we put them off until the last minute. The guilt communicates that we attribute the cause of the failure to lack of effort or another controllable cause. Because the cause is unstable and controllable, we expect to do better next time.

Shame is elicited when someone attributes his or her failure to an uncontrollable cause, such as lack of ability. Using the same example, if we fail to produce reports because we lack confidence in our ability to write, we are more likely to feel ashamed. In this case, our shame communicates that we attribute our failure to lack of ability or another uncontrollable cause. In attributing failure to a stable and uncontrollable cause, we do not expect to do better in the future.

> *How we think influences how we feel and what we do.*

There are other ways to communicate attributions. For example, we tend to punish those whom we believe to have ability and who fail because of lack of effort more than we punish those whom we believe to have less ability and who fail because of lack of effort. We would not be as likely to punish failure if we were to perceive the cause to be lack of ability, which is uncontrollable. In cases of success, we reward low ability more than we reward high ability. Again, we may be sending the wrong message if we reward someone for succeeding at a relatively easy task.

Applications in the Managerial Coaching Process

Even the most well-intentioned manager can attribute a subordinate's success or failure to a disadvantageous cause, which may contribute to the subordinate's lack of confidence and achievement. Managers can communicate their disadvantageous attributions verbally (e.g., "You were lucky this time") or nonverbally through their emotional responses to subordinates' successes or failures. At the same time, subordinates can cue the managers about their own attributions through their emotional response to success or failure.

When a subordinate expresses pride after an accomplishment, the pride may cue the manager that the subordinate attributes the success to ability and/or effort—advantageous attributions. If a subordinate does not express pride following an accomplishment, it may cue the manager that the subordinate attributes the success to external causes, such as luck or task ease—disadvantageous attributions. If this is the case, the manager should suggest that effort and ability caused the success. Attributing success to these causes will increase the subordinate's confidence and motivation.

If a manager becomes angry with a subordinate, the anger may indicate that the manager attributes a failure to a controllable factor, usually lack of effort. At the same time, it may cue the subordinate that the manager has confidence in the subordinate's ability. Because anger provides a cue to perception of high ability, it may be a more effective response to failure in many cases, particularly if the manager follows up with a statement such as, "How can you expect to be successful when you have not taken the time to understand this? You're good, but you will have to work harder to succeed with this."

A subordinate's emotions provide cues to the manager about the subordinate's perceived ability and efforts.

If a manager expresses pity when a subordinate fails, the pity may cue the subordinate that the manager lacks confidence in the subordinate's ability. Anger, followed by a suggested new strategy, may be a better response. This demonstrates confidence in the subordinate's ability and suggests an unstable factor—use of an ineffective strategy—as the cause of failure.

The subordinate's emotions also provide cues to the manager about the subordinate's perceived ability and effort. If the manager's anger elicits the subordinate's guilt, the guilt cues the manager that the subordinate has attributed the failure to a controllable cause and will probably be motivated to do better in the future. In this case, the subordinate and manager both attribute the failure to an internal, unstable, and controllable cause, such as lack of effort. Improvement is expected.

If the manager's anger elicits the subordinate's shame, the shame cues the manager that the subordinate attributes the failure to an uncontrollable cause such as lack of ability, and probably will not do better in the future unless the manager provides a more advantageous explanation. The manager could suggest that the cause of failure is lack of effort, demonstrated by a lack of prerequisite knowledge and experience. For example, if the subordinate fails to produce a report and expresses shame, the manager may say, "I have a good book on report writing that I use all the time. With that and a little experience, you'll do fine."

Often, finding an advantageous cause for failure is not enough. It also is important to search for the actual cause of failure. Attributing a subordinate's failure to the use of an ineffective strategy when, in fact, it was due to a lack of effort will not lead that subordinate to success. Even a new strategy without effort will likely end in failure, just as additional effort used with an ineffective strategy will seldom lead to success.

Managers need to be aware of their explanations of their subordinates' successes or failures as well as the subordinates' own explanations of their successes or failures. Understanding cues leads to asking subordinates, "Why do you think you failed?" or "Why do you think you succeeded?" The ability to identify disadvantageous attributions and the ability to suggest more advantageous attributions can be effective motivational strategies.

CONCLUSION

Bernard Weiner's (1986) attributional theory of motivation and emotion provides a rich resource for assisting HRD professionals in understanding individual, team, and organizational performance problems and in developing new motivational strategies for employees at all levels. It also provides the basis for an effective motivational strategy for managers to use in their own professional development as well as in the coaching process with subordinates.

Reference

Weiner, B. (1986). *An attributional theory of motivation and emotion.* New York: Springer-Verlag.

Craig VanHouten is the president of Knowledge First, in Escondido, California. He has applied many of the lessons found in attribution research through the "Success Path," a motivational training heuristic designed to change the way managers and subordinates think about success and failure. Mr. VanHouten and his associates provide seminars and consulting services to organizations on the use of the "Success Path" to increase motivation and improve performance.

STRESS MANAGEMENT FOR HRD PROFESSIONALS: TAKING TIME TO PRACTICE WHAT YOU PREACH

Herbert S. Kindler and Marilyn Ginsburg

Abstract: Professionals who teach stress management often neglect applying what they know to themselves. This failure is common among "helpers" whose chief focus is on the needs of clients rather than on concern for their own burnout. A three-phase stress management program appropriate to trainers is suggested: (1) understand your stress level in the context of an overall system; (2) assess where stress is excessive and deserves attention; and (3) design an action plan that you will commit to implementing.

Even trainers, consultants, and counselors who teach stress management as part of their jobs are not immune from excessive stress. In times of organizational restructuring, layoffs, and turbulent change, human resource development (HRD) professionals face an array of challenges: dealing with "downsizing" survivors, pursuing diversity initiatives, adding training programs with tighter budgets, and so on.

As the typical trainer scrambles to leave home on time, overwhelmed by thinking about the day's workload, he or she feels a twinge of conscience. How will he or she be able to attend that parent-teacher conference or that Little League game? This trainer has not even found time for that sixty-second "conscious breathing" exercise.

Trainers have promoted stress-management training in their organizations to lower health care costs, increase productivity, reduce absenteeism and accidents, and improve morale. How can they feel so stressed out and squeezed for time themselves?

Learning about exercise, nutrition, deep relaxation, play, rest, and even romance are not enough. The ingredients most frequently missing in stress-management programs are:

1. Knowing how stress management integrates into one's life,

2. Knowing how to assess how much stress you are currently experiencing and where it is coming from, and

3. A modest action plan.

This three-step program is recommended for trainers first and then, after it has proved successful, for their trainees.

STEP 1: GET THE BIG PICTURE

This step employs a cybernetic systems model. "Cybernetic" comes from the Greek word "to steer"; the model in Figure 1[1] enables you to manage stress by keeping you connected to your personal vision. An inspiring vision and a systems map help you to steer a safe and satisfying course through life without drifting.

---

[1] Used with permission from *Stress Training for Life*, by Herbert S. Kindler and Marilyn Ginsburg, New York: Nichols Publishing Company.

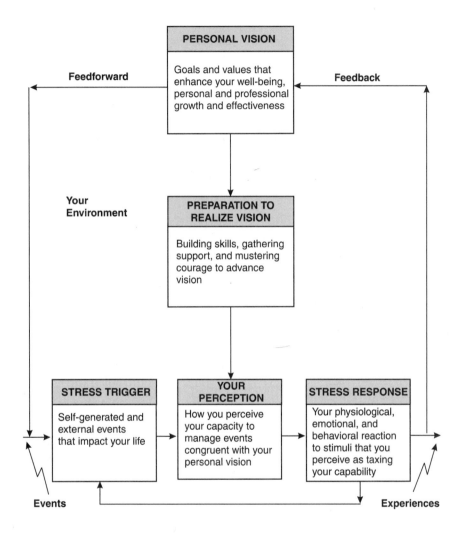

Figure 1. Cybernetic Systems Map for Stress Management

Personal Vision

To articulate your vision for this period in your life, do the following: turn your attention inward, stretch beyond where you are, dream, allow possibilities to gently unfold. See yourself healthy, radiant, enjoying life fully, and handling your job with mastery.

Feedforward

To move your vision from possibility to reality, share it with others. As you clearly communicate your aspirations and values, you are likely to attract people and resources helpful in advancing your personal vision.

Stress Trigger

A trigger or stress source is any impulse or event that has the potential to elicit a stress response. Typical triggers are:

- Outer events such as a demanding boss, an insensitive coworker, heavy traffic, a bounced check, a quarrel with a family member, and air pollution.
- Inner impulses such as the restimulation of a past trauma, and activation of an inner perfectionist, critic, or worrier.

Perception

Stress comes largely from the inside. Your interpretation of a stress trigger determines your stress reaction. For example, if a stranger brushes against you, the irritation you feel dissipates the moment you see that she is carrying a white cane. Perception is the intervening process in which you give meaning to outer events and inner dialogue. When you assign new meanings, you alter your stress response. Events that might otherwise evoke stress become challenges when perceived as opportunities to advance your personal vision.

Stress Response

Your body reacts to recurring triggers by sending you messages, such as headaches, indigestion, and rashes, to capture your attention. Chronic, continuing messages are asking for deeper examination. Until you identify the source of the problem, stress responses recur or escalate. When you consciously read early warning signals and begin managing stress with awareness, you empower yourself.

Feedback

Your own stress response to each trigger is valuable feedback.

- Notice if your reaction is appropriate to the triggering source. Rather than react automatically, consciously choose your response to each new circumstance.

- Call time out each day to ask yourself, "What are my stress responses trying to tell me?" Your body's signals are a gift.

Through comparing each stressful experience with your personal vision, you open the possibility of enlarging your self-concept.

Preparation to Realize Your Vision

The road to mastery requires patience, practice, and perseverance. On the path to attaining your vision, life's inevitable difficulties will be much less unsettling as you increase your competence.

STEP 2: ASSESS THE MAGNITUDE AND SOURCES OF YOUR STRESS

It is important to know exactly where your stress is coming from at this particular time and how great an effect it is having on your well-being. One way to obtain this information is through inventories such as the *Personal Stress Assessment Inventory*[2]. The inventory was developed from the conceptual model in Figure 2, which relates stress symptoms to three kinds of interacting variables: predisposition, resilience, and stress sources—occasional and ongoing, personal, and work related.

Predisposition to Stress

Some people have a predisposition to rush even without a compelling reason, to compete aggressively even when it is not necessary or is dysfunctional, and to be hostile in dealing with others. These are referred

---

[2] H.S. Kindler, *Personal Stress Assessment Inventory* (rev. ed). Pacific Palisades, CA: Center for Management Effectiveness, telephone 310-459-6052.

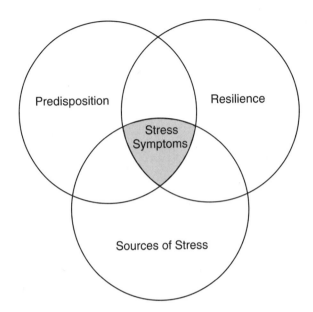

Figure 2: Stress-Symptom Model

to as "Type-A behaviors." People who manifest this predisposition are creating stress for themselves and others. If you have this predisposition, one concern is that you are putting your cardiovascular system at risk.

Resilience

Resilience is the capacity to bounce back from life's pitfalls. Its essence is balance. Unfortunately, most people develop a preference for one or more of four basic human dimensions—mental, emotional, physical, and spiritual—at the expense of others. Highly mental people may neglect their bodies; highly emotional people may ignore logic; highly physical people sometimes are insensitive to feelings; and spiritually oriented people may shun earthly passion. For resilience, we need to be grounded in all four areas.

Sources of Stress

The wear and tear of daily pressures, whether from internal or external sources, makes us more susceptible to chronic illness. The depletion of energy needed to adapt to intermittent life events further increases our vulnerability.

STEP 3: TRANSLATE YOUR VISION TO ACTION

Time is not money; it is a lot more valuable. Time is life. Time management boils down to two strategies: work smarter and do less. Trainers know how to work smarter; they teach it. Doing less, on the other hand, is a greater challenge. Use your personal vision to get the clarity to say "no" to activities that distract you from its realization, and "yes" to the few things that really make a difference.

As you draft your personal action plan, which areas in your life do you want to cultivate and which do you want to diminish? Balance your challenging career with a nurturing home life; balance excitement and adventure with quiet time for inner reflection and creativity. The following are ten options to consider in designing your action plan.

1. Clarify your personal vision. A prime cause of professional-helper burnout is losing the connection to goals you find personally satisfying. Keep a vision before you that is relevant to your needs, one that is realistic and rewarding.

2. Call "time out" every day. Spend time alone each day to review the day's events. Did you advance your personal and job visions? Do you see recurring patterns? What did you learn today?

3. Change Type-A behavior.

- Motivation: Appreciate how a serious illness would affect your life and others who love you.

- Awareness: When you hurry or compete aggressively, make your action a conscious, deliberate choice, not a knee-jerk reaction.

- Practice: Start modestly and congratulate yourself for small successes.

4. Play more. Do what you enjoy doing for its own sake, with no goal in mind. Start each day by asking, "What can I look forward to today?"

5. Keep humor in your life. Consider doing things such as placing a small sign on your bathroom mirror that says, "Don't take this person too seriously."

6. Celebrate. Break life-deadening routines. Create transcendent moments. What might you celebrate to keep your life fresh and exciting?

7. Empower yourself. Do not become a victim of circumstance. In a stressful situation, consider changing your perceptions, addressing the source of stress directly, or leaving.

8. Deal constructively with disagreement. Learn the core principles of conflict management and decide on a systematic process for dealing with disagreement and conflict. (See "Managing Conflict and Disagreement Constructively" by Herbert S. Kindler in *The 1995 Annual: Volume 1, Training,* pages 169-174.)

9. Monitor critical self-talk. If you have a harsh "inner critic," analyze the negative messages bemoaning your failings and incompetence. As you expose these messages to the light of who you really are and the true level of your professional competence, much of the negativity will be neutralized.

10. Be more self-caring. Develop an active network of close friends. Get adequate rest. Eat slowly and consciously. If you are not inclined to more vigorous exercise, at least walk briskly each day.

If you choose only one action option that makes your life feel better, you will have taken an important step. You may initiate other steps as you feel ready to make a further commitment. Good luck!

References

Kindler, H.S., & Ginsburg, M. (1994). *Measure & manage stress.* Menlo Park, CA: Crisp Publications.

Kindler, H.S. (1993). *Personal stress assessment inventory* (rev. ed.). Pacific Palisades, CA: Center for Management Effectiveness.

Herbert S. Kindler, Ph.D., is the director of the Center for Management Effectiveness, Pacific Palisades, California, and is emeritus professor of management and organization at Loyola Marymount University. He is the author or coauthor of five books currently in print and is the developer of the Personal Stress Assessment Inventory. *His past experience as a CEO enriches his training and consulting activities.*

Marilyn Ginsburg, M.F.C.C., is the associate director of the Center for Management Effectiveness and is a consultant to executives in entertainment, banking, advertising, health care, and telecommunications. She is a former editor for Glamour *magazine, an educational film writer and producer, and a psychotherapist who works with clients on transformational change.*

CUSTOMER VALUE:
THE STRATEGIC ADVANTAGE

Howard E. Butz, Jr., and Leonard D. Goodstein

Abstract: Building net customer value, establishing an emotional bond between a customer and a supplier, is an issue of building trust. However, it is difficult for a supplier to determine customers' true responses to its products and services, including how much of the customers' total budgets are spent with the supplier. The process of customer understanding is a way of examining the nature and extent of the trust established between the two parties.

This article presents a five-step customer-understanding process that provides a conceptual framework for converting raw data about transactions between the customer and the supplier into information. The framework makes the data meaningful and useful. There are two important kinds of information that the process should yield. First, what are the customer's present needs and how well is the supplier meeting them? Second, what are the customer's emerging needs and how can the supplier position itself to meet them?

The 1996 Annual: Volume 1, Training.
Copyright © 1996 by Pfeiffer & Company, San Diego, CA.

There is widespread understanding in U.S. business of the concept of "value added." The more a supplier adds value to a product or service, the more distinctive that product or service becomes. Distinctiveness can lead to higher prices and, presumably, to higher margins and greater profits. The unresolved issue, however, is who defines the value added.

In most organizations, the suppliers assume what the consumers will value and buy. Unfortunately, the history of U.S. business provides too many examples of suppliers' assumptions being erroneous. The Ford Edsel and the McLean Burger are notorious examples.

Many businesses have now realized that it is always the customer who decides whether there is value added. The emerging idea of customer value is the first attempt to understand the true meaning of value added and to use it to strategic advantage.

NET CUSTOMER VALUE

Customer value can be defined as the emotional bond established between a customer and a supplier. Such an emotional bond leads the customer to buy repeatedly and exclusively from that supplier, to recommend that supplier to friends and relatives, and to withstand the blandishments of other suppliers. This bond is established when the goods or services provided by the supplier regularly meet or exceed the customer's expectations. The customer believes that these goods or services produce more benefits to him or her than the costs incurred; this is net customer value.

Net customer value is not a simple concept. Value is intuitively calculated by the customer, based on that customer's values and beliefs. By way of example, one of the authors has bonded with a local carry-out seafood restaurant that has rude service people and an unattractive decor. The food, however, is so delicious and so moderately priced, and the restaurant is so convenient, that the author returns to it regularly. It would take a new supplier with the same convenience, the same low-priced, delicious food *and* with either better customer service or a more attractive decor to break this long-term bond. Suppliers rarely know which customers, if any, are receiving a sufficiently high net customer value to cause them to buy repeatedly.

Total quality management (TQM) has increased attention to providing customer satisfaction. Understanding net customer value fully, however, requires expanding on the usual approach to customer satisfaction. Simply pursuing customer satisfaction results in an incomplete understanding of customer value. Customer satisfaction is about *attitudes;* customer value is about *behavior.* The pursuit of quality initiatives must also be based on an understanding of customer value or one risks making improvements that are irrelevant to the customer and can even decrease customer value.

Increasing net customer value requires focusing attention on one's customers and understanding their wants and needs. For example, senior managers at Cathay Pacific Airways, the Hong Kong-based airline, "knew" that on-time arrivals and departures were key ingredients in customer value. Research, however, revealed that on long-haul flights of over ten hours, customers were not too concerned with on-time arrivals and departures. Customers were concerned, however, with the cleanliness of the on-board toilets, with the quality of the food, and with having continual information on the status of the flight.

Similarly, Goodman, Bargatze, and Grimm (1994) report that both management's intuition and its initial market research led an insurance company to believe that timeliness and accuracy of handling claims would increase net customer value. A later study, however, of over 5,000 actual customers who had filed claims revealed that the clarity of the company's explanations accompanying the claim settlement was far more important in increasing net customer value than either timeliness or accuracy. The earlier research either had not used the right customers, had not asked the right questions, or both. One can raise net customer value only by truly understanding the customer.

> *Increasing net customer value requires focusing attention on one's customers and understanding their needs.*

Those organizations that have been successful in establishing high net customer value—like MBNA, a leading credit card company—have built their entire business strategy on developing customer bonding. MBNA has recognized that retaining customers through bonding leads to increased market share, lower costs, and increased profitability. Reichheld (1993) estimates that every 5 percent increase in MBNA's retention rate increases its profits by 60 percent. Such retention, however, requires designing business systems that create bonding. Bonding cannot be achieved incidentally. For example, MBNA focuses on "affinity cards," with two groups of credit card customers. One group is recruited through professional groups and alumni associations, with the affiliative association receiving a small percentage of the revenue for its own use. The second group is recruited by businesses such as General Motors or American Airlines. The customer receives discounts on merchandise, frequent-flier miles, or other tangible benefits. These homogenous affinity groups allow MBNA to provide a customized package of services for each group, which increases MBNA's ability to meet customers' special needs. The latter is the hallmark of providing customer value. Because customers often cannot discriminate among products (e.g., gasoline), it is important that they bond to a system or brand and not to a specific product.

Management consultant Karl Albrecht (1994) defines customer value as "the customer's perception of specific need fulfillment...[it is] the outcome people seek, not the thing or experience they pay for" (p. 137). Such definitions of customer value highlight the fact that only customers themselves can supply clear and direct data regarding their needs, both manifest and latent, and the degree to which one has fulfilled them.

Customer Bonding

Customer bonding is related to actual behavior, both customer behavior and supplier behavior. Although brand recognition and attitudes about the brand are important components of customer bonding, observable customer behavior is more important. Customer bonding is not reflected in what customers say about the supplier; it is reflected in how they behave in their relationships with the supplier. Highly bonded customers will defend their choices to others, insisting that they have chosen the "best" products or services. Who has not had at least one discussion with an impassioned supporter of a particular fast-food restaurant or automobile manufacturer or retail store about why it was the "right" choice? It is the underlying emotional bond that leads to such a stance. This is customer bonding.

An organization can develop customer bonding. As we noted earlier, the entire organization must be truly, totally customer focused. Although many organizations include customer focus as part of their mission statements, only a handful of organizations truly behave in a customer-driven fashion. The development of customer bonding requires that the organization regularly meet or exceed the expectations of its customers.

The mission of Federal Express is to have a completely satisfied customer at the end of each transaction. The outstanding and continued success of FedEx is a direct result of the commitment of rank-and-file FedEx employees to make this concept a reality. This commitment also is supported by the FedEx systems and processes. For example, its tracking system enables employees to answer customers' queries, and its performance-appraisal system rewards customer focus.

As TQM impacts more and more organizations, it becomes more difficult for individual organizations to stand out from the pack and to create customer bonding. One unforeseen consequence of the quality revolution has been to reduce more products and services to the commodity level. To counteract this leveling effect, companies bend over backward to differentiate themselves by providing customer value. The development of frequent-flyer programs in the airline industry is an attempt at such differentiation. When American Airlines pioneered such programs, all U.S. carriers quickly followed. International carriers finally, reluctantly, joined as well. The current programs target business travelers who fly a specified number of miles annually. They are given special status: "AAdvantage Gold," "USAir Priority Gold," and so on. This special status not only provides bonus miles but, more importantly for many travelers, allows them to upgrade to a first-class seat for a minimum payment. Once a traveler achieves this special status, customer bonding has occurred.

> *One unforeseen consequence of the quality revolution has been to reduce more products and services to the commodity level.*

Another illustration is from customer-oriented Cathay Pacific Airways, whose top management determined that many travelers were avoiding Hong Kong because of lengthy delays at customs. Rather than assuming that this was a problem they could not solve, Cathay's senior staff asked the Hong Kong government how to avoid the customs delays. After lengthy negotiations, the airline agreed to make an annual grant-in-aid to the government to hire more customs inspectors, but these inspectors would service only the Cathay Pacific gates! This application of the notion of seamless service reduced the waiting period, reduced customer delays, and produced an increase in net customer value and greater customer bonding.

The California-based Chalone Wine Group has developed a unique approach to customer bonding. People who own one hundred or more shares of this company are invited to an annual celebration party at the vineyard, where they sample the new releases and feast on exotic delicacies. More importantly, these stockholders are the only ones who can purchase difficult-to-obtain cases of Chalone wines directly from the winery. Although the stock has never paid a dividend, this strategy has produced over 10,000 shareholders who are fanatically bonded to the company and its products. Of course, other vineyards have followed with their own approaches to building customer loyalty, primarily through winery-sponsored "clubs" that offer "member" discounts, access to limited-production wines, and newsletters.

What should be apparent from this discussion is that customer bonding is not easy to achieve. Successful companies now seem more than willing to go to elaborate lengths and find unique strategies to achieve customer bonding. Such bonding, however, provides a significant strategic advantage, assuring repeat sales and rendering the customer virtually impermeable to the competition.

Levels of Customer Value

There are at least three levels at which a customer's needs can be met. These are as follows.

Expected Level

The lowest level of meeting customers' needs is the "expected" or basic level, one that is normal or modal to the business or industry. At this level, the supplier provides goods and services at the level that customers have come to expect. For example, U.S. domestic airlines provide expected levels of service. They provide reasonably priced, more-or-less on-time travel service between most U.S. cities. There is nothing that is memorable in a positive way about their services and not much to distinguish one from another. Each airline's attempt to add customer value is quickly copied by competitors. Thus, there is little in the way of customer bonding (except for the true frequent flyers). The occasional traveler regards airline travel as a commodity, selecting a carrier based on price and convenience of schedule.

Southwest Airlines broke that mold by encouraging its cabin attendants to be innovative in their announcements and to engage passengers in less formal ways. These changes were intended to make flying Southwest a different, more pleasant experience. The fact that Southwest consistently proves to be the low-cost airline with the best on-time performance adds additional customer value.

Airport newsstands provide another example of organizations that typically provide expected customer value. They typically provide overpriced merchandise sold by undermotivated employees. The W H Smith Group, plc, a British news vendor, has made significant inroads on its competition by providing a wider range of products at downtown prices and with a clear sense of customer value. It is obviously attempting to live up to its motto, "There's more to discover at W H Smith."

Desired Level

The second level of customer value is the "desired" level. Desired features add value for the customer but are not expected because of company or industry standards. It does not require sophisticated market research to detect that customers wish that sales places were clean and attractive, that sales clerks were friendly and attentive, and that refunds were made on time. Customers have simply learned not to expect these features. They have bonded, however, with organizations that provide them.

An understanding of what customers truly value provides the organization with an opportunity to meet customers' needs. The degree to which the organization can find ways of increasing customer value enables it to distinguish itself from its competitors and to develop customer bonding.

The rise of sixty-minute photo finishing shops is an example of how an industry has been transformed by meeting the needs for a quick turnaround for personal photos. Similarly, Domino's "pizza in thirty minutes" also meets needs for quick service, although perhaps not for gourmet food. It is important to note that in these instances, what originally was the desired level has become the expected level. The integration of TQM into organizations has leveled the playing field and directly produced rising customer expectations. As this trend of rising expectations accelerates over the next few years, the desired level of customer value will become the baseline required to survive.

Unanticipated Level

The third and ultimate level of customer value is the unexpected or "unanticipated" level. Here the organization finds ways to add value beyond the customer's expectations or desires, at least on a conscious level. Value can be unusually prompt service, greater willingness to find a way to resolve a customer's problems, additional services, or anything else that unexpectedly meets customer needs.

The Seattle-based Nordstrom department stores have provided such unanticipated customer value so often that accounts of their service have become legendary. In one incident, a Nordstrom salesclerk stopped a customer and asked if the shoes that she was wearing had been bought there. When she was told that they had been, the salesclerk insisted on replacing them on the spot as "they had not worn as well as they should." The advertising for Nordstrom that results from the many times this story has been told more than covers the expense of the pair of shoes. Such unanticipated features produce strong customer bonding.

There is another way of thinking about unanticipated levels of customer satisfaction. Customers have many latent needs that are well below their thresholds of awareness. Who knew that we needed VCRs before they were commercially available? How many of us thought that we needed a fax machine or a cellular telephone ten years ago? Were we aware that we needed on-line computer services such as Compuserve and America Online before they appeared? Knowing the answers to future needs would allow us to increase customer value.

The development of the disposable diaper provides a good case study in meeting latent needs. In the late 1950s, there was no stated need for disposable diapers because they did not exist. However, Procter and Gamble had learned in its ongoing market research that a major source of unhappiness for its customers was dealing with soiled diapers. Procter and Gamble recognized that this unhappiness provided a market opportunity and turned the problem over to its research and development staff. The rest, as the saying goes, is history. A $3.5 billion annual business is a direct result of finding a solution that reduced a source of dissatisfaction.

The moral of the story should be clear. In order to reach the unanticipated level of customer value, we need not only to find new and different ways of providing already established goods and services to our customers; we need also to develop products and services that fill our customers' latent needs. Organizations that genuinely listen to their customers and understand customers' problems are those that will find solutions for their customers' problems and, in so doing, provide customer value and develop bonding.

Up to this point, the examples presented have been about consumer products. This does not mean, however, that customer value is important only in the direct consumer marketplace; everything in this article applies to those who have internal customers and to those who have other businesses as customers.

Internal Customers

Relationships between suppliers and internal customers often are troubled. The requirement to use the internal legal staff or print shop or machine shop leads to intensive bonds that frequently are experienced as chains by the in-house customers. Internal service suppliers often are perceived as overpriced, unresponsive suppliers of shoddy services and goods—ones that do not provide net customer value. Such negative views are heightened by internal cross-charges, especially when such costs are seen as noncompetitive with the external marketplace.

The growing trend toward outsourcing services is a result of these dissatisfactions.

Internal service suppliers can prosper only when internal customers are pleased. This means approaching the job with a view toward increasing net customer value. This should be quite easy. Based on their closeness in both background and geography, internal suppliers should know their customers, understand their problems, and be able to help the customers solve the problems quickly, economically, and better than anyone else. When this is done, the threat of outsourcing recedes because net customer value is provided.

The question is how to develop an understanding of one's customers and their values. The approach we advocate is very different from the typical market-research approach that has served as the basis for most current understanding of customers and their needs.

STEPS IN CUSTOMER UNDERSTANDING

Defining customer value and the various levels at which it can be provided leads to the issue of its measurement. Because of the complexity of this process and the general lack of knowledge of its application, we have termed this process "customer understanding."

Step 1. Customer Identification

The customer must be clearly identified, and everyone who affects the "buy decision" must be included as the customer. This is not as straightforward as it may seem. Especially when other businesses are one's customers, the decision-to-buy process typically is more complex. Even simple consumer purchases can involve multiple decision makers but, in business-to-business relationships, these tend to be complex and hierarchical. Procurement agents, contracting officers, multiple layers of management, and even boards of directors may become involved. Thus, the customer-identification process is critical in understanding business-to-business relationships.

Nearly all businesses can immediately identify their primary customers; but other strategically important people in the decision-making process often are overlooked. A defense contractor must consider not only the procurement agency or the contracting agency as the customer but also the research laboratories that developed the specifications, the end user(s), and any number of sponsors in the government agency and in the Congress. Because many of these customers will value various aspects of the product differently, a complete understanding of these numerous customers and what each values is necessary.

Consider as a further example a manufacturer of hand tools that has two product lines: one nationally branded and a second, lower-priced, private-label line. In both cases there are end users and a variety of others—such as chain-store buyers and store managers—involved in the buying decision. The end user is far more important to the nationally branded line than to the private label. A customer who is bonded to a nationally branded product—who sees that product as having high customer value—will continue to shop for that product, even if it requires additional effort. For the privately labeled product, however, the views of the chain's hand-tool buyer about customer value will probably be more important in making purchasing decisions. In both cases, the views of the end user are important. The question here, as always, is one of relative importance.

> Anyone who influences the decision to buy is a customer.

Today, a single decision maker in any decision is very rare. Even most children have input about where to stop for fast food and which breakfast cereals to buy. Every supplier must recognize that anyone who can exert positive or negative influence on the decision to buy must be included as a customer. Initially, the influence of some of these participants in the decision-making process may not be known. Many current management strategies (e.g., empowerment, employee involvement, and self-directed work teams) will expand the pool of decision makers. As our knowledge of the process of customer understanding evolves, it is important to be on the lookout for these yet-unknown influences and to begin to study them systematically.

The list of customers must then be put into priority order based on the degree of influence each has on the "buy decision." Developing the priority list requires input from all those in the business who regularly deal with the customers; thus, arriving at a priority list may be more difficult than initially assumed. The needs of each of the customers must be identified. Then a relative weight must be assigned to how important that need is to that customer's decision to buy. At the very least, one needs to identify the key decision makers—those who can derail any decision—and make certain that one meets their needs.

Step 2. Planning

Conducting a complete customer-understanding process is both a time-consuming and expensive activity. It also can disrupt the often-fragile relationship between the customer and the supplier. By inquiring about how well one is serving the customer, one implicitly raises the customer's expectations about one's service. Therefore, there needs to be explicit support for this process at the very top of the organization. This support requires not only an understanding of the process—its risks and its benefits—but also a commitment to using the results of the analysis in developing the strategic plan of the organization. We recommend against even beginning the process without this legitimization.

Developing customer understanding invariably involves actually visiting customers in their usual places of business. It is simply not possible to develop an adequate understanding of customers and their needs without such visits. Playing golf with the customer, buying the customer a meal, or asking the customer to complete a satisfaction questionnaire will not lead to the kind of customer understanding that provides strategic direction and long-term success.

Before any customer visit is scheduled, careful planning is required. One question to be answered is the level at which the visit will be conducted. Although there needs to be dialogue at the most senior levels of management, there are great advantages to broader interactions as well. DuPont recently has reorganized in an effort to become closer to its customer—to increase its net customer value. As part of this process, DuPont has begun to send operators from its nylon spinning mills to visit those factories where DuPont nylon is transformed into swimsuits and bras. The DuPont operators talk to the customer operators about the quality problems they experience in using DuPont nylon.

Another planning question is how customers will benefit from participating in such a process. One possible benefit is that the supplier will be better positioned to meet both present and emerging customer needs. Another is reduction of problems in the regular customer/supplier interface. It is important to have answers for customers when they ask why they should participate in a process that initially appears to be of advantage only to the supplier. The answer(s) offered should be tailored to an understanding of the customer and what would appeal to him or her as a benefit to offset the costs involved in entertaining such a visit.

Each customer/supplier interface is unique. The goal of customer visits is to understand this unique interaction in two ways. The first is to learn how the customer decides today's "best value"; the second is to discover how to provide unanticipated value in the future. The former addresses the current competitive environment and how to increase market share. The latter leads to strategies for creating new customer relations in the future.

One must begin the planning process by collecting and analyzing whatever data already is available about the customer. This in-house review should focus on understanding the customer's core values. This means reviewing the customer's annual reports and other relevant documents, the customer's mission statement, and so on. One needs to understand the customer's corporate goals, culture, driving forces, etc. This understanding will give the planning team insight into the customer and allow the team to begin to understand the customer's perspective. The goal of this analysis is to better see the world through the customer's eyes. One must be clear about what one is looking for before asking for the customer's cooperation.

Following the in-house review is planning the data-collection phase, including deciding exactly what questions to ask during the visit with the customer. Beside any questions that have emerged from the in-house review, the supplier needs to understand how the customer uses the product (preferably by direct observation). Then the supplier needs to figure out how to increase the value of the product to the customer, how the customer measures his or her success, and what factors might change the customer's use of the product. The focus of planning the visit should be on discovering the fundamental needs of the customer and how the product is actually used.

A data-collection checklist should be prepared before every visit. Such a checklist should help focus the discussion on issues of customer value. Because each customer relationship is unique, each checklist will be unique. A sample checklist is provided in Figure 1. The actual questions asked of the customer, of course, should appear more spontaneous. For example, to explore product use, one might ask the customer, "How do you use our...?" or "Can you show me how you install our...?" It is important not to ask vague questions such as, "How do you like our...?" It is vital to understand the current customer/product interface as well as the customer's more general problems and goals as all can lead to ideas for creating increased customer value in the future.

Step 3. Data Collection

Typically, many people are involved in making the decision to buy a product or service. To fully understand how to increase customer value, it is imperative to include each of the people who play a role in making the buying decision as a source of data. This often is not simple. Organ-

Understanding the Customer/Product Interaction
- Why does this customer use our product?
- How does this customer use our product?
- What customer problem does our product solve?
- What additional or new problems does our product create?
- How could our product be easier for this customer to use?
- How could we expand our service(s) to reduce this customer's problems?

Understanding the Customer's Values
- How does this customer define success?
- What does this customer see as its distinctive competence?
- What are this customer's problems?
- How can we make this customer more successful?
- What does this customer value?
- What changes does this customer see coming in its environment?

Understanding the Customer Bond
- How does this customer make its selection decision?
- How much of the total product budget does this customer spend with us?
- What would we have to do to increase our percentage of this customer's budget?
- How do we compare to our competition?
- What does this customer see as our distinctive competence?
- Under what circumstances might we lose this customer?

**Figure 1. Sample Checklist for Planning a
Customer-Understanding Process**

izational hierarchies, politics, and naive views of who makes decisions may make it difficult to obtain access to the full range of decision makers. Nevertheless, it is very important that this be done, despite whatever difficulties are encountered.

The planners must decide which customers to include in the analysis. Clearly loyal, current customers will provide important information, but so will former customers—those who have been lost over the years for one reason or another. They will provide different kinds of data. Also important are the competitors' customers—those who have been implicitly saying that another firm meets their needs. Talking candidly to these customers is very important, as their opinion is too often discounted. "They only care about price" or "They really aren't interested in quality" are ways of rationalizing the loss of their business. If, however, a supplier can hear the underlying reasons that a customer uses a competitor, the supplier often can learn a good bit about how he or she has failed to meet the needs of significant parts of the marketplace.

The data-collection process is guided by a data-collection checklist. If the checklist has been carefully prepared, the actual data-collection process should be straightforward. Collecting data of this type is quite different from doing a typical customer survey. The topics on the checklist guide the discussion with the customer. The customer's responses require follow-up questions and interpretation to develop full understanding of customer value. A checklist is only a guide to keep the discussion focused on the customer's fundamental needs.

The purpose of collecting data is to learn what one's product should do from the customer's point of view, i.e., what attributes of a product meet the customer's needs or provide the best value to that customer. The answers will be complex and multifaceted. They should include not only specific performance characteristics such as reliability, ease of use, and the like, but also such aspects as price, delivery, service, and so on. Getting such information from a customer is not an easy task.

Black and Decker is a supplier that listens to its customers. Several years ago, Black and Decker's data showed an erosion of its industrial power-tool business to foreign competitors such as Makita and Ryobi. What the customers were saying was that Black and Decker needed to distinguish its industrial line from the entry-point line sold by the mass retailers. By listening carefully, Black and Decker realized that it could not meet this customer need without abandoning the cherished B&D label. It did recognize, however, that the industrial customers were still bonded to the then dormant DeWalt brand name. Therefore, Black and Decker introduced an enhanced DeWalt line of industrial-quality power tools to the market. This move was phenomenally successful, with sales growing from zero to over $250 million in less than three years. This story is an illustration of the power of listening to one's customers (and using that information) and how important bonding can be as a driver of buying decisions.

Data collection requires skill and sophistication in interviewing.

Data collection requires skill and sophistication in interviewing, skills that many persons do not have. There also is a tendency by customers to sugar coat their answer in their direct contacts with a supplier. Selecting the right persons to conduct these customers visits is critical to the success of this process. We recommend using senior people, perhaps accompanied by a consultant who is familiar with the company and has outstanding listening and interpretative skills. What is clear is that this is not a task to be delegated to the traditionally oriented market-research group.

In asking questions, one must recognize that people tend to give socially acceptable answers to many questions. For example, McDonald's developed the McLean Burger because it believed its market research reports that customers wanted "healthy" food—the socially acceptable response. However, when confronted by the choice between the new, healthy product and the traditional Big Mac, the customers' true preference was the Big Mac. One way to avoid such false leads is to ask customers comparative questions. For example, "Under what circumstances would you choose Product A over Product B or Product C?" "What kind of price difference would lead you to change that choice?" The interviewer must remember that the purpose of the interview is to gather information on the customer's values, not to change them.

Step 4. Measurement

Nothing is so critical to organizational success as increasing the value provided to customers. Thus, measuring increases in customer value provides a critical success indicator of organizational vitality. There are two elements to consider in any measurement of customer value: short-term selection and long-term bonding.

- Selection as the customer's supplier depends on how well one provides current customer value, as can be measured by market share, sales, orders, and so on.

- Bonding refers to the depth of one's relationship with the customer and the customer's future selection behavior.

As we have noted earlier, bonding is critical to retaining customers in the face of competitive challenges. An organization not only must know how loyal its customers are but also must develop strategies to maintain and solidify that bond.

It is useful to think of five ever-increasing levels of bonding:

1. Preferential: "Us over them this time."
2. Favorite: "All things being equal, we get the order."
3. Committed: "We are their supplier."
4. Referential: "They tell other people to buy from us."
5. Exclusive: "No one else has a chance to get their order."

Although one would prefer all of one's customers to be at the fifth level of bonding, that generally is impossible, given the nature of most marketplaces. It is important, however, to discover the current level of bonding and then develop strategies for increasing it.

The levels of bonding represent increasing levels of trust. People make recommendations based on their confidence that the value received is not unique to their experience but is representative of the general quality of the supplier's product and service. Exclusivity is like leaving home without first checking the weather because you know you will be taken care of by the particular supplier regardless of how inclement the weather may be.

Several of the levels of bonding involve retaining customers. However, there are dangers inherent in focusing on customer retention, as one can overlook how much of a total budget for the product or service a customer is spending with one's organization. One may retain customers over a long period, but they may be spending most of their budgets elsewhere. Fay (1994) reports that in the retail industry, those customers retained the longest were the least profitable. These long-term customers had learned how to shop the stores for sales and bargains, picking the least-profitable mix of merchandise. It is important to learn how much of the total budget the customer spends with one's company, as that is the most significant measure of bonding.

It typically is necessary to use external resources to reveal the extent of customer bonding. Customers rarely will give accurate information about their level of bonding to their suppliers. It is far too confrontational. Some indicators of bonding, such as referrals or repeat orders (a measure of commitment), may be readily apparent but also may give an incomplete picture of the level of bonding.

Step 5. Implementation

The payoff for customer understanding is its application to strategy development and implementation. Once the customer-understanding process is complete, the organization's strategic planning team needs to receive, digest, and apply the findings of the analysis.

One way to think about customer understanding in the context of strategic planning is to regard it as one way of conducting the SWOT analysis (Goodstein, Nolan, & Pfeiffer, 1993). That is, the customer-understanding analysis can provide a unique view of the organization's Strengths, Weaknesses, Opportunities, and Threats—from the customer's point of view.

CONCLUSION

Maintaining and solidifying current customer value and developing tactics for meeting unanticipated emerging needs provides the basis for either developing or modifying an organization's strategic plan. It is this application that makes the customer-understanding analysis pay off.

References

Albrecht, K. (1994). *The northbound train.* New York: AMACOM.

Fay, C.J. (1994). Royalties from loyalties. *Journal of Business Strategies, 15,* 47-51.

Goodman, J.A., Bargatze, G.F., & Grimm, C. (1994, January). The key problem with TQM. *Quality Progress,* pp. 45-48.

Goodstein, L.D., Nolan, T.M., & Pfeiffer, J.W. (1993). *Applied strategic planning: How to develop a plan that really works.* New York: McGraw-Hill.

Reichheld, F.F. (1993). Loyalty-based management. *Harvard Business Review, 71,* 64-73.

Howard E. Butz, Jr., is director of total quality for AAI Corporation, located in Hunt Valley, Maryland. He consults internally in the areas of quality, process improvement, and strategic planning. Mr. Butz founded the Maryland TQM Directors' Council and cofounded TQM/100, a strategic benchmarking alliance of aerospace and electronics manufacturers. In addition, he serves on the board of directors for the Mid-Atlantic Planning Association. Mr. Butz is the author of "Strategic Planning: The Missing Link in TQM."

Leonard D. Goodstein, Ph.D., is a consulting psychologist based in Washington, D.C., as well as a senior vice president for Pfeiffer & Company. After more than thirty years as an academic, he joined Pfeiffer & Company (then University Associates) as president and later chairman of the board. Subsequently, he served as chief executive officer of the American Psychological Association. Currently he consults with multinational organizations, specializing in organizational and executive development as well as strategic planning. He is a frequent contributor to the professional literature, including the Annuals *and is one of the coauthors of* Applied Strategic Planning: A Comprehensive Guide, *copublished by Pfeiffer & Company and McGraw-Hill in 1993.*

FROM VISION TO ACTION: DETERMINING THE IMPACT OF A MISSION STATEMENT

John Geirland and Eva Sonesh-Kedar

Abstract: A successful, thriving organization is created to fulfill a specific purpose and is sustained by a vision. Often the purpose and vision are incorporated into a mission statement intended to provide behavioral guidance for the members of the organization.

But how does an organization know whether employees are interpreting the mission correctly and consistently and whether they are translating it into appropriate action?

This article defines potential difficulties associated with a mission statement, presents a case study describing how employees in one organization interpreted its mission, and offers a step-by-step procedure for creating and administering a survey similar to the one used in the case study.

The 1996 Annual: Volume 1, Training.
Copyright © 1996 by Pfeiffer & Company, San Diego, CA.

A mission statement is intended to be the guiding force behind an organization, providing employees with a direction, purpose, and context for their activities. But how can an organization determine whether its mission statement meets this intended goal?

In this article, we offer a powerful tool that organizational leaders can use to assess whether employee behavior is aligned with the organization's mission.

POTENTIAL DIFFICULTIES

The task associated with aligning employees and mission consists of much more than writing a good mission statement, distributing it, and explaining it carefully. The mission statement and its fulfillment present several potential difficulties that must be taken into account:

1. *A mission statement is necessarily general and, thus, open to interpretation.* Well-intentioned individuals may interpret the mission statement differently and end up working at cross-purposes. For example, consider an organization whose mission is to produce state-of-the-art computer technology. Given this mission, which activity carries more value, generating new designs or refining current designs? Both activities are important and have value; both are consistent with the organization's mission. How do employees decide which activity should be emphasized?

2. *A mission statement involves one-way communication.* As a result, management may have difficulty in determining whether employees have perceived the message as intended.

3. *Strategies for fulfilling the mission must change over time, in accordance with changing circumstances.* For instance, new strategies may be needed to deal with marketplace changes. And during a transition in top leadership, the new leader may define strategies that are strikingly different from those of his or her predecessor. Strategy changes, although necessary, often conflict with deeply ingrained organizational attitudes and behaviors. Consequently, they may be met with resistance.

These potential difficulties give rise to some important questions that an organization needs to answer:

- How is the mission statement being interpreted by employees? Are employees at different levels interpreting the mission statement differently?
- How are employees translating the mission statement into specific activities?
- How are employees incorporating new strategies into their understanding of the organization's mission?

One way to obtain answers (and subsequently provide corrective feedback) is to develop and administer a survey. The remainder of this article describes our intervention in a particular organization, which led to the creation of such a survey, and our recommendations for organizations that want to try the same kind of survey approach.

A CASE STUDY

New Leadership, New Strategies

We were asked to assist in the transition of leadership in a firm located in southern California. This organization was managed for over twenty-five years by David Pynchon,[1] a competent, no-nonsense leader with extensive experience and technical knowledge.

After David retired, Karen Pizzi was brought on board as David's replacement. Karen was a highly talented professional with years of experience working for a large consulting firm. She was considered an innovator in her field.

Karen soon discovered that although the general mission was well understood, the organization's basic structure and strategies had changed little during the past ten or fifteen years. Many members of the management team had been in their jobs for ten, fifteen, even twenty years. None had ever been expected to think innovatively, and Karen wondered if they knew how. Karen wanted to introduce new strategies for fulfilling the existing mission.

Karen was convinced that all employees needed to be more proactive in dealing with clients, building relationships, and solving problems. She also believed that the organization's current management practices and attitudes reinforced specialization and fragmentation of effort; as a result, only a few managers had the kind of larger business perspective

---
[1] All the names in this case study have been changed. Details about the nature of the company's work have also been kept vague to protect confidentiality.

that she thought was vital. Karen wanted the managers to adopt the larger perspective, and she wanted both managerial and nonmanagerial employees to provide clients with a more integrated set of services.

In a series of meetings with employees, Karen began espousing the organization's mission and her strategies for achieving that mission. These meetings were well received and useful. But later, in subsequent meetings and interactions, Karen found that many employees were still thinking and working in the old ways.

Survey Development

We began to work with Karen to develop a survey that would clarify how people were interpreting the mission statement and translating it into action. Our first task was to identify activities that were general enough to be relevant to most employees, but specific enough to be easily identified and related to everyday work experience. We used information from our previous interviews with employees to generate a representative sample of activities.

Then we worked with Karen to revise and refine the list. We made an effort to include activities that varied in their consistency with and support of Karen's strategies. Some activities represented behaviors that Karen wanted to see more widely adopted, while other activities represented older practices that Karen wished to deemphasize.

We decided that respondents would be asked two questions with regard to each activity:

- How is the activity currently valued in the organization?
- How should the activity be valued in the organization?

Survey Administration

We had asked Karen to complete the survey first, as we intended to use her value scores for comparison to those of other groups and levels in the organization.

Subsequently, everyone in the organization was given an opportunity to complete the survey. Participation was voluntary, and responses were kept confidential. The response rate was close to 90 percent.

After the surveys were completed, we were able to show Karen how well (or how poorly) her message was getting across. We broke out the data according to levels of the organization and departments. What we discovered was that, not surprisingly, the managers who reported directly to Karen were more in alignment with her values than were front-line employees. However, we also found several important activities for which there were dramatic differences between Karen's value scores and those of her top managers. As a result of our analysis, Karen knew which parts of her message she needed to emphasize and with which groups.

As can be seen in Table 1, Karen placed very little value on consistency with past practices and methods, whereas her managers placed somewhat greater value on consistency and the staff (nonmanagerial employees) highly valued consistency. Karen showed that she highly valued risk taking, whereas her managers and staff were far more risk averse. It was clear that for employees to be more proactive in dealing with clients, building relationships, and solving problems, they needed to abandon old practices and take more risks.

Table 1. How Activities Should Be Valued
Scale: 1 = Low Value; 10 = High Value

Activities	Karen	Managers	Staff
Remaining consistent with past practices and methods	1.00	2.29	6.14
Being cautious in decision making	3.00	4.57	7.40
Taking risks	9.00	7.00	5.93

CREATING A CUSTOMIZED SURVEY

The development of a customized survey similar to the one used in our case study involves the following steps:

1. *Review the organization's mission statement.* If the organization has a written mission statement, review it and any memos or documents relating to how the mission statement was developed. Interview the organizational leader to clarify current thinking about the mission, vision, and values to be promoted.

2. *Generate a pool of activities.* Conduct interviews with organizational managers and nonmanagerial employees. Ask general questions about what people do on a daily basis, how they spend their time, and what activities they feel are important.

3. *Create a survey form.* Activities will vary in their specificity, but try to end up with ones that are general enough to apply to most people in the

organization, yet specific enough to be easily identifiable. Include activities that are consistent with the leader's espoused strategies as well as ones that are inconsistent. Also include some past practices that the leader suspects are still being pursued, despite adding little value in light of the leader's desired strategies. Work closely with the leader in developing and refining this survey. A sample survey form is provided in Figure 1.

4. *Have the organizational leader complete the survey, assigning numerical values to the activities.* The leader should indicate how he or she feels each activity is *currently valued* in the organization as a whole and how it *should be valued.* We recommend a ten-point scale, where 1 = "Low Value" and 10 = "High Value."

5. *Administer the survey throughout the organization.* The survey may be administered in the form of a stand-alone instrument; or, as in the case study, the items may be incorporated into a larger survey instrument. Results may be summarized for different levels, departments, functions, or job classifications—usually in the form of mean (average) value scores. Compare these mean scores to the scores obtained from the organizational leader. Small differences indicate areas in which employees and the leader are in alignment; large differences indicate areas in which the leader's message may not be getting through.

6. *Discuss value scores in a series of feedback sessions with managers and nonmanagerial employees.* Feedback sessions provide an opportunity to reinforce those activities that are aligned with the leader's vision and to point out activities that should be deemphasized or abandoned. Include action planning in these sessions, when appropriate.

CONCLUSION

The results we obtained in Karen's organization stimulated a lively and productive discussion about the need to abandon or deemphasize some older practices and embrace new ones. Subsequently, the organization moved in a direction that was closer to Karen's strategies but still in keeping with the organization's mission. She later told us, "I think they got the message."

The methods described in this article offer the following potential benefits to organizations:

- A powerful tool for communicating a leader's strategies and priorities throughout the organization;

Instructions: Rate each of the following fourteen activities on a scale from 1 to 10, where 1 represents *low* value and 10 represents *high* value. Be sure to assign a rating in each column, showing how each activity *is currently valued* and how it *should be valued.*

Activities	How Activities Are Currently Valued in the Organization	How Activities Should Be Valued in the Organization
1. Remaining consistent with past practices and methods	_____	_____
2. Being cautious in decision making	_____	_____
3. Writing reports	_____	_____
4. Meeting deadlines	_____	_____
5. Being friendly	_____	_____
6. Collaborating with other departments	_____	_____
7. Making suggestions for improvements	_____	_____
8. Being accurate	_____	_____
9. Taking risks	_____	_____
10. Helping clients solve problems	_____	_____
11. Challenging existing work practices	_____	_____
12. Developing a broad business perspective	_____	_____
13. Taking initiative	_____	_____
14. Doing quality work	_____	_____

Figure 1. Sample Survey Form

- Feedback on people's alignment with the organization's mission, vision, and values;
- A clear idea of which parts of the organization are "getting the message" and which parts need help or attention; and
- The basis for creating a performance-review instrument.

Suggested Reading

Foster, T. (1993). *101 great mission statements: How the world's leading companies run their businesses.* London: Kogan Page.

John Geirland, Ph.D., *heads up Geirland & Associates, an organization and management consulting firm based in Studio City, California, specializing in individual and organizational assessment, team development, managing change, and organizational design. Dr. Geirland has consulted to a wide range of public and private organizations, including Amgen, U.S. West, Blue Cross/Blue Shield of Florida, General Dynamics, Great Western Bank, and the Los Angeles County Department of Mental Health, among others. He has published papers on organizational design, the impact of technology in organizations, leadership and values, and creativity. He can be reached at jgeirland@aol.com.*

Eva Sonesh-Kedar, Ph.D., *is a management and organization development consultant. She assists executives and middle-level managers to develop strategies for managing organizational change, innovation and creativity, and team development. Dr. Sonesh-Kedar consulted for several years to Great Western Bank, and currently is working as a consultant for Apple Computer. Other clients include CBS Inc., First Interstate Bank, Adizes Institute, and others. She has published papers on organization values and creativity.*

DIVERSITY AND TEAM DEVELOPMENT

Claire B. Halverson and Guillermo Cuéllar

Abstract: The changing nature of work, coupled with the changing composition of the work force, has put a great deal of pressure on organizations to adapt. A major response is the formation of diverse, interdependent work teams. This article discusses the complexities of the development of a team through three stages: infancy, adolescence, and adulthood (Weber, 1992). The climate issues, interpersonal issues, task issues, and leadership issues that face a multicultural team at each stage of development are described and contrasted with those of monocultural teams. The focus is on diversity of race, gender, and nationality as it applies to team members at different stages of development of their social identity. Other issues, such as sexual orientation, physical/developmental ability, and socioeconomic class are equally as important, but, for purposes of brevity, will not be the focus of this article. Issues that need to be addressed by consultants and team leaders who are helping teams to overcome the threats—and benefit from the challenges—of diversity are identified.

The 1996 Annual: Volume 1, Training.
Copyright © 1996 by Pfeiffer & Company, San Diego, CA.

T he changing nature of work has put a great deal of pressure on organizations to adapt. This change is a result of the following factors:

- specialization of human resources;
- limited physical resources, which requires increased synergy and coordination;
- increased complexity of problems, which demands high-quality creative solutions; and
- rapidly changing markets and technologies.

To respond to these factors, organizations are changing from depending on individuals to perform discrete tasks to utilizing high-performance teams that accomplish work interdependently.

The composition of the work force also is changing; it is increasingly diverse. This is the result of changes in immigration patterns, lifestyles, economic pressures, and legal demands.

Although there historically has been diversity of race[1], gender, and/or ethnicity/nationality in many organizations, roles generally were segregated so that teams were homogeneous. An example of this is the Bell Telephone Company, which, in the 1960s, was the first corporation brought before the U.S. Supreme Court for a violation of affirmative action. Its record was not worse than other corporations at the time, but it was the largest employer. At that time, EuroAmerican men who worked at Bell were technicians, African American men were janitors, and EuroAmerican females were operators. Later, EuroAmerican women moved to clerical positions, and African American women became operators. Today at Bell, as at many other organizations, jobs are integrated into teams that are diverse in terms of race, gender, nationality, sexual orientation, age, and physical ability.

DEVELOPMENTAL STAGES OF SOCIAL IDENTITY

A multicultural team is likely to be confronted with issues related to the developmental stages of social identity of members and their consciousness of racism and sexism (Halverson, 1982; Jackson and Hardiman,

---

[1] The authors wish to acknowledge that "race" is a sociological construct based on people's perceptions, not a biological reality, inasmuch as no one characteristic can group people of the world according to distinct racial categories.

1983). These stages can be generalized to other types of social diversity. The stages are described as follows.

Dependent

The team members who have dominant status in society (whites, men) and those who have subordinate status (people of color, women) accept the standards and judgments of the dominant status group. Racism and sexism are ignored, and problems are perceived as resulting from actions of individual members of the subordinate-status group or the overt bigot/chauvinist. Relationships are "one up-one down," reflecting the power dimensions of society.

Counterdependent

Dominant-status group members realize the institutional nature of oppression and their privileged status. This is often accompanied by guilt and inability to be authentic with members of subordinate-status groups. People of color, women, and foreign-born nationals redefine themselves according to the standards and values of the group. They usually experience anger at what they have given up and how they have been treated during their dependent stage. Their choices often are in reaction to the norms of the dominant group.

Independent

At this stage, both dominant- and subordinate-status group members actively work against the established values of oppression. Relationships are authentic and collaborative across groups. There is open dialogue about problems related to diversity.

Multicultural teams often are composed of individuals who are at different stages of development in their consciousness of their social identity. This affects the development of the team.

DEVELOPMENTAL STAGES OF TEAMS

Stage I: Infancy

Climate

During this forming stage, individuals seek to create a safe environment for their interactions and they establish basic criteria for membership. As they form, multicultural teams must manage a more complex range of issues than monocultural teams. The familiar patterns of compatibility are layered with an array of cultural differences and values. For example, simple things that individuals take for granted in a homogeneous group, such as common norms related to the pacing of speech, use of silence, and type of emotional expression may not be present in a diverse group.

If dominant- or subordinate-status team members are in the dependent stage, they may be unaware of the complexities of diversity and assume that all members should conform to the dominant-status norms. Subordinate-status members in the counterdependent stage may be angry at attempts to establish conformity. Others may be aware of the complexities but feel awkward and confused about how to work with the differences. In monocultural teams the climate is polite; in multicultural ones politeness can be exaggerated to awkwardness.

Interpersonal Issues

Individuals usually are tentative and polite in order to be included in a team. In multicultural teams, they progressively discover more complex and difficult issues that affect inclusion. They look for solutions to ease the uncertainty of their interactions.

Dominant-status members are easily included, and subordinate-status members may be consciously or unconsciously excluded. Members of subordinate status (e.g., people of color, women, recent immigrants) may need a longer period of time in which to develop trust. This is because they may have been excluded in the past, their abilities may have been questioned, and they may be struggling with the cost of relinquishing their cultural norms and values in order to be accepted. They may tend to take a low participatory role, either to observe the stage of consciousness of dominant-status members and ascertain their own safety or, if they are new to the country, to understand the cultural norms.

If members of the dominant culture attempt to include others in their participation, their actions may be perceived as insensitive and impolite because they do not understand the perceptions, values, and cultural behavioral patterns of the subordinate-status members. For example, they may not understand the preference of many Asians to hold back on participation, to speak only if something important needs to be said, and to allow intervals of silence.

Cultural differences related to individualism/collectivism and task/relationship are crucial here. For example, individualism and task orientation have been documented (Halverson, 1993; Hofstede, 1984) as being deep cultural values in the dominant-status group in the United States. Team members with these values find it difficult to join with others and often prefer to work by themselves. They want to start on the task right away and consider time spent in developing relationships to be time wasted. Members from more collectivist and relationship-oriented cultures assume that the group has a higher value than individual needs and preferences. They consider it important to spend time connecting at the beginning of meetings. EuroAmericans who try this often find that the task can be accomplished in the same amount of time. Differences such as these represent cultural patterns.

Cultural patterns are different from stereotypes because groups are not rigidly categorized; preferences, not innate characteristics, are identified. Even if a person has a preference for one thing, he or she is capable of the alternative.

Task Issues

In the first stage, little work is done, and that which is accomplished often is not of good quality. If decisions are made, they are often rushed and represent the desires of the dominant culture.

In Stage I, it is important for the team to agree on its goals and purpose. For a multicultural team, a compelling goal that transcends individual differences is even more crucial than it is for a monocultural group.

Identifying the skills of individual members also is important. Assumptions and stereotypes may exist about roles members should take in accomplishing the work. For example, it may be assumed that Asian Americans may be good technicians but not good leaders.

Leadership Issues

In Stage I, team members are uncomfortable with ambiguity and need to establish leadership. Multicultural teams often follow a path of least resistance and form around the leadership of the dominant-culture members. Group members collude with the leadership to ignore differences and to suppress discomfort. A dynamic of social conformity or "groupthink" emerges, and members choose loyalty to the team even if the leadership is not providing a realistic appraisal or an effective course of action. The degree to which these dynamics occur varies according to the extent of diversity in the team and the developmental stages of consciousness of the leader and team members.

Leadership is critical to creating an environment that is either inclusive or exclusive. When leadership fails to address inclusion needs, the team will not achieve the level of safety necessary to move past the stage of infancy. A "revolving door syndrome" may occur as subordinate-status members join the team and then leave.

Stage II: Adolescence

Climate

During the second stage, politeness wears off and conflict emerges openly or is hidden under the surface. In multicultural teams, members of the dominant-status group (e.g., whites and men) are apt to be unaware of the conflicts felt by members of the subordinate-status groups (e.g., people of color and women).

Interpersonal Issues

In any team, issues of subgrouping, alliances, and infighting occur in Stage II. In multicultural teams, subordinate-status members frequently are excluded from forming effective relationships with dominant-status members. They may be excluded because they do not share the same jokes, language, style of communicating, social habits, or work style. Or they may be excluded because of feelings of hostility and unwillingness to accept them. Men, whites, and U.S. nationals may fear that they will have to change because of the subordinate-status group members, but they often do not believe they *should* have to change.

Issues of sub-grouping, alliances, and infighting occur in Stage II.

If members of subordinate-status groups form relationships among themselves, they are accused of subgrouping and of not becoming part of the team. Subordinate-status group members can experience anxiety and stress if there is pressure to conform in order to belong to the team.

Task Issues

In the adolescent stage, a team needs to focus on how realistic its goals are and what norms and procedures should be used in accomplishing them. Creating common norms is more complicated in multicultural teams because of culturally different patterns of behavior regarding decision making, conducting meetings, communication, and conflict management. For example, the dominant cultural style of problem solving in the United States is linear and emphasizes rational thought processes; however, many other cultures value circular and holistic processes that include intuition.

Pfeiffer & Company

A team often will find it easier to continue with business as usual and use norms that reflect the culture of the dominant-status group. This happens particularly when there is only token representation of subordinate-status groups. However, differences need to be addressed in a way that allows all to contribute and the team to benefit from the richness of diversity.

Leadership Issues

In the adolescent stage, leadership is resisted by most teams. In multicultural teams, this struggle is apt to be less overt. Because white male leadership may be taken for granted, it may be harder to challenge it. In self-directed teams, it may seem easy and natural to have the leadership fall to, or be taken over by, white men. White women frequently assume traditional roles and support white male leadership. If the leader is a member of a subordinate-status group, for example, a Hispanic female, she may be bypassed or ignored, or there may be a rebellion against her leadership.

Stage III: Adulthood

Climate

The third stage is characterized by interpersonal support and high energy for accomplishing the task. The energy and creativity can be higher in a multicultural team than in a monocultural one (Adler, 1991).

Interpersonal Issues

Emotional conflict in this stage is reduced by patching up previously conflicting relationships. There is a strong sense of group identity and expression of interpersonal support. Differences continue to be expressed, but there are agreed-on methods for managing them. Relationships are functional.

Task Issues

The team may be harmonious but unproductive after it has faced the issues of conflict in the adolescent stage. If so, the team must be realigned with its goals. When this is accomplished, it can be highly productive, drawing on the diverse skills of all team members and no longer hindered by stereotypes and assumptions.

Multicultural teams at this stage can be more productive than monocultural teams because they can benefit from the following:

- increased creativity from different points of view,
- a decreased tendency to conform to ideas without questioning their validity,
- special insights and observations resulting from the previous exclusion of subordinate-status members,
- the opportunity to rethink norms and processes, and
- strengths stemming from cultural patterns of members of subordinate status as well as those of dominant-status members.

Increased creativity is particularly important when the team is working on tasks that require an expanded understanding of the problem and new solutions. For example, one team with a member who spoke English as a second language finally recognized its need to slow down and to paraphrase and summarize more frequently so the member could understand. When it adopted this norm for the non-English speaker, the team found that all benefited with increased understanding.

Leadership Issues

In the adult stage, there is less attention to status hierarchy, and the leadership skills of various team members are utilized. Lines of authority are followed, not circumvented. Different styles of leadership are recognized and valued. For example, women's experience in listening and supporting is recognized and valued as important to team building and coaching.

CONCLUSION

Many multicultural teams do not move beyond the initial stage of infancy and, thus, are less effective than monocultural teams. Stereotypes abound, and differences are treated as problems rather than as potential benefits. Whites and men, at the dependent stage in their consciousness of racism and sexism, may not realize that people of color and women do not feel included and that their skills are not being used.

In working with multicultural teams, the team leader or consultant needs a high level of awareness relative to the issues of a diverse work force. A clear vision is needed of what diversity and equality mean in a team and how the dynamics related to dominant- and subordinate-status groups can negatively impact the team. Specific guidelines around safety and participation need to be developed so that members of subordinate groups can be included as full participants on their own terms. Members' differing needs for addressing task and interpersonal issues should be acknowledged.

The adolescent stage is more intense and complex in multicultural teams than in monocultural teams, because of the difficult issues of racism, sexism, and other forms of discrimination. The team leader or an outside consultant must help the team to resolve conflicting needs in order to develop synergistic norms.

The team needs to set aside time to discuss its processes relative to diversity. Addressing conflict is complicated by differences in individual and cultural styles of conflict management. For example, whites and men may be reluctant to accept direct feedback from people of color and women. Differences in emotional expression also may abound. Skills in giving and receiving feedback, process observation, active listening, and problem solving may need to be developed.

Multicultural teams in the adult stage often will perform better than monocultural teams. The danger for multicultural teams is that differences will be ignored and conflict will be unresolved; the opportunity is their high potential to be creative and productive.

References

Adler, N. (1991). *International dimensions of organizational behavior.* Boston, MA: Kent.

Halverson, C.B. (1982). *Training and stages of consciousness of racism and sexism in the world of work.* Paper presented at the OD Network 1982 Conference, Breakthroughs: Creating a World That Works, Lake Geneva, WI.

Halverson, C.B. (1993). Cultural context inventory. In J.W. Pfeiffer (Ed.), *The 1993 annual: Developing human resources.* San Diego, CA: Pfeiffer & Company.

Hofstede, G. (1984). Motivation, leadership, and organization: Do American theories apply abroad? In D.A. Kolb, I.M. Rubin, & J.M. McIntyre (Eds.), *Organizational psychology.* Englewood Cliffs, NJ: Prentice-Hall.

Jackson, B.W., & Hardiman, R. (1983). Racial identity development: Implications for managing the multiracial work force. In R.A. Ritvo & A.G. Sargent (Eds.), *The NTL managers' handbook.* Arlington, VA: NTL Institute.

Jackson, B.W., & Holvino, E. (1986). *Working with multicultural organizations: Matching theory and practice.* Proceedings of the OD Network 1986 Conference, New York.

Weber, R.C. (1982). The group: A cycle from birth to death. In L. Porter & B. Mohr (Eds.), *NTL readings book for human relations training.* Arlington, VA: NTL Institute.

Claire B. Halverson, Ph.D., *is a professor of diversity and organizational behavior in the Master's Program of Intercultural Management at the School for International Training in Brattleboro, Vermont. She consults in the areas of diversity and multicultural team building, working with a variety of organizations in the public, private, and not-for-profit sectors. Dr. Halverson has been director of the Southeastern Wisconsin Sex-Equity Training Institute and of the Southeastern Wisconsin Race Desegregation Training Institute. She is a member of the NTL Institute.*

Guillermo Cuéllar, Ed.D., *is an organization development consultant with more than sixteen years of experience. He also serves as an adjunct faculty member at the School for International Training in Brattleboro, Vermont. His areas of expertise include diversity, multicultural development, planning, systems change and innovation, creativity, leadership, communication skills, mediation, conflict resolution, and stress management. Dr. Cuéllar provides professional services in both English and Spanish.*

VALUES-BASED LEADERSHIP
FOR THE 21ST CENTURY

Robert C. Preziosi

Abstract: In this article the author concentrates on
what a leader needs to *believe* and *do* in order to
promote the high performance that will be required
for organizational success in the 21st Century. His
premise is that leader values are the guiding principles
that determine leader behavior, which, in turn, motivates and inspires follower behavior. The author describes twenty attitudes and associated behaviors that
the effective leader needs to exhibit. In addition, he
presents an example of how a leader might generate
behavioral options stemming from one of the essential
values.

$\mathbf{M}$anagement in the 21st Century will focus on the well-documented values-based theory of leadership (DePree, 1992; Tichy & Sherman, 1993). The companies that DePree and Tichy and Sherman have written about offer powerful examples of the practical impact of this new theory: Leader values are the guiding principles that determine leader behavior, which, in turn, motivates and inspires follower behavior. The end result is the high performance required for an organization to achieve competitive advantage and future success.

THE CONNECTION BETWEEN LEADER VALUES AND HIGH PERFORMANCE

Several authors have helped to identify the specific leader values and associated behaviors that foster high follower performance: Covey, 1991; Garfield, 1986, 1991; and Leonard, 1991. What I have learned from these authors is consistent with my own experience with high-performance organizations.

There is no magic involved in promoting high performance, although the phenomenal success of some organizations might lead others to wonder if there is. Instead, the same kind of performance is within the reach of virtually any organization.

What exactly does a leader need to *believe* and *do* in order to promote high performance?

1. *Attend intently.* Regardless of the setting, the situation, and the characters involved, the leader needs to demonstrate the same totality of focus—physical, mental, and emotional—until closure is achieved.

2. *Build on success.* All successful leadership situations share certain elements. The leader needs to identify those elements and consciously repeat them as a foundation for building increasingly better leadership performance.

3. *Champion the shared vision.* The assumption underlying this point is that the leader has worked with followers to develop such a vision. Then the leader's responsibility is to serve as the energizing force behind that vision—so much so that every follower acts in support of the vision.

4. *Generate renewal.* The organizational world of the 21st Century will be characterized by continual, rapid change. Constantly adapting to changing organizational circumstances requires that the leader not only be creative, but also encourage creativity on the part of followers. It is the leader's example of creative behavior that allows the organization to

renew itself continually and flourish, regardless of the stage of organizational development involved.

5. *Embrace diversity.* Increasing diversity within organizations will lead to an important opportunity for organizational redefinition. The successful leader will honor many different sets of values in order to take advantage of this opportunity.

6. *Energize oneself.* With so many responsibilities, a leader may forgo tasks that he or she feels passionately about in order to take care of more pressing matters. It is important to note, though, that leaders maintain high levels of physical and emotional energy by including activities they love in their daily schedules.

7. *Learn from others.* Heroes, mentors, and instructors all provide opportunities for learning. Regardless of success in past performance, the effective leader is always ready, willing, and able to learn and to apply that learning.

8. *Listen to internal prompts.* Often a leader is placed in a situation involving conflicting information or conflicting interpretations of that information. Although the successful leader carefully considers and compares all positions, he or she is most influenced by internal directives.

9. *Honor the environment.* The old cliché about the environment is still true: "It's the only one we have." The successful leader knows how important it is to replenish a resource before it is entirely depleted.

10. *Measure all activities.* The leader must know the state of everything in the organization, and the only way to stay informed is to measure all human activity.

11. *Offer learning resources.* Every person in an organization must be as self-renewing as the organization itself. As self-renewal is dependent on learning, the leader must develop and implement a total learning system consisting of accessible resources. With such a system, each person can learn whatever needs to be learned, whenever it needs to be learned, in the most effective way.[1]

12. *Acknowledge everyone's value.* Superior service, quality, and productivity are dependent on employees' self-esteem. The leader must first recognize people's value. Then he or she must exhibit and promote behaviors that build esteem and must work to rid the organization of behaviors that destroy esteem.

---

[1] For more information about organizational learning, see *The Faster Learning Organization: Gain and Sustain the Competitive Edge* by Bob Guns, 1996, San Diego, CA: Pfeiffer & Company. This book is scheduled to be published in 1996.

13. *Practice effective leadership behavior.* Leadership, like other behavior, is learned. The leader's responsibility in learning a new, effective leadership behavior is to practice that behavior until it becomes habit.

14. *Provide opportunities for people to succeed.* The leader's task is to create opportunities so that each person will be limited only by his or her own behavior and not by the fact that opportunities do not exist.

15. *Put followers first.* This is perhaps the most difficult of the leader values and behaviors; it asks that the leader subjugate personal objectives. But the leader's foremost responsibility is to provide followers with the resources they need—at his or her own expense, if necessary.

16. *See the "big picture."* The leader must be able to see how all organizational elements interconnect in a single entity. This entity must be viewed in past, present, and future terms.

17. *Extend the boundaries.* The leader is obligated to take the organization and its members beyond the current boundaries of performance. Consequently, the successful leader is always inspiring people by painting new pictures of the organization's desired state. Higher and higher levels of performance are the result.

18. *Encourage team development.* Teams are becoming a natural part of the organizational landscape. Employees at all levels are finding that collaboration is preferable to conflict and frequently even to individual effort. The effective leader encourages team development and uses it as a force for greater productivity and quality.

19. *Exercise mental agility.* Organizational functioning leads to a lot of surprises. Responding appropriately requires that the leader be able to switch gears, see a surprise as an opportunity, and act quickly on that opportunity. This ability is dependent on mental agility and flexibility.

20. *Use mental rehearsal.* Sports champions are not the only ones who mentally rehearse activities in order to enhance performance; many successful leaders do, too. In effect, the leader creates a mental video for replay in a real situation in the future. The shorter the time between rehearsal and actual performance, the greater the impact of the rehearsal.

HOW TO USE VALUES

The role of a value is to trigger behavioral options, and in choosing options the leader develops a personal behavior system. The leader may act alone in response to his or her own values or may consult others—followers, for instance—and lead them in a brainstorming session to increase the number of options.

For example, "generate renewal," a value/behavior discussed in the previous section, might lead to a group-brainstormed list of options like the following:

1. Develop and conduct a three-day training session on creativity for all employees;

2. Design a program for recognizing and rewarding individual and group creativity;

3. Hire a creativity consultant to identify which organizational activities suffer from a lack of creativity;

4. Hold an annual creativity fair at which organizational members present the products of their creativity;

5. Train all employees in stress-management techniques so that they feel free to release their creativity;

6. Start a creativity newsletter to provide organizational members with tools and techniques for enhancing creativity;

7. Stop all normal organizational activity for two hours once a week so that people can concentrate on unleashing their creativity;

8. Require every member of senior management to develop an annual creativity plan for his or her part of the organization;

9. Build a library of books and tapes for all employees to use;

10. Place posters about creativity in every room in the building;

11. Attend a creativity conference for senior executives;

12. Purchase computer software that assists the creative process and have it installed in every PC;

13. Have each member of the organization develop a personal creativity plan with a checklist to measure conformance to the standards of the plan; and

14. Incorporate a requirement of one new product (or service) per quarter for each business unit.

Choosing from these options will depend on the following variables:

- The requirements of the work unit;
- The participative process that is used to determine choices;
- The results desired;
- The leader's ability; and
- The organization's capacity.

There may be other variables that come into play, depending on the leader, the organization, and the specific group members involved. The important thing is to be aware of which variables to consider.

Conclusion

Values-based leadership has a significant impact on an organization. Each organization needs to decide which leadership values will drive its functioning. Once these values have been established, specific behavioral options present themselves. After options have been taken, the results can be measured to determine whether the organization is headed in the direction it desires.

References

Covey, S.R. (1991). *The seven habits of highly effective leaders.* New York: Simon & Schuster.

DePree, M. (1992). *Leadership jazz.* New York: Doubleday.

Garfield, C. (1986). *Peak performers.* New York: William Morrow.

Garfield, C. (1991). *Second to none.* Burr Ridge, IL: Irwin.

Leonard, G. (1991). *Mastery.* New York: Dutton.

Tichy, N.M., & Sherman, S. (1993). *Control your destiny or someone else will.* New York: Doubleday.

Robert C. Preziosi, D.P.A., is a professor of management education in the School of Business and Entrepreneurship at Nova Southeastern University in Fort Lauderdale, Florida. He is also the president of Management Associates, a consulting firm. He has worked as a human resources director, a line manager, and a leadership-training administrator and has consulted with all levels of management in many organizations, including American Express, the Department of Health and Human Services, John Alden Life Insurance, Siemens, and a number of hospitals and banks. Dr. Preziosi has been training trainers since the 1970s; his areas of interest include leadership, adult learning, and all aspects of management and executive development. In 1984 he was given the Outstanding Contribution to HRD Award by ASTD; in 1990 he received the Torch Award, the highest leadership award that ASTD gives.

GETTING YOUR MESSAGE THROUGH: A GUIDE FOR CEOS

Robert Hargrove

Abstract: It is important that every CEO know how to get a message through a complex organization so that it produces not only dramatic results but also a fundamental shift in corporate culture. This article tells how a CEO can structure communication and use top executives to create a force field for realizing the CEO's vision and goals for the organization.

Seven factors that restrain the communication of desired organizational change are described, and the solutions to them are discussed. Seven factors that amplify the CEO's message and enable action are then presented, with guidelines for creating them in an organization.

The 1996 Annual: Volume 1, Training.
Copyright © 1996 by Pfeiffer & Company, San Diego, CA.

Imagine that you are the newly hired CEO of a bank that was transformed to a global custodian of pension funds under your predecessor. The bank has made record profits over the past ten years. You are trying to convince your ten fiercely autonomous, highly successful business-unit heads that the bank's future lies in eliminating boundaries between divisions and doing more cross-selling. You have held meetings, solicited nods, and have sent memos, yet you are not sure whether anyone has heard you or not. What should you do now?

COMMITTED SPEAKING AND LISTENING

In most organizations, there is a great deal of speaking and listening; yet, 99.9 percent of it fails to make any difference. Because a chief executive's message often heralds significant change and must bring about a new order in the organization, it must "get through" to its audience. An executive message should fall into the 00.1 percent of communications that make a difference, that have an impact, that break the spell of the past, alter the present, and create a new future.

Most senior executives are good at the administrative parts of their jobs; some are good at formulating strategic visions; but few know what it takes to get a message through a large organization so that it becomes the vision, climate, and spirit of the company. Many CEOs are good communicators in the conventional sense—speaking clearly and listening with understanding and empathy. Yet communication in most organizations is so commonplace that CEOs often do not realize that it is a powerful tool that can impact the organization's vision, culture, and bottom line.

This involves interweaving the message into every aspect of the organization—its strategy, operating policies, employee relationships, customer interfaces—until everything that happens in the organization occurs within its boundaries. Brilliant CEO's like Jack Welch of General Electric, Paul Allaire of Xerox, and Bill Gates of Microsoft have an intuitive understanding of how to do this. They spend huge amounts of their time putting out basic messages that not only become forces in people's minds and hearts but also shape, limit, and define everything that happens in their organizations.

CREATING A FORCE FIELD

Although most managers dedicate themselves to thinking about strategy and operations, exceptional CEOs realize that they have the power to create a force field when they speak and listen, by speaking and listening from a stand, a real commitment. This can exert a powerful and even transforming influence on employees, customers, and suppliers. It has been said that in designing a building, architects create a context that shapes, limits, and defines the way we live. Effective CEOs are social architects who create a context through their speaking, listening, and actions. The context is usually based on preaching and practicing governing values like innovation, quality, service, or learning. Their messages eventually become self-sustaining and exist independently of them.

"Getting a message through" is defined by the following criteria:

- The message is clear and has been communicated to all who need to hear it.

- People are able to see something in a new way as a result of the message. When people see things in new ways, they generally act in new ways.

- People change their underlying ways of thinking and behaving as a result of the message. This is evident in the ways planning is done, decisions are made, and actions are taken.

- Organizational results are different and can be measured through performance criteria.

To explain the force field, we can focus on two categories: "amplifying factors" and "restraining factors." Amplifying factors are factors that help get the message through; restraining factors are those that cause it to fall on deaf ears. We will start by looking at the restraining factors, which are numerous, powerful, and subtle. By understanding the restraining factors, it will be easier to understand the amplifying factors and their implications.

RESTRAINING FACTORS

Restraining Factor 1: Most Leaders Come from Backgrounds in Finance, Marketing, Operations, or Technical Disciplines and Are Not Experts in Human Nature

When people talk in general terms about changing the culture of an organization, everybody agrees; but when changes are cast in terms of

Restraining Factors

1. Most leaders come from backgrounds in finance, marketing, operations, or technical disciplines and are not experts in human nature.

2. The message does not represent a true personal calling and is stated in a way that does not capture people's imaginations.

3. A credibility gap is created when the CEO backs the message but the senior managers are viewed with suspicion because they don't walk their talk.

4. The goals, objectives, and reward systems are not aligned with the message that the CEO is trying to send.

5. There is often a massive amount of resignation or "giving up" in the organization, which makes it difficult or impossible to communicate a new message.

6. Managers may talk about change but stay in the comfort zone.

7. Leaders underestimate the degree of difficulty involved in communicating a new message and tend to give up too soon when confronted with the reality of what it takes.

changing individuals, it becomes much more difficult. Yet, if individuals do not change, nothing changes.

The ability to impact human beings does not come from having an MBA but from an understanding of human nature. Company leaders are generally most comfortable in changing organizational structures. One of the reasons for this is that they have no background in human relations. However, in attempting to change the culture and behavior in an organization, executives often find that "people" issues are the real issues.

As Thurow (1992) points out, most CEOs in the United States come from backgrounds in marketing, finance, and operations. Human resource management is considered "soft," and rarely does a human resource manager become a chief executive. In Japan, by contrast, the opposite occurs: no one becomes a CEO without serving as human resource manager. The human resource function is not just administrative (salary and benefits), it is geared to creating and maintaining a high level of alignment between the organization and the people in it. In order to do this, one has to become—to some degree—a master of human nature.

Although thinking about improving their functions or their departments might come naturally for many executives, the idea of communicating a message so that it becomes a force in people's minds and hearts is a challenge. The tendency is for executives to apply solutions to people issues that reflect their functional prejudices. Thus, when confronted with the issue of getting a new message through, the finance manager tends to translate the vision into numbers. The marketing manager tends to broadcast his message verbally and in writing, as a kind of advertisement, without taking responsibility for whether people get the message or not. The engineering manager tends to communicate the message with an emphasis on cold facts and with the idea of "fixing" people who do not comply. Although these may sound like stereotypes, they often hold true.

Many executives need to learn that you cannot treat people in the same way that you treat a finance, marketing, or engineering problem. For one thing, people are full of idiosyncrasies, not the least of which is that they are not rational. In order to communicate effectively to people, one has to understand not only "what to communicate" but also "to whom to communicate."

The first question to ask is "What are people's concerns?" People may listen to whatever a CEO says, but they are listening primarily in terms of whether the message speaks to their concerns (fears, hopes, etc.). The mistake that most executives make is that they speak from their own concerns, not the people's concerns, and often address these in the most superficial way, e.g., "If we don't make a profit here, we will be out of business, and you will all lose your jobs." People may be influenced by such negative communications but they are more powerfully influenced by positive communications that represent a chance to realize their aspirations, and when they can sense the speaker's commitment. The effective CEO is one who finds out what is in people's minds and hearts, speaks to their concerns, and, at the same time, addresses the concerns of the organization.

One of the reasons for the success of the total quality movement is that most people want to work in a way that represents a commitment to excellence and quality. When a company leader provides people an opportunity to do something that represents a personal calling and gives them passion and pride, he or she creates a powerful alignment between the purposes and goals of the individual and the purposes and goals of the organizations.

Messages that are consistent with human nature are:

- Messages that represent an opportunity to be part of a team or to build something (e.g., a great organization).

- Messages that reflect an opportunity to realize one's personal visions and goals. People always listen for the opportunity in it for them (to be who they want to be, to do what they want to do).

- Messages that speak to people's values (e.g., justice, fairness, integrity, achievement).

- Messages that communicate positive recognition and rewards. The desire for recognition is one of the most powerful forces in human nature and human history.

Restraining Factor 2: The Message Does Not Represent a True Personal Calling and Is Stated in a Way That Does Not Capture People's Imaginations

Several years ago, the executives of a company in the Midwest were told that the employees were unclear about what the company's vision was and that maybe the executives should address that issue. The response of all ten top managers was, "We would have a vision if we only followed those ten goals that we decided on at the last planning meeting." When we asked the general manager what those goals were, he looked embarrassed and said, "I can't remember." In fact, none of the other managers could remember any of the ten goals.

This type of situation is more common than might be expected. It exemplifies the inability of many managers to distinguish between a vision that is a personal calling (one that is a force in people's minds and hearts) and a typical vision statement. Many management teams have gone off for a two- or three-day retreat to develop a company vision, mission statement, etc. What often is produced at such meetings is a statement full of apple pie and motherhood, but not something that anyone really believes or can be held accountable to.

For example, the number of CEOs who supposedly had a quasireligious conversion to total quality management (TQM) must be astronomical, but the number of organizations that really practice TQM are few and far between. Sometimes this is a way of saying, "We don't want any real change around here." At other times, it shows that the company is merely being pushed along by the momentum of the marketplace and does not know what it stands for.

Another frequent problem is that an organization tries to focus on too many things. "Our mission statement," one manager said, "was like the omelettes that we used to make in college where we dumped every spice from the pantry into the frying pan. It didn't highlight the one or two issues that we were serious about."

The CEO needs to focus on one or two key messages (sales, profits, or whatever) if he or she is going to communicate them effectively. These issues must be urgent and compelling, and there must be an existing readiness to do something about them. The CEO also has to construct his or her message in a way that captures people's imaginations and tells them what actually needs to be done.

An excellent example of this is when President Kennedy said in 1960, "We will put a man on the moon by the end of the decade." This is a lot different from saying, "We will be the leader in space exploration." Yet, this is what many organizational mission statements sound like, i.e., "We will be the leader in customer responsiveness in our industry." Such generic statements need to be accompanied by something that tells employees what to work on or customers what to expect. One company had a vision that was expressed as "55555," but most of its 10,000 employees did not know what the numbers stood for. A large insurance company had an operations plan that said, "We plan to shrink and maintain profits." Although this made sense in economic terms, in human terms it went over like a lead balloon.

> *A vision that is a personal calling becomes a force in people's minds and hearts.*

Thus, one of the most important keys to getting a message through is not only to have it be a true calling but also to recognize that language is fundamental. The words chosen need to be precise and effective, both in setting direction and in saying something that people can relate to and find uplifting.

It is also important to surround the message with drama and symbols in a way that gets attention and leaves an indelible impression on people's minds. A few years back, Sam Walton told his employees that if Wal-Mart's stock reached a certain number, he would dance the hula on Wall Street. The stock exceeded that number, and Sam kept his promise.

A final key element is the use of stories. These can be an excellent way to communicate the underlying purpose of the organization or to enhance the specific message you are trying to get across. There are incidents of breakthrough, innovation, commitment to quality, or heroic service in every organization that are just waiting to be enshrined in history.

Restraining Factor 3: A Credibility Gap Is Created When the CEO Backs the Message but the Senior Managers Are Viewed with Suspicion Because They Don't Walk Their Talk

In many cases, the CEO is authentically committed to a vision and to the substantive changes that will be necessary to realize it, but the executive team that reports to the CEO is not really behind it. Executives may agree in principle to the changes and may say that they are committed to them, but they seem to lack conviction when they deliver the message and they don't "walk their talk."

This is a very difficult issue for a CEO to deal with as it is difficult to measure commitment, conviction, and behavior on an absolute scale. The executives in question would probably say that they are committed to the change and they may even be taking some action. Yet the CEO may feel that he or she cannot really count on their support. As time goes by, and projects are delayed, it becomes clear that there is passive resistance to the change.

The situation requires that the CEO really look at himself or herself and the executive team and ask, "What is my driving principle, what is my vision, and what kind of organization do I need to create to realize it?"

"What is my driving principle and what kind of organization do I need to create to realize it?"

In many cases, some members of the top management team may just not fit. This does not mean that people do not perform their functional roles well, or that they are not "nice" people, or that they could not make a powerful contribution to another company; it means that they may not be a good match for the particular CEO, his or her vision for the organization, and what he or she wants to accomplish. Such people will tend to pay lip service to the CEO's message and become nonplayers who clutter up the field.

The solution to this restraining factor is to *get the nonplayers off the field,* to acknowledge what is occurring and ask them to leave. Then replace them with people who fit the CEO's personality, who share his or her vision, and who will actively contribute to building the kind of organization the CEO desires.

Most people do not like to deal with the degree of discomfort involved in firing someone, especially if the person is performing the functional aspects of his or her job. However, in many cases this is exactly what needs to be done—the sooner the better.

There are several other approaches a CEO can take to deal with this situation. The first is to bring up the issues that everyone else is avoiding. For example, although everyone in an organization may agree intellectually that going from a functionally driven to a process-driven organization may be a good idea, when it comes time to actually implementing the change, it means that people have to give up some of their control. It is obvious that a voluntary, emotional commitment to move to this new kind of organization just might not exist. It is the CEO's job to dig below the superficial agreement and explore the issues that are of concern to people, even though it may mean discussing how the change affects people's self-interests. It is important to acknowledge and honor what people may have to give up in order to make the transition to the future.

The goal is to engage in a dialogue, not just to argue for one's point of view, but for the individuals and the group to learn something. For this to happen, everyone needs to stop perceiving opposition as something to crush and begin to embrace it as a necessary part of transformation. Engaging in dialogue, with the assistance of a good facilitator, is an opportunity to reduce friction and gain valuable information that allows people to correct their courses and transform their beliefs.

At some point in the dialogue, it is important that the CEO simply ask for support. A personal appeal that cuts below the intellectual level can be astonishingly powerful. The request for support should be followed by other explicit requests that involve implementing the CEOs strategy.

One way to get the ball rolling is to create a near-term objective based on the issues, making it clear who will do what, by when. By monitoring this tightly, a CEO can do a lot to move people through their personal considerations and push the project along. As actions often speak louder than words, this can go a long way toward closing the credibility gap.

Restraining Factor 4: The Goals, Objectives, and Reward Systems Are Not Aligned with the Message That the CEO Is Trying to Send

It has been said that an organization is as powerful as it is in alignment. Alignment is the degree to which an organization functions as a whole. Strategy, structure, systems, goals, plans, and—most importantly—people have to be aligned. A crucial factor is the performance-measurement and reward system. It is the organizational leader's chief responsibility to create alignment between these critical factors, and this must happen by design rather than by accident.

A recent experience with a Fortune 500 firm illustrates what happens when critical factors are out of alignment. The CEO, at the start of his term, took a stand for two things: total quality and a 30 percent reduction in fixed costs. The CEO went all around the world spreading the message of finding opportunities in change and total quality. Everyone agreed to these goals, but people were expected to achieve them at the same time that they achieved the cost reduction, within one year. Although the total quality initiative would be difficult to implement on its own, the reward system actually worked against it. The performance of the division general managers was measured on sales, profits, and cost reduction. There was no measurement of total quality implementation, and engineers who normally would have been responsible for quality were fired as part of the restructuring process. Thus, when defective products showed up, the order to the distribution center was "ship it." The CEO had communicated a positive message successfully, yet because the organization was not aligned in terms of goals, performance measures, and rewards, the message produced a great deal of cynicism.

As Paul Allaire, chairman of Xerox has said, "One of the things I learned a long time ago is that if you talk about change and you leave the reward and recognition system exactly the same, nothing changes" (Howard, 1992). People quite rationally say, "I hear what he is saying, but it's not what I get paid to do or what I get promoted for. So what's in it for me?" A similar case could be built for any of the other key factors that a CEO must align.

Restraining Factor 5: There Often Is a Massive Amount of Resignation or "Giving Up" in the Organization, Which Makes It Difficult or Impossible to Communicate a New Message

In the past ten years, organizations have instituted change programs of every conceivable description, including quality circles, restructuring, participative management, reengineering, encouraging team work, interdepartmental cooperation, and highly autonomous profit centers. Yet, in many cases, the more things change, the more they stay the same. Management does not change its ways, the results often are not improvements, and people become cynical and demoralized as a result. This is compounded by the fact that many organizations have a corporate culture and management system that is autocratic, bureaucratic, and deadening to the human spirit, despite what it is called. As one middle manager said, "People feel betrayed by leaders who do not help them realize their goals and by an organization that does not help them realize their potential."

In most organizations there is a massive amount of resignation that the organization's leaders are unaware of when they talk about the latest change effort. Ask people about the change and they are likely to respond with, "This place is like a 747 without a pilot"; "This company is focused on turf wars, not on the competition"; "Nothing will change until management changes"; "The last time I tried to make a constructive suggestion, I was hit in the knees with a lead pipe"; or "TQM is just the 'flavor of the month'—this, too, shall pass." When a CEO goes to deliver a message to employees, he or she is walking into a "minefield" that is likely to blow up.

Employees have their own views of the organization, based on their experiences in it. They listen to what the boss has to say through their own filters, which often distort the message. People who are disillusioned tend to collect evidence for their points of view and treat anything else with hostility.

What is needed are not more inspirational appeals, persuasive arguments, facts, or information but for the CEO and other executives to interact with people in a way that alters their underlying assumptions and leaves them open to receiving new messages. Engaging employees in dialogue is an excellent way to do this; the CEO has a chance to deliver his or her message and the employees have an opportunity to express themselves.

The key to the success of such communication is not how well the CEO and executives present their message but how well they listen to the managers and employees. This is often difficult for CEOs who think that their thoughts are more important than anyone else's, who have built-in prejudices about "marketing" or "manufacturing," or who feel that other people "just don't understand." They need to understand that they are there not only to help people express their concerns and opinions but also to help them shift their underlying points of view. Behind what people are saying are get-out strategies, give-up strategies, or get-up strategies (i.e., promotions). Practice in listening reveals not only what people are saying but the emotions behind it.

If the CEO takes responsibility for how the organization has been in the past (good, bad, or indifferent) and also takes the position that a difference can be made, he or she can break the grip of resignation and stir the human spirit toward action. In this process there is a dance between engaging people in new ideas and listening to what they have to say. Being a committed speaker and listener requires staying at it until there is a shift in attitudes and behavior.

Success breeds resignation, too. Although resignation frequently is a symptom of poor organizational performance, cutbacks, thwarted attempts at positive change, or treating people without respect, there is another variety that is seen in organizations that are fat, dumb, and happy. It often is difficult to get a message through an organization that has been highly successful, as managers point to their outstanding results and say, "We don't need to change anything." In reality, these people are resting on their laurels and have "given up" because they do not have any idea how to take the organization to the next level.

Restraining Factor 6: Managers May Talk About Change But Stay in the Comfort Zone

Many executives paralyze their organizations by being more committed to staying in the comfort zone than they are to implementing change. They often fail to generate sufficient actions and decisions to create momentum, to make anything happen. The typical scenario is to go through an endless process of consensus testing. This is followed by an interminable phase of planning, analysis, and preparation. Then, when everyone is frustrated and says, "We need to take some action," the demand for action made is very low (this includes what the executives demand of themselves as well as what they demand of others).

For example, when we asked a general manager of a large European company about the fact that his implementation of manufacturing resource planning (MRPII) was almost a year late, he responded that all of his unit managers were "for the implementation or at least not against it." When we asked him further what he was doing to create a sense of urgency for the project, he said, "we are taking small steps" and that many of these would lead to the objective.

The small-step approach, which usually follows a path of convoluted, political detours, often results in the manager losing his credibility or the employees losing interest. Instead of the conversation being about what can be done to move the change process forward, it is about whether management really supports it or not.

If an executive wants to get a message through, he or she has to find appropriate ways to bypass office politics, shorten the gearing-up phase by focusing on producing some near-term results, and increase the level of demand made on people. Although people like to stay with what is safe, comfortable, and familiar, they often jump eagerly at the opportunity for a challenge. A breakthrough in organizational excellence is not possible without risk, and people respond to risk with inspiration, commitment, and enthusiasm.

The following ideas may be useful in creating motivation:

Challenge. Motivate people by showing that you believe in who they are and what they are capable of: "You are capable of achieving much higher results. I am confident that you can do it. I expect much more from you."

Confront with support. Be clear and specific about what results will be required. Let people know that you are available to support them: "This is exactly what I want you to do. You have two days in which to do it. I'll be here if you need me."

Hold people accountable. Assess progress in terms of measurable results: "This is what you and your group agreed to be accountable for. The results so far are not meeting that goal. You either have the results or you have the reasons."

Restraining Factor 7: Leaders Underestimate the Degree of Difficulty Involved in Communicating a New Message and Tend to Give Up Too Soon When Confronted with the Reality of What It Takes

"But I told them three times!" These were the words of a former CEO who was exasperated that employees had not implemented zero-based budgeting. They had not done it because they did not know what he expected. Several weeks later there was a quotation in *The Wall Street Journal* by Ren MacPherson, former chairman of the Dana Corporation, who said, "By the time I tell them thirty-four times, they start to listen a little." These two statements exemplify the discrepancy between the common perception of what it takes to get a message through a large, complex organization and the reality.

Communicating a message that heralds organizational change and demands that people break out of old patterns is not a part-time job but a full-time job. Unfortunately, this does not fit the concept of CEOs and executives who think of themselves as administrators who read reports and hold meetings. There is a slot in most executives' minds that says, "I am a strategist," another that says, "I am the guardian of operations," and another that says, "My job is to keep shareholders happy." There often is no slot that says, "I am chief communicator." It is time for CEOs to think of communication as a vehicle of creation and generation. The CEO's communication is a tool by which he or she creates the future of the organization. Obviously, large-scale change cannot be achieved merely by sending a memo or holding a kickoff meeting. It takes discipline, consistency, and perseverance in communicating the message to all parts of the organization.

A CEO's job is to speak and listen and then speak and listen again and again, adjusting both until people begin to see things in new ways and act in new ways. This requires drawing out individuals who are intimidated by the CEO's position and listening to things that help to create a picture of what the organization is really like for the people in it. This type of communication is not a one-time event but a process. The objective is to make the communication exist independently of the CEO—to have it assimilated into the organization, rather than merely implemented when someone is watching because it is mandated.

Amplifying Factors

1. All executive communication is created in terms of a context— one that becomes the vision, culture, and spirit of the organization.

2. The generation of "new" conversations moves people beyond fear and the comfort zone, eliciting their commitment to make a difference, to bring forth a breakthrough.

3. New conversations are based on a big idea that shapes products, services, and organizational processes.

4. When top executives dare to take a stand, their speaking and listening can make a difference.

5. Spearheading a breakthrough creates a structure for fulfillment for the message.

6. An idea picks up force and speed to the extent that it is translated into action.

7. A rigorous, active inquiry into the organization's issues makes the message sustainable once it is delivered, understood, and acted on.

AMPLIFYING FACTORS

Amplifying Factor 1: All Executive Communication Is Created in Terms of a Context—One That Becomes the Vision, Culture, and Spirit of the Organization

Max DePree (1989), former Chairman of Herman Miller, says that a leader's primary responsibility is to define reality. This involves accurately interpreting the business environment, developing the right strategy, and setting limits, but it also involves communicating the governing ideas—the purpose, vision, and values by which people live. It involves using language to create a structure of interpretation for people in the organization that helps them to determine what to consider important, what to work on, and how to interact.

Although they may have had different words for it, the business geniuses of the Twentieth Century, such as Thomas J. Watson, General Johnson, and Walt Disney, realized that the purpose of executive communication is not only being understood, making decisions, and causing action but also creating a context. At IBM the message was "think"; at Johnson and Johnson it was "unfailing responsibility to doctors, nurses, and patients"; at Disney it was "every person is called a guest with a capital G." The institutions became great not because their governing ideas were inscribed on bronze plaques or office posters but because their leaders used them to shape, limit, and define every aspect of their organizations.

Although the context of an organization is largely unseen, it is felt and it has a direct impact on innovative ideas, productivity, morale, and profits. When Air Force General Bill Creech arrived at Tactical Air Command (TAC), he found that pilots were complaining about the state of repair of the airplanes and that sorties (the flying of an airplane on a combat mission) were at an all-time low. Instead of indulging in finger pointing and fear tactics, he motivated, celebrated, and virtually canonized the support people in all of his communications. "The airplane is our customer," he said. He made heroes out of people whose mundane chores contributed to getting the airplanes in the air.

If we liken "context" to a bowl and "content" to what is inside the bowl, many managers tend to concern themselves with rearranging the content—fiddling with the strategy, structure, and systems, as if that were an end in itself. Real leaders recognize that the greatest opportunity to impact their organization is to create a context that becomes the vision, climate, and spirit of the company. As a president of a high-tech company once said, "I'll tell you how to create a great marketing organization. It has to do with creating an atmosphere in the company where the man or woman on the loading dock decides not to drop the damned box into the back of the truck."

Although generating a context may seem soft when compared to the yearly plan, budget, and performance reviews, more often than not, it determines whether there will be hard results. Many managers are not aware of the context they are unconsciously creating through their speaking, listening, and actions. However, an organization always fulfills the context that is created for it, whether it is good, bad, or indifferent.

The issue often is how to create a shift in context, given what was created in the past or inherited from a predecessor.

When Jack Welch became CEO of General Electric, he sold off businesses, cut costs to the bone, and fired a lot of people, earning himself the nickname of "Neutron Jack." In so doing, he created a context in which people headed for shelter and waited for the next bomb to drop. Since that time, he has been trying to create a shift in context to a context of leadership, risk taking, and worker empowerment.

As has been noted previously, creating a shift in context involves speaking and listening with the intention of inspiring and enabling people to see things in a new way. This involves using even routine occasions (frequent, informal, face-to-face communication) to interact with people on issues such as being innovative, creating more cross-functional teamwork, or reducing costs. When a critical mass of people begins to see things in a new way and act in a new way, a shift in context will occur and people, actions, and circumstances will begin to move into alignment with the desired context.

The following can help to create a shift in context that becomes a force field in an organization:

1. Label the existing context (e.g., business as usual).

2. Understand the consequences of the existing context in terms of what it creates.

3. Create a new context consistent with the new vision and desired change.

4. Look for opportunities to get the message through while weaving it into organizational strategies and operating procedures.

5. Take bold and unreasonable action when called for to let people know that the message is serious.

Amplifying Factor 2: The Generation of "New" Conversations Moves People Beyond Fear and the Comfort Zone, Eliciting Their Commitment to Make a Difference, to Bring Forth a Breakthrough

Executives are often engaged in the work of organizational transformation, setting the strategic vision, establishing the core organizational values, and giving substance to a network of primary beliefs. The single most powerful vehicle through which an executive accomplishes this is language. One of the most powerful factors in being able to shape, limit, and define the future of an organization is through speaking and listening. These two functions are so commonplace, we often fail to recognize how vital they are and how important it is to use them purposefully. As Hegel (1951) once said, "While our speaking and listening are often thought to merely represent things, they are actually like the chisel of the carver, they have the power to free an idea from the general formlessness of the outside and call it forth in reality."

An organization can be viewed as a network of conversations that shape, limit, and define its strategies, structures, and systems, as well as its assumptions, attitudes, and behaviors. Generating a new conversation involves using the forward force of an idea to introduce a new order, to alter ideas and habits. Before the U.S. Declaration of Independence, human rights as a concept of government did not really exist. Yet the words "all men are created equal and they are endowed by their creator with certain unalienable rights, amongst these life, liberty, and the pursuit of happiness" generated a network of conversations that became a force in people's minds and hearts, a force that changed half the world. We can see from this example that generating a new conversation is a potent form of action. It may be of much greater significance as a management technology than a staff, plan, or budget, which is what executives usually are focused on.

An executive shapes the organization not just through the formal strategy statement, but through the numerous informal conversations that he or she has with people every day. The idea is to recognize each of these occasions as an opportunity to make a difference, keeping in mind that "as a man speaks, not only is his language in a state of birth, but also the very thing about which he is talking" (Hegel, 1951).

If we look at the organizations that have been most successful in the past decade, their success may be more a function of the ability of their leaders to generate a new conversation than of the traditional things leaders do. Steve Jobs of Apple Computer redefined the marketplace when he made the distinction of "the world's first intuitive computer." John Watts of AT&T came up with the idea of the fax machine and transformed business communications. Fred Smith of Federal Express declared that his company would deliver packages within twenty-four hours and brought to mind visions of the Pony Express.

A typical example of an "old" conversation is as follows: Americans are more interested in cars with big fins and pointed taillights than they are in quality or gas mileage. John Pederson, former CEO of the Ford Motor Company, showed that a new conversation can play a vital role in breaking the grip of old paradigms and habits. He spent almost every day for two years preaching that "Quality is Job 1." This was not just a slogan; it resulted in a whole new mindset—Team Taurus—and dramatically different ways of working at Ford.

Old Conversations	New Conversations
■ Obsolete answers to the question "What business are we in?"	■ Conversations that set a new direction for the organization and become its vision, climate, and spirit.
■ Conversations that reinforce the old paradigm, management system, attitudes, and behaviors.	■ Conversations that provide the answers to what is missing in the organization or marketplace that could make a difference.
■ Conversations that reinforce old products, product cycles, and marketing strategies.	■ Conversations that introduce new possibilities or create new market niches and powerful new product cycles.
■ Conversations of mere opinion that do not forward the action.	■ Conversations that generate a new paradigm, attitudes, and behaviors that forward the action.
■ Conversations that express cynicism based on the past.	■ Conversations that leave people feeling inspired and empowered.

Generating a new conversation is difficult and complex, because it is hard for organizations to overcome their histories. Yet, there are some relatively simple things to keep in mind that can help:

Clarity is power. The clearer, simpler, and more thought-provoking a message is, the more likely it is that it will get through.

Dialogue is more effective than monologue. Asking people what they think involves them. The idea is to interact with people in a way that allows everyone to see something they did not see before.

Do not indulge in old conversations about how discouragingly complex the situation is or about how other people and departments have failed.

Speak and listen from a commitment to enrolling people in new ideas, to empowering and enabling others to forward the action.

Pfeiffer & Company

Use generative language, not "I hope," "I'll try," or "Maybe." As J.L. Austin (1962) says, leaders must speak in the language of performatives—language that defines what is possible, achievable, and makes something happen.

A new conversation is generated by certain kinds of language that can be placed in five categories:

Declarations declare new possibilities as open. "We declare these truths to be self-evident, that all men are created equal."

Commissives commit the speaker to a future course of action. "We will put a man on the moon by the end of the decade."

Expressives add meaning and emotion to the message and connect with the human part of those to whom you are speaking. "I am very proud of all of you customer-service people and I want to tell you what your success means to me."

Assertives state a belief, without immediate proof or evidence. "We will be number one in our field within five years."

Directives attempt to get the listener to do something. "Please do whatever is necessary to increase the quality of service in your group's relationship to the customer."

Amplifying Factor 3: New Conversations Are Based on a Big Idea That Shapes Products, Services, and Organizational Processes

Dr. Jonas Salk (1981) says, "Ideas are themselves substantive entities which like food, vaccines, and DNA have the power to influence and transform human life." The ability to get one's message through is less a function of being a brilliant speaker than of having a bold, inventive, and effective idea that shakes people out of their complacency. A big idea expressed in plain language has communicative power, not only because it catches people by surprise but also because it has the power to change an existing point of view or habit. The appeal of any big idea is that it offers people an exciting new possibility. The personal computer, fax machine, and total quality movement are all examples of this.

The genuinely talented executive is armed with the belief that the bothersome issues and problems of organization can be solved with a big idea—a surprising solution, an idea that can be communicated with simple, stunning imagery and richness of meaning. Yet, all too often, instead of getting to the heart of the problem and searching for an exciting, breakthrough solution, organizational leaders use patent solutions: "hire and fire," "cut costs to the bone," or "break the company into autonomous divisions." Although these may be useful and ultimately necessary, what is required in many cases is a new way of thinking.

The companies that have rocketed to success in recent years were not based on linear, logical, formula thinking but on inquiry into problems, blending together emerging concepts in people's minds, and coming up with a brilliant flashes of insight. This is how Scott McNeally, CEO of Sun Microsystems, came up with the idea of open systems and created one of the fastest-growing success stories in U.S. industry. This is how Les Wexner came up with the idea of The Gap and The Limited, based on a new kind of marketing and on bringing products from concept to market in one month rather than the traditional six. This is how Nucor Steel got the idea of rolling process mills rather than traditional foundries.

The above breakthroughs were the result of leadership commitment and communication that produced commitment, passion, and zeal from followers. One generates new ideas and new insights by cultivating new ways of thinking and acting. Company leaders have to start to see themselves outside their administrative roles and as sources of creativity and imagination. They can do this is several ways:

1. *By reflection and inquiry.* CEOs are often so busy thinking in terms of organizational politics, the planning process, and budget reviews that they do not nurture the skill of reflection and inquiry. The organization's greatest problem should be regarded as something to be reflected on and inquired into until a moment of true insight emerges, not as grist for the mill of standard operating procedures.

2. *By listening to new ideas throughout the organization.* Ideas can come from engaging people in dialogue. The objective of such communication is to stimulate ideas and to learn rather than to win points.

3. *By reading a variety of magazines and books that facilitate a cross-fertilization of ideas.* As advertising genius George Lois (1991), who came up with the idea of "Lean Cuisine," comments, "I read because I have an insatiable hunger to see, hear, taste, and experience as much stimuli as my mind and body can absorb." The greatest error that many CEOs make is that they do not read enough. Reading often results in putting one idea together with another over time until a synthesis is created that has breakthrough capacity.

Another thing to keep in mind when thinking in terms of generating a new conversation based on a big, powerful, new idea is the impact of a big idea on how other people speak and listen. People generally have a structure of listening that filters in certain communications and filters out others. Those that are filtered out include politically derived promises and executive communications that talk about change but are really hot air. Those that are accepted include personal communications, opportunities for personal growth or advancement, and big new ideas that solve practical and immediate problems. Communicating effectively includes intentionally designing, packaging, and delivering a message so that it is accepted.

Amplifying Factor 4: When Top Executives Dare to Take a Stand, Their Speaking and Listening Can Make a Difference

> I am of the impression that nine out of ten cases that I deal with are windbags, who do not speak in a way where they take anything upon themselves. From a human point of view, their ideas and opinions do not move me very profoundly. However, it is immensely moving when a mature man...acts by following the ethic of reasonability and somewhere reaches the point where he says here is where I stand; I can do no other.
>
> —*Max Weber*

No one listens for very long to someone who never takes a stand and who never really takes any actions. It has been said that nothing is as powerful as a good idea whose time has come. Yet what makes an idea's time come may be the individual who is standing behind it. In many organizations there are lots of ideas, opinions, and experts but few people who are willing to take a risk. Too frequently, organizational life breeds politicians, negotiators, and compromisers. In order to succeed, people accommodate themselves to the need to look good, play it safe, and do whatever the situation demands.

Taking a stand does not mean being a dictator, issuing ultimatums, or banging a shoe on the table. It means speaking, listening, and taking action with the belief that a difference can be made from embracing a possibility. It means living by one's word rather than one's desires, moods, and the dictates of circumstance. Once a CEO takes a stand, that stand must be nonnegotiable; the flexibility is not in "what" or "by when," but in "how." Commitments made in this way have a much greater chance of being achieved than do mere hopes, wishes, and dreams.

People who take a stand make a commitment that indicates their vision, goals, and intended course of action; their identity shifts to what they stand for. When we think of Lee Iacocca, Jack Welch, and W. Edwards Deming, we realize that who these men are and what they stand for are inseparable. Leaders who authentically take a stand are believable. Others can say of them, "This person commands my respect." This is a lot different from adopting the latest trend, saying one thing and doing another, or sending conflicting messages.

Taking a stand does not mean becoming rigid and dogmatic. One must be willing to "embrace the enemy"—learning how to speak and listen to people in a way that elicits their voluntary commitment rather than trying to convince them through force of argument or pressure. When this is done, commonplace meetings and routine events take on unexpected potency. One discovers a shift in the way one converses with others and even in the way one "is" in the communication process. Others tend to respond with the same commitment-based, action-oriented, no-nonsense communication. Greater access opens to relationships, accomplishments, and satisfaction.

Amplifying Factor 5: Spearheading a Breakthrough Creates a Structure for Fulfillment for the Message

For many executives the ability to generate a new conversation is brought forward by emerging issues and opportunities. Thus, the greater the speed with which we create visions, goals, and ideas, the more there is a need to manage our commitments and conversations. The more there is a need to make our dreams come true, the more urgent the need for a structure by which we can accomplish this. A structure for fulfillment gives substance to the possibilities that we have called forth. A leader can use communication to create such a structure for fulfillment. Although people may express genuine understanding of the new message, as well as commitment and a desire for involvement, they may lack a reliable path to accomplish the goals. The structure works like a road map—a route to generating appropriate and effective action.

For example, John Akers got the idea that IBM had become too big and bloated and that it was time to do things in a more entrepreneurial fashion. He asked each of his senior executives to be accountable for a breakthrough goal for IBM and for his or her own area. At the same time, he broke the company into autonomous divisions. He also introduced a market-driven quality program. This became the structure for fulfillment.

Often executives abdicate responsibility for creating a transformative idea and a structure of fulfillment and attempt to use a packaged change program. Executives who adopt management trends such as total quality, participative management, and worker empowerment often come up with general goals such as "excellence through innovation," "continuous improvement in everything we do," or "talk back to the boss." Employees are expected to translate ideas into concrete actions. Although the intention may be positive, without a common goal, management direction, and real accountability, effort tends to become dispersed. For example, "Everyone in the company was expected to have his or her own total-quality project. The problem was that we had so many projects, the whole effort lost focus, and it was difficult to demonstrate any bottom-line results."

One approach for getting a message through while creating a structure for fulfillment is to spearhead a breakthrough in an area of the company where accomplishing something significant could provide the opening or opportunity for the whole company to move a huge step forward. A spearhead is pointed and powerful; it is aimed at a leverage point where a small change can radiate throughout the system and make a big difference. The starting point is to look the message that one is trying to communicate and to ask what would be different if it were successful. Is there an area in which spearheading a breakthrough would not only help to get the message across but also act as a catalyst for people to begin to think, plan, and act in a new way?

These additional guidelines may be useful:

1. Enroll the management group in the big idea. If some of them oppose it, embrace their objections as an opportunity to open conversation.

2. Set a breakthrough goal that is based on current resources and authority.

3. Create a set of "mandates" that represent the key issues involved—whatever really needs to be accomplished for the breakthrough goal to be realized.

4. Ask each department or unit manager to sign a contract regarding what he or she will accomplish, with specific, measurable criteria and performance consequences.

5. Immediately start focusing on what can be done right now.

Amplifying Factor 6: An Idea Picks Up Force and Speed to the Extent That It Is Translated into Action

One of the problems in most organizations is that situations often appear so discouragingly complex that people do not take action. Thus, when the CEO delivers his or her message, people tend to hear it through a number of filters such as, "I'll do this after it's clear who is going to be our next CEO," or "It's a good idea, but it can't happen under this organizational structure and without a single sales force," or "Fine, just give me more people and a bigger budget." Against this background, it is up to the CEO and the executives to get the message across and to forward the action.

The problem is that people do not act until there is a suitable climate. Creating a climate that calls for action does not start with soul searching or taking an attitude survey. It starts with distinguishing three different kinds of conversations. First are conversations of mere facts and opinion. For the most part, people spend the majority of their time indulging in these conversations. Second, there are conversations of possibility—those that fuel visions of a new future. Finally, there are conversations of action.

Once the idea and breakthrough goal are set, it is up to the leaders to generate a conversation for action that actually makes something happen. This is not as difficult as it might appear. A key point to deal with is that one has to work with what one has. Generating a conversation for action involves asking people questions such as "What can you do now to get this message across and accomplish something around it, within your present resources and authority?"; "Where can we produce a success in the next three weeks to generate some momentum?"; "What can you do right now to get the ball rolling?"

A structure of fulfillment in line with these questions is the "planned breakthrough project." This involves working from a break-through goal (or major objective). The idea is to create a widening circle of quick successes and a rallying momentum that results in new management confidence and new management skills.

Some criteria for a planned breakthrough project are as follows:

1. Focus on bottom-line results. What is urgent and compelling?

2. Exploit existing readiness. (Don't try to create new readiness.) What really needs to be done that everybody wants to get on with?

3. Success must be near and clear. The objective of the small breakthrough project is to be accomplished in weeks, not months.

4. Stay within current resources and authority.

5. Build on a widening circle of successes. Initial results create new openings for action.

Amplifying Factor 7: A Rigorous, Active Inquiry into the Organization's Issues Makes the Message Sustainable Once It Is Delivered, Understood, and Acted On

There is an old Japanese saying that what has a front has a back, and the bigger the front the bigger the back. This applies to most management nostrums as well as to much of what has been said here. No matter how well something works in the front, there is a back side to it. The difference between a highly effective CEO and a not-so-effective one is that the effective one takes time to think about both the front and the back.

For example, a high-tech company started a reengineering program. The program was so successful that it eliminated many defects, improved work processes, and set higher improvement goals. The back side was that it worked so well that it resulted in over 150 people being let go. The following year, the employees became so frightened of the program that they virtually abandoned everything that had anything to do with it. As a result, the traditional problems between departments appeared again, processes deteriorated, and defects dramatically increased. Before long, the company was in trouble, and its employees were so cynical about what had happened that when management asked for help, the employees basically thumbed their noses.

What this example demonstrates is that for any new message to be introduced to an organization, management needs to consider not just the front but the back that it is likely to create. For a message to have a sustainable impact, it is important that the executives consider what is missing before making promises, implementing changes, or taking actions that may backfire. This is not to suggest that one should shrink from the challenge of creating a better organization; rather, it is to suggest that one of the most overlooked factors in getting a message through so that it is sustainable has to do with rigorous inquiry. A well-designed inquiry allows executives not only to step back and see the big picture but also to see what is missing and to take more powerful action.

Rigorous inquiry has to do not only with getting a message through in the short to midterm future, but also with creating the organization by design, so that strategy is consistent with it, structures are congruent, and systems are aligned. This is not something that can be accomplished tomorrow or next week, but in the next four-to-six months or a year or more. Thinking things through and gathering the necessary insights is a creative process that takes diligence.

One tactic is to assign a team of managers who have strong opinions and are not afraid to express them to look at the organization's current strategies over a period of months and to begin the process of designing the organization around them. This approach gives people the time to come into alignment intellectually about the best way to implement these strategies, as well as to break through the barriers to expressing emotional commitment.

Inquiry must not be casual but must be rigorous, active, and targeted to a specific result. There is a way of inquiring, of asking questions, that is actually empowering with respect to the question—not the power of understanding, but the power of transformation.

References

Austin, J.L. (1962). *How to do things with words.* Boston, MA: Harvard University Press.

DePree, M. (1989). *Leadership is an art.* New York: Doubleday.

Hegel, G.W.F. (1969). *Science of logic.* (A.V. Miller, Trans.). Atlantic Highlands, NJ: Humanities.

Howard, R. (1992, September-October). The CEO as organizational architect: An interview with Xerox's Paul Allaire, *Harvard Business Review.*

Lois, G. (1991). *What's the big idea?* New York: Doubleday.

Salk, J. (1981). *World population and human values: A new reality.* New York: Harper & Row.

Thurow, L. (1992). *Head to head.* New York: Morrow.

Weber, M. (1967). *Ancient Judaism.* New York: Free Press.

Robert Hargrove is the founder of Transformational Learning Inc., in Brookline, Massachusetts offering consulting and training services. He is the author of Masterful Coaching: Extraordinary Results by Impacting People and the Way They Think and Work Together. *As an internationally sought-after speaker on the topics of stewardship, executive reinvention, collaboration and communication, building learning organizations and communities of commitment, he laces his talks with wisdom, compassion, and humor. Mr. Hargrove and his colleagues offer in-depth coaching programs that are based on transformational learning. These programs enable people to see themselves and their situations in new ways and enable them to learn new skills and capabilities.*

LEADERSHIP FROM THE GESTALT PERSPECTIVE

H.B. Karp

Abstract: The current trend in organization development is toward large-system interventions. Although
nothing is wrong with this trend, it is important that
individual growth and effectiveness not be ignored.

This article explores the following definition of
leadership: *Leadership is the art of getting people to perform
a task willingly.* However, two key factors affect leader
effectiveness: competence and comfort. A leader can
achieve maximum effectiveness first by being aware of
what and how he or she thinks and second by considering options for any specific situation. Leadership
then becomes the ability to adapt one's authentic style
to the circumstances of a particular situation.

The 1996 Annual: Volume 1, Training.
Copyright © 1996 by Pfeiffer & Company, San Diego, CA.

In recent years, the trend in organization development (OD) has been focused on large-system interventions. Strategies such as self-directed work teams, right-sizing, and organizational reengineering are just a few examples of this trend. Although this direction is not wrong, individual growth and effectiveness may be downplayed, if not completely lost, in the attempt to evolve larger and more comprehensive interventions. Whether within the context of a major system-wide change strategy or cast in an individual's daily work routine, a consistent and pragmatic means of developing leadership is needed—one that will respond to what is occurring right here, right now.

The one theory base that has consistently responded to this demand is Gestalt. Gestalt originated with Fritz Perls in the field of psychotherapy in the mid-1930s. Described as "therapy for normals," the Gestalt theory base has more recently been used to define an effective and healthy organization, just as it has been used to describe a healthy and functioning individual.

In recent years, Gestalt has provided a unique perspective to organizations while maintaining the prime OD objective of increasing individual and group effectiveness through intervention in group processes.

TERMINOLOGY

Prior to presenting the Gestalt leadership model, it will be helpful to clarify several terms and to show how they relate to leadership and, in some cases, to each other.

Leadership

Leadership is the art of getting people to perform a task, willingly. This definition is clearly different from "management," which can be defined as "the science of the allocation of resources." This definition of leadership has three operative terms: *art, task,* and *willingly.*

Art indicates that leadership is a combination of both talent and skills. Leadership talent is distributed normally throughout the population. Not everyone has the talent to be an effective leader, just as not everyone has the talent to be a concert pianist. The opposite side of the coin also implies that very few people either have no talent or have all the talent.

One way to actualize the talent that exists within an individual is by way of skill development, through training, education, and experience. *Art* also implies that each leader performs individually. Just as no two singers sing alike, no two authors write alike, and no two sculptors sculpt alike, no two leaders lead alike. It is impossible to teach people to be good leaders. They can only be taught what leadership is about and then assisted in adapting that knowledge to their own individual styles. In the end, people will be effective leaders only to the extent that their potential for individual creativity and uniqueness of expression will allow.

The second term, *task,* means that leadership does not occur in a vacuum. Two structural elements must exist before a leadership function can occur. First, at least two individuals must be involved: a leader and at least one follower. Second, leadership must have an objective. The task may be work oriented, such as manufacturing a product, solving a problem, or designing a new widget; or it may be socially oriented, such as planning a party. Regardless, leadership is a process that affects how the task finally will be accomplished.

Willingly, the third element, means that leadership precludes the use of threat or coercion as a means of getting the job done. The use of threats, monetary rewards, or promises of future promotion to control another's performance requires neither skill nor talent and is not leadership. *Willingly* implies that another person will perform the task without resenting having to do it or resenting you for having assigned it.

It is safe to say that no one is capable of being a maximally effective leader 100 percent of the time and that sometimes it is a lot easier to be a good leader than it is at other times. In this light, the definition for leadership can be converted into the following pragmatic statement: To whatever extent an individual can get others to perform a task willingly in a given situation, to that extent the person can be judged an effective leader.

Leadership Effectiveness

Leadership effectiveness depends on two basic and essential criteria: *competence* and *comfort.*[1]

Competence, which is the more observable and measurable of the two criteria, refers to the leader's ability to get the work done willingly by

---

[1] Note that the term *comfort* refers to comfort with self and style and does not refer to what might be called situational discomfort, i.e., the discomfort that arises from dealing with situational ambiguity, tough choices, or painful situations.

others; it can be measured through attitude surveys, critical incident analysis, and, of course, the quality of the work itself.

Comfort refers to a leader's comfort with himself or herself and with his or her individual leadership style. The importance of this criterion is that it clearly implies that *there is no one best way to lead.* For example, any accomplished art student can copy a master effectively. It is not until the student takes that skill and creates *something unique* that he or she is considered to be an artist. As it is with painters, so it is with leaders or anyone else who practices an art for a living.

Therefore, if a leader is judged to be competent by observable measures and is comfortable with his or her leadership style, that person has every right to resist the demands of others to alter *how* he or she leads. Like artists, only they themselves know best how to uniquely express their art.

If, on the other hand, the person is comfortable but not terribly competent or competent but not very comfortable, it may be wise to consider making a career change to something that will easily provide both comfort and competence. It is here that that person stands to make the greatest contribution and simultaneously gain the most satisfaction and growth from the work.

Boundary

One additional Gestalt term, *boundary,* needs to be surfaced because it also has major impact on the leadership model. The essence of Gestalt theory holds that each human being is separate and distinct from all others. A person's individuality, or *I-Boundary,* is made of many sub-boundaries such as attitudes, values, tastes, assumptions, abilities, and so forth. All of these combine to make each person absolutely unique. In a practical sense, each sub-boundary carries the explicit message, "For me, this far and no farther." Thus, boundaries, as the word implies, define and give each individual his or her identifiable personality characteristics, just as its geographic borders give a nation its identifiable configuration.

Human characteristics can be seen as operating in polarities, such as good-bad, strong-weak, introvert-extrovert, or tough-tender. Each sub-boundary then can be seen as an area that is defined by a range within that polarity. For example, in Figure 1, the polarity ranges from "Mistrust" to "Trust." The range that is indicated between the points labeled "a" and "b" is my sub-boundary on this dimension and defines the extent to which I have the capacity to authentically mistrust and trust others. Note that this makes no statement about how other people are, only my capacity on this dimension. The positions at each extreme represent the maximum potential for human experience for this characteristic, i.e., being as mistrusting and trusting as it is humanly possible to be. The configuration in Figure 1 shows that at point a, I am mistrusting enough to always lock my car, no matter where I am parked; at the other extreme, point b, I am trustful enough to take most people at their word the first time I meet them. My range of effectiveness and self-confidence, in terms of mistrusting and trusting others, lies between points a and b. If I try to operate outside these parameters, chances are that I will be tentative, lacking in confidence, and marginally effective at best. All sub-boundaries operate in this way. A person's sub-boundary can also be thought of as one's "Zone of Present Effectiveness" or "Zone of Comfort."

Figure 1. The Mistrust-Trust Polarity

An individual's I-Boundary can be represented by the pattern intersecting the various sub-boundaries, as shown in Figure 2.[2]

Each person's I-Boundary is intact. It is essential that each individual recognize, accept, and value his or her personal I-Boundary. The simplest step toward increasing your effectiveness and comfort with self, in leadership or any other area, is to have your *perceived* boundary, (where you think it is or should be) correspond to your *actual* boundary (where it actually is).

THE GESTALT LEADERSHIP MODEL

Leadership effectiveness is most influenced by two highly individualistic variables: the need for *congruence* and the need for *integration*.

---

[2] For a more detailed discussion of boundaries and how they work see Polster and Polster (1973), p. 107 or Karp (1995), pp. 9-23.

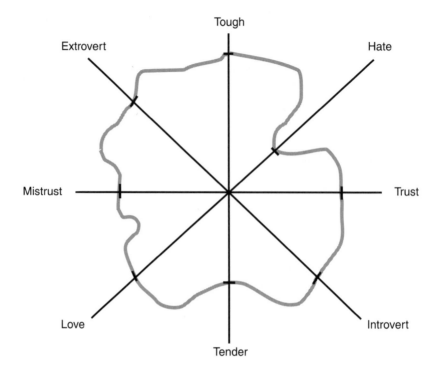

Figure 2: I-Boundary

The Need for Congruence

Congruence, or authenticity, can be viewed as having one's *perceived* boundary correspond to one's *actual* boundary. Regardless of who the person is, a leader will be judged by what he or she *does*. As suggested earlier, leadership effectiveness can only be determined by the appropriateness of the specific actions taken to get others willingly to comply to work.

Because it is highly unlikely that any leader will be able to get willing compliance in every situation, increasing leadership effectiveness becomes a matter of increasing one's "success rate" in choosing the effective and appropriate actions when responding to each new and different situation. It is not so much a matter of *what* the leader elects to do as much as it is a matter of *how* the selection is made.

In Figure 3, the top broken line is designated as "Actions." It represents the nearly infinite range of specific behaviors available to every leader to attempt to get willing compliance to work (planning, supporting, reprimanding, encouraging, training, coaching, and so on).

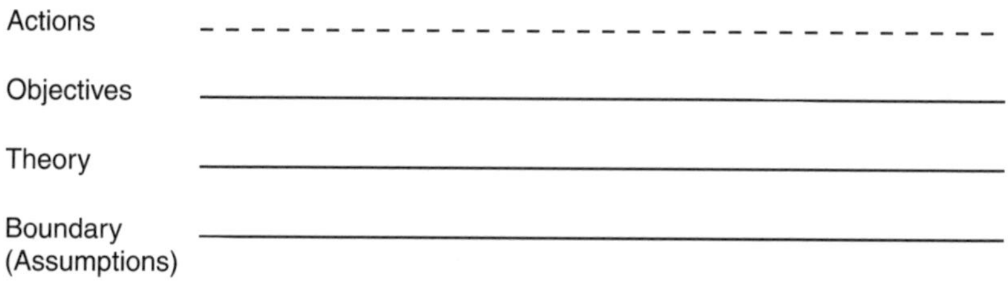

Actions   –

Objectives   _____

Theory   _____

Boundary   _____
(Assumptions)

Figure 3. Four Levels of Leadership

No specific action, in and of itself, is either good or bad. It is only functional or nonfunctional in getting compliance from another person in a given situation. Again, these actions and their results are the only things that can be observed and judged by anyone else.

Directly below the "Actions" line, however, are three lower levels, all of which are internal to the individual. These levels are not observable or subject to the judgment of others; understanding these levels is clearly the best means by which leaders can increase their own effectiveness.

Boundary

The lowest level, "Boundary," is not only the most general of the three levels, it also is the most basic and important determinant of effective leadership behavior. In this case "Boundary" is synonymous with one's assumptions about people. It refers to how the individual leader experiences self as well as others. Because a leader works exclusively with people, as opposed to cabinet makers who work with wood or masons who work with stone, it is both essential and primary that leaders be clear about the assumptions they make about people. The single most important question that a leader must answer is "What are people like?"

I would like to point out that the only person I can ever know, to any extent, is myself. My interactions with everyone else, to greater or lesser degree, are based only on my assumptions of how they are. Because I do not share a common nervous system with anyone else, I can never really know how people are merely through observation. Therefore, the more I know about me—who I am and how I see things—the more I am able accurately to check out my assumptions with and about others.

Many theorists, most notably Douglas McGregor (1960), make this point quite strongly. However, the difference between the Gestalt view and other views is that the Gestalt view is much more concerned with *how* the assumptions are made and clarified than it is with *what* the assumptions actually are.

To state the premise simply:

*The more clear and the more confident leaders are about their assumptions concerning people, **regardless of what those assumptions are**, the higher the probability that they will be effective leaders.*

Theory

Once leaders are clear and comfortable with the assumptions they hold, the next level to be addressed is "Theory." "Boundary" asks the single question, "What are people like?" In contrast, "Theory" asks the single question, "What is leadership about?" Just as there is an infinite range of assumptions about people, so there is an infinitive range of leadership theories. I would suggest that there are just about as many leadership theories as there are individual leaders and theorists. The real question being asked is, "What is leadership theory about for me?"

Whether an individual ascribes to an established theory, chooses to modify an established theory, or devises an original theory, the important points to remember are as follows:

- The theory must be clear and explicit; and

- The theory must be consonant with the leader's own assumptions about people.

To be explicit, suppose I were to ask a large random sample of people the following question: "Who was the more effective leader—General Douglas MacArthur or Martin Luther King?" My guess would be that most people would judge them as comparable within the contexts of their specific situations. It requires only a passing knowledge of the history of these two men to realize that probably the only thing they had in common was that each held a very clear, defined, and different view of what people were like, themselves included. Not only was each man clear about his assumptions, but each operated out of a style of leadership that was highly consonant with how he saw things. Had MacArthur tried to lead like King or King like MacArthur, neither would have been effective.

Objectives

The third, and last, of the internal levels deals with objectives. This level also addresses a single question: "What do I want?" Objectives can be viewed in two ways. The first and most subjective view relates to personal objectives. Whether these objectives are general and long range ("I want to be successful" or "I want to be highly regarded by my superiors") or short range and specific ("I want a corner office" or "I want the promotion that's coming up"), the more clear and the more concise the individual is about what is wanted, the higher the probability that he or she will succeed.

Secondly, objectives must also be viewed from the organizational perspective. Here the organization's demands become a guideline for the individual's objectives. The more people are clear and comfortable with wanting whatever they want, the higher the probability that they will be able to integrate their personal objectives with the organizational objectives so that pursuing either one will have a positive impact on getting the other. For example, if I am clear about wanting the promotion and clear about what the organizational demand for productivity is, pursuing either one will work toward getting the other. The most important aspects of "Objectives" are the following:

- The individual leader is clear about and "owns" each objective; and

- The "Objectives" are consonant with the leader's "Boundary."

On the surface it would seem that the leader must spend an appreciable amount of time and energy struggling with each of the three lower levels. Paradoxically, this is not the case at all. Actually, the situation simply calls for increasing one's awareness. Clarity on any level is a matter of having one's *perceived* position, i.e., where one thinks one is or should be, accurately reflect one's *actual* position, i.e., where one is.

Actions

The last level literally is where all of the action is. It is here that a leader's effectiveness ultimately is determined. Although no one ever is accountable to anyone else for what happens on any of the three lower levels, a leader is totally accountable for the choices made at the fourth level.

The assumption here is that at any given moment, any one of myriad possible actions are available to attempt to get willing compliance to work from others. The broader the range or the greater the number of authentic choices that fit for the leader at any given moment, the higher the probability that the leader will be able to respond appropriately.

In this case, increasing leadership effectiveness is only a matter of answering the following question: "Given an almost infinite number of choices, how do I select an action that will work best for me in getting willing compliance in this situation, versus selecting one that just barely makes it or doesn't make it at all?"

Most people attempt to answer this question by going outside of themselves (asking a colleague, reading a book, or attending a seminar). There is nothing wrong with this approach; however, I suggest that there is a better place to go, at least at first: Go inside. Herein lies the Gestalt perspective to leadership.

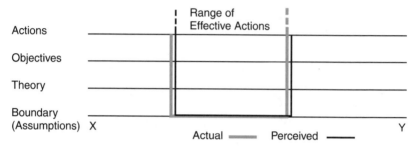

Figure 4a. Manager "A"—Congruence

Having worked with this model for a number of years, I see that the clearer the individual is about his or her assumptions concerning self and others, the higher the probability that it will be easy to develop a theory of leadership and a set of objectives that are consistent with and clearly reflect those assumptions. Most important, it is from this position that the leader will be able, with confidence, to select the leadership actions that will enable him or her to deal easily and effectively with most situations.

Using Theory X/Theory Y as a convenient set of assumptions to illustrate the premise in Figure 4a, "A" is clear about how she sees herself, others, and the work setting.[3] From this point of clarity and comfort, she

---

[3] The focus of this piece is not yet another reworking of Theory X/Theory Y. "X" and "Y" are being used solely because they represent one very familiar and clear example of a relevant sub-boundary. Equally relevant, but less workable, would be the sub-boundary of mistrust/trust of others. In this case, the "growing edge" of the cynic would be to learn to trust others more appropriately; the "growing edge" for the naive individual would be to learn to mistrust others to the point that that response would be appropriate. Growth can occur in either direction, as opposed to the more conventional view that growth only occurs toward the right or "trust" (Theory Y) end of the continuum. Gestalt theory does not imply that one "should" move toward either pole, that is, that the capacity for trusting is any more valuable than the capacity for mistrusting. The thrust of Gestalt theory is on the individual's being clear about where he or she is on this dimension right now and then being able to move in the direction that is most responsive to getting what is wanted.

Pfeiffer & Company

is more able to develop ways in which to work more confidently and comfortably and she is more able to surface and state clear long- and short-term objectives that are important for her. She is clearer about what is important to her, freer to give her commitments openly and unhesitatingly, more willing to state disagreement with things that are dissonant for her, and much more available for effective collaboration when that is what is called for in the situation (Karp, 1976).

Leader "B," on the other hand, is unclear about his assumptions. For him there is little or no awareness of what people are like, including himself. His tendency is to confuse a changing situation with the notion that the characteristics of people are changing on a moment-by-moment basis. Therefore, no theory ever fits well, no objectives are ever tested, and, more to the point, very few actions are ever wholly trusted by him. Simply stated, nothing ever fits for "B." His purgatory is one of constantly plaguing himself with questions such as, "What will my boss think?" "What should I do next?" "What would my predecessor do in this situation?" and "Is it fair for me to ask for this?"

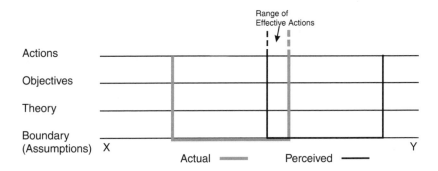

Figure 4b. Manager "B"—Incongruence

Because "B" has no clear sense of what he wants, how he sees things, what is or is not important for him, and little ability to support himself, he has no choice but to rely heavily on other people's views, judgments, and suggestions. This does not provide a healthy prescription for increasing leadership effectiveness.

In Figure 4b, leader "B" actually is somewhere nearer the "X" side of the continuum; however, because of his lack of awareness of this or the social unacceptability of being seen as an "X" type, a surface conversion to human-relations training has occurred, and he perceives himself as being much more toward the "Y" side. This usually takes the form of such thoughts as, "I should be more open (or participative or collaborative or caring)." His assumptions generally are derived from theorists, bosses, and consultants who tell him how he should see other people. From this position, both his theory and objectives are cast in terms of others' views and values.

The result is that his *actions,* although usually adequate, are rarely creative and rarely fully responsive to the situation; frequently, these actions are low risk. The actions he allows himself, that is, those arising from the perceived boundary, are not compatible with who he really is and how he sees things. Those actions that would fit for him and be responsive to the present challenging conditions he rejects for fear of being seen as an autocrat, or Theory X type leader.

As opposed to leader "A," who brings all she has to the work situation, leader "B" brings only the shadow of others. As long as this condition exists, he will never be able to fully maximize his potential for personal growth and creativity, nor will the organization be able to realize the full extent of his ability to contribute effectively. Even more damaging, although more subtle, is that by being incongruent, he models incongruity as his leadership style to those he is attempting to influence. This sets a bad example and tends to increase the probability that the next "generation" of leaders will be even more likely to look to others for guidance and direction first, before attempting to rely on their own knowledge, internal strength, and sense of what is appropriate. His only area for real, effective action is the small area in "Actions" where his actual and his perceived capacities overlap.

The key to increased leadership effectiveness is first to get as much overlap as possible between where you are and where you think you are. The greater the amount of overlap on the "Boundary" level, the more congruence and choices that fit on all other levels, particularly on the "Actions" line.

The Need for Integration

Gestalt theory maintains that every human being is born with the capacity to experience his or her full range of human characteristics. Furthermore, competence and effectiveness are held to be the natural state. What has occurred in most cases is that, because of societal norms, parenting, education, or religious guidance, we have learned to disvalue certain parts of ourselves. With much help from others, we even have attempted to amputate many of these parts. This can have a strong negative impact on leadership behaviors later on in life. For example, suppose that as a young child I was taught never to speak ill of others. Although the value may be a fine one, believing it completely as a child could result in my being a supervisor who is unwilling or unable to give my direct reports clear, corrective feedback on the job.

Integration is the process through which we begin to regain and re-own these lost parts. Integration also serves the function of effectively expanding one's I-Boundary. Casting this into the organizational setting, the premise is as follows:

The more effective leader will be the one who can generate the most alternatives in any given situation.

Each and every leadership situation that one encounters is, to some degree, unique. A leader's effectiveness will be increased to the extent that he or she can (1) be fully aware of the uniqueness of this particular situation and (2) be able to respond to the situation authentically. This implies that a leader must have more than a single way of approaching and dealing with contingencies.

For example, suppose that I describe and experience myself as being "easygoing" and "thoughtful." Furthermore, suppose that I have been fairly effective overall in consistently coming from this position. People like me this way and reinforce my behavior. However, what happens when there is a crisis or I am attacked in some way? Because over time I have eliminated the tougher, more aggressive parts of myself in order to please others, where do I find the toughness needed to respond to the present situation? In the absence of toughness, I find myself with one of two possible alternatives. I could attempt to restructure the situation so that I could somehow respond to the situation from my comfort zone (attempt to reason with a bully) or I could choose simply not to respond. However, the more authentic ways I have to be—easygoing, tough, thoughtful, aggressive, supportive, angry, humorous, or logical—the more responsive I can be to any ongoing situation.

Note that this does not preclude the reality and the rightness of choosing to spend the greatest majority of my time in my most comfortable stance. It does mean that I can readily leave this stance when the situation calls for it and be just as comfortable for as long as it takes to accomplish what needs to be accomplished from a different position. If leaders would give up their self-demand to be consistent and replace it with a self-demand to be optimally effective, they would be better leaders.

One way of defining alternatives is "ways of being." A second, and equally important, definition refers to the ability to create choices of action before committing to a specific course of action. Managers frequently limit the generation of workable alternatives because of fear of negative reactions from others or a fear of being seen as unfair. When first viewing the situation, responding to these concerns is definitely counterproductive. However, when it is time to make the conscious choice of what to do, then it is appropriate to consider these restrictions.

For example, I can choose not to implement a certain alternative because it would be unfair to another person. However, unless I am free enough to generate that alternative and am willing to consider it, I have consciously denied myself the option of choosing for or against it. In addition, this particular alternative, although unfair to a single individual, might be the best way to avert an overall crisis.

This view of alternatives underscores the premise that there is no one best way to be. It also suggests that, in most cases, there are several potentially effective ways to attack most problems and pursue most objectives. Each effective leader brings a totally unique being (himself or herself) to each organizational decision point, and the most valuable contribution made is his or her unique perspective.

> *Each and every leadership situation that one encounters is, to some degree, unique.*

In attaining organizational objectives, the more diverse the originating pool of opinion, the higher the probability that an optimally effective choice will emerge. Anything that discourages a broader range of alternatives limits the potential for a successful outcome. Once again, using Theory X/Theory Y as a convenient reference point, integration can be viewed in terms of how the four levels of leadership contribute to individual leadership effectiveness.

Much recent literature alleges that organizations that operate from a Theory Y set of assumptions and values are more effective than those that operate from a Theory X set. Certainly self-directed work teams and total quality management programs rest solidly in the Theory Y assumptions about people. Although this allegation may be true in many cases, it is not always true. Many organizations are maximally effective operating from a clear set of Theory X assumptions, such as Marine Corps boot camps, certain religious organizations, and almost all penal institutions. The issue is not so much one of *what* the underlying assumptions are, but rather one of *how* clearly those assumptions are stated and owned by the leadership and membership of the respective organizations.

Given, as a necessary precondition, congruence between a leader's actual and perceived boundaries, the more encompassing the boundary, the broader the effective range of "Actions" available.

In Figure 5, leader "A" is operating authentically from the position on the X/Y sub-boundary in Time Period 1 (TP1). She is clear about the assumptions she holds, i.e., that people tend to be lazy, will avoid responsibility, and mostly are not to be trusted. However, she is using that awareness as a means of selecting the appropriate leadership approaches, objectives, and actions that fit best for her.

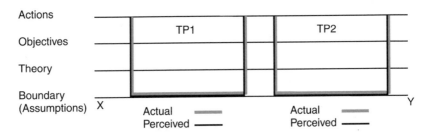

Figure 5. Change

Assume that she is doing very well and decides that she wants to increase her leadership effectiveness. She attends some workshops in team building and total quality management, does some personal growth work to increase her communication and listening skills, and develops a more genuine concern for her people. A year later, at Time Period 2 (TP2), she is holding a more authentic Theory Y set of assumptions at the indicated point in Figure 5. Is this growth? Most people would say that it is; however, I disagree. It is not growth...it is change!

At TP1, leader "A" only has the capacity to view people as potentially lazy, unmotivated, and averse to responsibility. At TP2 she only has the capacity to see them as potential opportunities for growth, motivated, and open to responsibility. At TP1, she might have made a good Marine stockade commander but not a very effective supervisor of a social work unit. In TP2, the situation would be reversed. The secret in increasing leadership effectiveness is to be able to do as much of both as you can!

As Figure 5 suggests, growth for "A" in TP1 would be toward the right, or the Theory Y, side of the scale. For whatever reason, she has limited her capacity for supportiveness and trust. Growth for her in TP2 would be toward the left, or Theory X, side of the scale in order to regain her capacity for toughness and mistrust.

Whether speaking of personal growth in the group setting or of leadership effectiveness in the organizational setting, the premise is as follows:

Growth is not changing existing positions but rather expanding them.

Growth, or effectiveness, is best depicted in Figures 6a, 6b, and 6c for leader "B."

Time Period 1 in Figure 6a indicates the starting position, in which the perceived position and actual positions for "B" are congruent. This is the same point that "A" began in Figure 5.

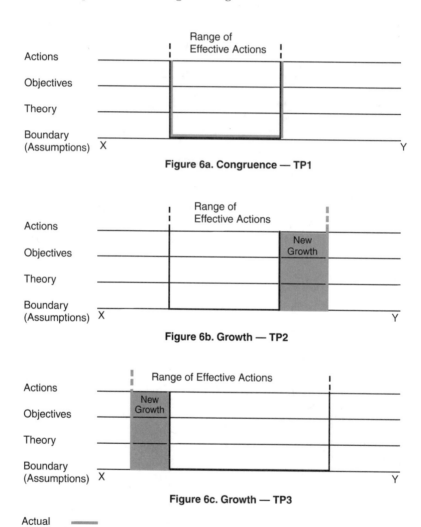

Figure 6a. Congruence — TP1

Figure 6b. Growth — TP2

Figure 6c. Growth — TP3

"B" is precisely where he thinks he is. He is clear and unapologetic about where he is and how he sees things and maintains enough flexibility to be willing to learn.

He is now faced with a leadership challenge that requires a more supportive set of assumptions and approaches than he presently possesses. By working out of the extreme congruent position (getting some coaching in communications and listening skills, going to seminars on team building and participative management, and experimenting with some new collaborative techniques that stretch him), he succeeds in overcoming the challenge. Figure 6b, TP2, indicates where he is at the point of successfully responding to the challenge.

He has done such a good job that he is given a promotion to a new location. On his first day at the new location, he discovers to his consternation that each of his new direct reports is either an ex-convict or would like to become one. His growth opportunity now is in the opposite direction. He needs to increase his capacity for mistrust, provide unilateral direction, be willing to discipline, and so forth. These skills are what the new position requires, and growth is now in the opposite direction, toward the X—the more controlling—side of the continuum. "B" loses no capacities in the process. Figure 6c then depicts his capacities after successfully responding to these conditions.

This model suggests three axioms for increasing personal and leadership effectiveness:

1. When growth occurs on any continuum, in either direction, the far boundary stays fixed. The implication is that anything that ever worked for you in the past has a capacity to work for you again. It just needs to be tested and adapted to the present conditions.

2. Growth, or any increase in effectiveness, always occurs at the boundary. A leader's best position in the face of new challenge is at the very edge of his or her Zone of Comfort.

3. As one nears the edge of a sub-boundary and the probability for growth increases, the probability of discomfort, risk, and diminished self-confidence increases proportionally.

CONCLUSION

Regardless of the setting in which it is employed, the Gestalt approach relies heavily on the use of paradox. Several such paradoxes may be very helpful in increasing leadership effectiveness.

Paradox I. The best way to build an effective team is to focus on the individual. The concept of synergy suggests that because the whole (team) is greater than and different from the sum of its component parts (individuals), the stronger each individual member is, the higher the potential for the maximum strength of the team. When the leader focuses on and legitimizes the value of individual differences and common goals, each group member is encouraged to develop the best way to be and to work. Once this differentiation process is established and is well under way, linkages are formed among strong, confident individuals, each of whom is able and more willing to contribute uniquely to the organizational objective.

Paradox II. The best way to change is not to change (Beisser, 1970). The Gestalt approach focuses heavily on what is rather than on what should be. Assisting a leader to be more aware and appreciative of how she is rather than how she should be puts that person in better position to make a conscious decision to remain in this position or to try something different. In short, once the effective Theory X leader is told, "It's really okay to be how you are," she no longer has to expend effort in defending her position or hiding it. Making it genuinely safe for her to relax and experience her present position more fully is a change! Any modification in her approach that she makes from this position is because she chooses to do so; if successful, the change will become permanent change. Permanent change is the only kind of change that has lasting impact on increasing the effectiveness of the individual and the organization.

Paradox III. No "One Best Way" is the one best way. People are much more different from each other than they are similar, and the same can be said for organizations. The range of uniqueness is infinite and is limited only by an inability to recognize the differences that do exist. No single approach, theory, or set of assumptions is going to be universally applicable to the individual's or the organization's needs—this one included.

If, for example, after reading this article, you reject it, you have, paradoxically, acted in consonance with the approach. That is, you have allowed yourself to try something new, have weighed it carefully, and have then consciously chosen to reject it in favor of an existing position. In this process, you have become more aware of your existing position and how it is of more service to you than the one presented here. You are more aware of how our respective theories and assumptions differ, and at least for now, you are more sure that your position is more useful and correct for you than is mine. At the very minimum, you have gained another alternative that might be useful to you at some later date.

Some direct implications can be shown for the future training and development for the leaders of today's and tomorrow's organizations. Currently, most leadership training and development programs are geared specifically to the expansion of theory, the pursuit of objectives, and the learning of new techniques. What has been missing is the essential first step—assisting individual leaders in becoming more clear and more confident in the assumptions they make about themselves and others and in their ability to provide the necessary leadership to get the organization where it needs to go.

References

Beisser, A.R. (1970). The paradoxical theory of change. In J. Fagan & I.L. Shepherd (Eds.), *Gestalt therapy now*. Palo Alto, CA: Science and Behavior.

Bennis, W.G. (1969). *Organization development: Its nature and origins and prospects*. Reading, MA: Addison-Wesley.

Herman, S.M. (1974). The shadow of organization development. In J.W. Pfeiffer & J.E. Jones (Eds.), *The 1974 annual handbook for group facilitators*. San Diego, CA: Pfeiffer & Company.

Herman, S.M. (1976). The shouldist manager. In J.W. Pfeiffer & J.E. Jones (Eds.), *The 1976 annual handbook for group facilitators*. San Diego, CA: Pfeiffer & Company.

Karp, H.B. (1976). A gestalt approach to collaboration in organizations. In J.W. Pfeiffer & J.E. Jones (Eds.), *The 1976 annual handbook for group facilitators*. San Diego, CA: Pfeiffer & Company.

Karp, H.B. (1995). *Personal power: An unorthodox guide to success*. Lake Worth, FL: Gardner Press.

McGregor, D.M. (1960). *The human side of enterprise*. New York: McGraw-Hill.

Perls, F.S. (1969). *In and out the garbage pail*. Moab, UT: Real People Press.

Polster, E., & Polster, M. (1973). *Gestalt theory integrated*. New York: Brunner/Mazel.

H.B. Karp, Ph.D., *is the owner of Personal Growth Systems, a management consulting firm in Virginia Beach, Virginia. He consults with a variety of Fortune 500 and government organizations in the areas of leadership development, team building, conflict management, and executive coaching. He specializes in bringing Gestalt applications to issues of individual growth and organizational effectiveness. In addition to many articles, he is the author of* Personal Power: An Unorthodox Guide to Success *and* The Change Leader: Using a Gestalt Approach with Work Groups, *published by Pfeiffer & Company in 1995.*

REIGNITING SPIRIT IN THE WORK PLACE

Laura Hauser

Abstract: Reengineering and downsizing—the change initiatives of the 1990s—have caused a serious dip in employee morale, which, in turn, has decreased productivity. Yet the pace at which business changes will only accelerate in the future, and organizations must be able to implement change initiatives without undermining morale even further.

The author suggests that executives, managers, and other change agents must integrate both the tangible and intangible dimensions of business. How? By speaking not only to people's heads but also to their hearts, and by aligning structures, systems, and technology in a way that promotes human potential. Hauser believes that by integrating the tangible and intangible dimensions of business, organizations can not only survive but can thrive in today's competitive business environment.

The 1996 Annual: Volume 1, Training.
Copyright © 1996 by Pfeiffer & Company, San Diego, CA.

$\mathbf{R}$eengineering and downsizing, the cost-cutting strategies of the 1990s, are taking fierce tolls on organizations. More and more, we are learning that downsizing depletes employee morale. Low morale, in turn, diminishes productivity, which causes the very monetary losses that management was trying to avoid by downsizing.

As a result of widespread staff reductions, the remaining employees often feel overwhelmed by their increased work loads and have had to lengthen their working hours to as many as ten to sixteen per day. Both managerial and nonmanagerial employees feel devalued and understandably discouraged; they no longer find their work satisfying and meaningful. People feel a loss of energy; they feel psychologically empty and distanced from their work and the organization.

The fast pace of change is only going to accelerate in the future, and organizations still have to be able to respond with changes of their own. So how can management effect change without disengaging and overextending employees in the process? At a recent conference for PIHRA, the Professionals in Human Resources Association, I presented what I believe is the answer: reigniting spirit in the work place. My thesis was that sparking organizational energy is an emerging critical success factor for leaders who are responsible for planning and implementing strategic-change initiatives.

When people are asked to implement change but their spirits are not engaged, they take whatever action is required of them, but they do not offer their loyalty, support, concern, and special efforts. Consequently, the change itself often fizzles and gives way to anxiety and frustration. And if the organization's own employees do not adapt to the new situation, how can the organization survive and thrive in a rapidly changing world?

THE CONNECTION BETWEEN SPIRIT AND THE BOTTOM LINE

An individual's "spirit" is the source of positive, creative energy—the center of his or her being. Spirit is an intangible but powerful aspect of individual and organizational success. When people's spirit is evoked, they feel energetic, attuned to their work, and committed to achieving desired business results.

Although many organizational leaders are proficient at dealing with the tangible dimension of success (how to focus on profits, how to

298   *Pfeiffer & Company*

implement new systems, structures, technologies, and processes), they either forget or do not know how to deal with the intangible dimensions of business (the human spirit). But a leadership that integrates the tangible and intangible dimensions into the planning and implementing of strategic change guides the organization toward dynamic business results (see Figure 1). Such a leadership understands that employee support and enthusiasm play an important role in achieving a positive bottom line.

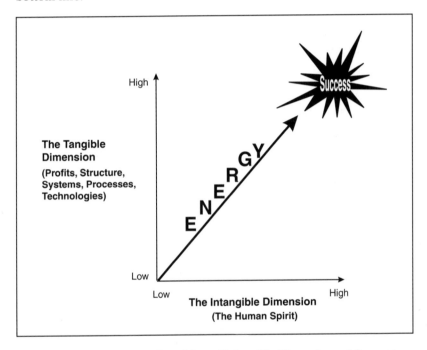

Figure 1. Integrating the Tangible and Intangible Dimensions of Success

Every employee needs to see meaning in a job in order to get that job done; the importance of purpose, values, and ethics in work cannot be overstated. Consequently, a CEO who is able to speak sincerely, not only to heads but also to hearts, is in a position to access powerful energy and creativity. In addition, the organization's management must "walk the talk" by aligning structures and systems in a way that promotes human potential.

A Case Study in Reigniting Spirit

The following case study illustrates how to reignite the spirit of an organization during a reengineering change initiative by integrating the tangible and intangible dimensions of success.

The Situation

The new president of the mortgage division of a major U.S. bank was under pressure from the corporate office to significantly improve financial results, increase market share, and enhance customer satisfaction. During his first year, the division was running behind its financial plan, the processing of residential loans was backlogged, and there was a high level of customer dissatisfaction. Most processes were manual; employees did not trust one another to do things right the first time, so they regularly double-checked one another's work.

The division embarked on reengineering, designing and implementing a new work-flow process and significantly changing the structure of the enterprise. Employees held the unrealistic expectation that a "reengineering switch" would be flipped and conditions would magically change overnight. When the magic did not happen, the employees were disillusioned.

The Intervention

The president realized that to turn the reengineering effort into a success, he would have to integrate the tangible dimension of producing positive bottom-line results with the intangible dimension of engaging the human spirit. I consulted with the president and his human resources manager about how to accomplish this integration. A key intervention used was the creation of two cross-functional teams. The first, the *project team*, was responsible for coordinating and overseeing the technical aspects of the new work-flow design. The second team, the *transition team*, served as a mirror and pulse-check of people's spirits as the changes were implemented.

The transition team's primary goal was to provide top management and the project team with honest feedback as the organizational changes were implemented, much as an anesthesiologist informs a surgeon of a patient's condition as an operation progresses. The members of the transition team followed this pattern of action:

Pfeiffer & Company

- They identified critical human and operational issues that were impeding the reengineering effort;
- They made recommendations to the president and key executives about how to address these issues;
- They monitored the implementation of approved recommendations; and
- They scheduled similar meetings to follow up on the implementation of recommendations and to address any new issues.

"Just-in-Time" Problem Solving

The transition team's meetings offer an excellent example of integrating nuts-and-bolts business issues with human concerns, engaging the spirits of the employees, and communicating with employees at a heart level as well as a head level.

In each case, I facilitated monthly meetings in which the team members met for half a day without top managers, identifying the successes and problems associated with reengineering thus far and creating solutions to recommend to top management. Then, in the afternoon, the president and key vice presidents joined the transition team.

A dialogue ensued. The members of the transition team and the executives openly and honestly talked about the positive responses as well as the pain and problems associated with the organizational changes. The executives listened to the team's recommendations and engaged in "just-in-time" problem solving. As all of the organization's key decision makers were present, decisions could be made on the spot.

Although approval of the team's recommendations was not always automatic, the executives were careful to communicate their belief that the team members were presenting realistic solutions based on an understanding of the organization's operational concerns. The team members were empowered in that they were able to have an impact on human issues; top management was able to convey its concern about human issues as well as ensure the stability of the reengineering effort.

With each subsequent meeting, the transition team followed up with the executives, asking for an update on the agreements made during the previous meeting before proceeding to new issues.

In addition to bestowing empowerment, conveying trust, and demonstrating top management's concern for people's feelings, these meetings reignited people's spirits in other ways. For example, the meeting structure created a forum for interaction among people who ordinarily would not have interacted. For the first time in the division's history, the "process owners" consistently sat together to understand how their departments interacted and how they could better help one another.

Also, the team members were able to see the big picture, which, in turn, initiated a process of effective, cross-functional communication. People's language changed from divisive and blaming terminology ("We are not the problem; they are the problem") to inclusive and problem-solving terminology ("We're all in this together; let's figure out how to make things better"). Team members left the meetings with a sense of satisfaction, feeling that they had made an impact on managerial thinking, decision making, and the quality of work life for everyone. And they had.

Results

The division was expecting a 75-percent success rate in implementing the new work-flow design. However, due to increased employee commitment, job satisfaction, and quick resolutions of problems, the division achieved an amazing 95-percent success rate.

Other benefits also were realized, as expressed in the president's words:

> Without the team interventions, I think we would have only been at 80 percent of our financial goal. But more important is the positive change in the satisfaction rating of our major customer base and our increase in market share. I am very, very satisfied with the turn. I think what we really learned is the power of the human spirit in the equation. The first half year, I was talking to people's heads by emphasizing the numerical targets, but my message just wasn't sinking in. I said to myself, "I have to switch—I have to talk to their hearts."

CONCLUSION

The integration of the tangible and intangible dimensions of organizational success during times of strategic change is the key to positive results. Human resource managers are in a unique position to become the architects of this integration, building bridges between top management and employees as well as between the bottom line and the human spirit. The way to begin is by raising the question "How can we tap into individual and team spirit to unleash new energy to contribute to individual and organizational success?"

Using the bank division's successful implementation of a reengineering effort, we can extrapolate the following guidelines for reigniting spirit and promoting success in a strategic change initiative:

1. Deal with the intangible dimension of change as seriously as the tangible dimension.
2. Speak not only to people's heads but also to their hearts.
3. Involve employees in the design and execution of the change.
4. Allow for the emotions, intuitions, and qualities of relationships to enter the design and implementation process.
5. Align structures, technologies, and systems in a way that promotes human potential and engages people's spirits.
6. Create an environment for organizational learning and for talking honestly about the pain and difficulties associated with organizational change.
7. Implement mechanisms for cross-functional communication and interaction and just-in-time problem solving.
8. Acknowledge and trust people's abilities to come up with realistic solutions to organizational problems related to the change initiative.
9. Maintain a constancy of purpose and sense of urgency.
10. Check continually on the emotional climate of the organization during the change period.

Laura Hauser, M.S.O.D., *is founder of Leadership Strategies International, a consulting and training firm that specializes in the diagnosis and resolution of workplace problems so people and organizations can achieve greater effectiveness and performance. She is an expert in interpersonal communication and in engaging the creativity of individuals, teams, and organizations to proactively create their future. This involves her in strategic planning, business process reengineering, and team and leadership development. Ms. Hauser is a published author in the areas of valuing workplace diversity and the role of executive leadership in affecting customer satisfaction.*

CONTRIBUTORS

Mary Sue Barry
Principal
Full-Circle Training and Consulting
114 27th Avenue North
St. Petersburg, FL 33704
(813) 823-3604

Howard E. Butz, Jr.
Director, Total Quality
AAI Corporation
P.O. Box 126
Hunt Valley, MD 21030
(410) 628-3355
fax: (410) 683-6498

Greg H. Cripple
Manager, HR Planning & Development
John Deere Credit Company
John Deere Road
Moline, IL 61265
(309) 765-5358
fax: (309) 765-4947

Guillermo Cuéllar, Ed.D.
Organization Development Consultant
216 Silver Lane
Sunderland, MA 01375
(413) 665-3288

Patrick Doyle
Principal
High Impact Training Services
R.R. #2
Perth Road, Ontario K0H 2I0
Canada
(613) 544-5400
fax: (613) 353-6517

Maureen Wilson Dücker
Academic Adviser
Educational Policy & Leadership—
   Higher Education & Student Affairs
Ohio State University
154 West 12th Avenue
015 Enarson Hall
Columbus, OH 43210
(614) 292-0646
fax: (614) 292-2124
e-mail: mducker@mgate.uvc.ohio-
   state.edu

Caela Farren, Ph.D.
President
Career Systems, Inc.
900 James Avenue
Scranton, PA 18510
(800) 283-8839

Peter R. Garber
Manager, Teamwork Development
PPG Industries, Inc.
One PPG Place
Pittsburgh, PA 15272
(412) 434-3417
fax: (412) 434-3490

John Geirland, Ph.D.
President
Geirland & Associates
4335 Beck Avenue
Studio City, CA 91604
(818) 760-4978
fax: (818) 760-0348
e-mail: jgeirland@aol.com

Gary Gemmill, Ph.D.
Professor Emeritus
School of Management
Syracuse University
Syracuse, NY 13244
(315) 443-2961

Tom G. Geurts
Department of Insurance and Real Estate
Pennsylvania State University
409C Business Administration Building
University Park, PA 16802
(814) 865-0614
fax: (814) 865-6284

Marilyn Ginsburg, M.F.C.C.
Associate Director
Center for Management Effectiveness
427 Beirut Avenue
Pacific Palisades, CA 90272
(310) 459-6080
fax: (310) 459-9307

Leonard D. Goodstein, Ph.D.
Consulting Psychologist
4815 Foxhall Crescent NW
Washington, DC 20007-1052
(202) 333-3134
fax: (202) 333-8519

W. Norman Gustafson
Chair, Department of Social Sciences
Sanger Unified School District
1905 7th Street
Sanger, CA 93657
(209) 875-6521

Claire B. Halverson, Ph.D.
Professor
Master's Program in Intercultural
  Management
School for International Training
Brattleboro, VT 05301
(802) 254-6098
fax: (802) 258-3248

Robert Hargrove
CEO/President
Hargrove & Partners, Inc.
39 Harvard Street
Brookline, MA 02146
(617) 739-3300
fax: (617) 738-9149

Laura Hauser
President
Leadership Strategies International
15555 Bronco Drive, Suite 101
Santa Clarita, CA 91351
(805) 251-0641
fax: (805) 251-5062

Tom Henschel
Founder
Essential Communications
14253 Weddington Street
Van Nuys, CA 91401
(818) 788-5357

Jane Mitchell Howard
Center for Applied Cognitive Studies
719 Romany Road
Charlotte, NC 28203-4849
(704) 331-0926
fax: (704) 331-9408
e-mail: centacs@vnet.net

Pierce J. Howard, Ph.D.
Director of Research
Center for Applied Cognitive Studies
719 Romany Road
Charlotte, NC 28203-4849
(704) 331-0926
fax: (704) 331-9408
e-mail: centacs@vnet.net

Austin J. Jaffe, Ph.D.
Department of Insurance and Real Estate
Pennsylvania State University
409A Business Administration Building
University Park, PA 16802
(814) 865-1938
fax: (814) 865-6284

H.B. Karp, Ph.D.
Principal
Personal Growth Systems
109 82nd Street
Virginia Beach, VA 23451
(804) 425-8203
fax: (804) 425-8203

Beverly L. Kaye, Ph.D.
President
Beverly Kaye & Associates, Inc.
3545 Alana Drive
Sherman Oaks, CA 91403
(818) 995-6454
fax: (818) 995-0984

Herbert S. Kindler, Ph.D.
Director
Center for Management Effectiveness
427 Beirut Avenue
Pacific Palisades, CA 90272
(310) 459-6052
fax: (310) 459-9307

James W. Kinneer
Support Services Supervisor
Indiana Hospital
Hospital Road
Indiana, PA 15701
(412) 357-7089
fax: (412) 357-7241

Michael R. Larsen
TRW, Mesa 1 Facility
4051 North Higley Road
Mesa, AZ 85215
(602) 396-1482
fax: (602) 830-3647

Robert William Lucas
Manager, Professional Development
American Automobile Association,
National Office
1000 AAA Drive
Heathrow, FL 32746-0563
(407) 444-7520
fax: (407) 696-7205

Michael L. Mazzarese, Ph.D.
President
Mazzarese & Associates
330 Benson Place
Westfield, NJ 07090-1302
(908) 518-0406
fax: (908) 518-0412

Phyllis L. Medina, Ph.D.
Center for Applied Cognitive Studies
719 Romany Road
Charlotte, NC 28203-4849
(704) 331-0926
fax: (704) 331-9408
e-mail: centacs@vnet.net

Robert C. Preziosi, D.P.A.
Professor of Management Education
School of Business and Entrepreneurship
Nova Southeastern University
3301 College Avenue
Ft. Lauderdale, FL 33314
(305) 476-8912
fax: (305) 370-5637

Eva Sonesh-Kedar, Ph.D.
Apple Computer
Infinite Loop, MS: 75-6AV
Cupertino, CA 95014
(408) 974-6769
fax: (408) 974-4920

J. Craig VanHouten
President
Knowledge First
2311 Country View Glen
Escondido, CA 92026
(619) 471-4755

Gary Wagenheim
Associate Professor
Organizational Leadership
Purdue University
1420 Knoy Hall of Technology
West Lafayette, IN 47907
(317) 494-5613
fax: (317) 496-2519

CONTENTS OF THE COMPANION VOLUME, THE 1996 ANNUAL: VOLUME 2, CONSULTING

---

*See Experiential Learning Activities Categories, p. 5, for an explanation of the numbering system.

INVENTORIES, QUESTIONNAIRES, AND SURVEYS

PRESENTATION AND DISCUSSION RESOURCES